D1608466

Practical COMPACT JAPANESE-ENGLISH DICTIONARY ON TRADE & BUSINESS

コンパクト

貿易英語活用辞典

三好章六編

北 星 堂 書 店

Published by The Hokuseido Press
3-12, Kanda-Nishikicho, Chiyoda-ku, Tokyo

まえがき

　日本経済は世界経済の 10% を担うところまで成長を遂げた。人口1億2,000万人(世界人口の3％)，国土面積37万平方キロ（世界陸地の0.3%)を占めるにすぎない日本が，これだけの経済力を保有するにいたっている。世界の貿易に占める日本の地位を見ると，世界の輸出の 8.2%，輸入の 7.4% を占めている。

　この日本の経済力を可能にし，かつ支えているのが貿易であり，貿易立国が叫ばれている理由もここにある。それだけに最近の貿易取引は多様化しており，通常の原材料，製品の輸出入のほかに三国間貿易，プラント輸出，技術輸出・輸入もますます増えている。したがって，それに用いられる英語も広範にわたり，時に時事英語あり，経済英語あり，法律英語あり，工業英語ありで，相互に密着・関連している。このような視点から本書を作るに当っては広く vocabulary を選び，これを活用できるように配慮した。

　携帯に便利で使いやすいコンパクト版とするため必要度に応じて単語，活用文の分量を定めた。活用文の作成に当っては新進の同学2氏の協力を得，さらに米人教師2名，豪州人教師1名の native speaker に英文の検討を受けた。また北星堂編集部の一方ならぬ助力を得た。ここに謝意を表したい。本書を出すに当り，内容については編者の力が及ばず，不適当な箇所もあるかと思われるので，お気付きの点は何卒御指導，御叱正を賜わりたい。

　1984年1月

　　　　　　　　　　　　　　　　　　　　　　　編　者

執筆協力者　　柳平友平（前橋育英短大講師）
　　　　　　　松為信文（前神田外語学院講師）

凡　　例

1.　見出しの日本語
　　50音順にゴシックで配列し，ローマ字表記はヘボン式に従い，
　　【　】の中にイタリックで示した。
　　囫　あいさつ【*aisatsu*】greeting; best wishes

2.　見出し語の中の配列
　　見出し語に対する訳語を与え，囫で例文を示し，それぞれの訳
　　語(句)はイタリックで表した。次に見出し語に関連する語句・
　　熟語も例文とともに並べた。

3.　各種の記号
　　：　見出し語に補足した語句を示す場合。
　　　　囫　せい【*sei*】：—である　　「せいである」

　　—　見出し語を示す。
　　　　囫　更新【*kōshin*】renewal‖—する renew　　「更新する」

　　；　訳語(句)の区切りを示す。

　　[　]直前の語(句)に入れ換えることができることを示す。
　　　　囫　決済［算］　　「決済」または「決算」
　　　　invite [call] attention　　'invite attention' または
　　　　'call attention'

　　(　) 省略可能ないし補足的説明を示す。
　　　　囫　送り状を作る (make an) invoice　　'make an in-
　　　　voice' または 'invoice'
　　　　確認する acknowledge (他人の書面); confirm (自己
　　　　の書面)
　　　　日本語(句)と訳語(句)との対応を示す。
　　　　囫　高(安)く買う buy dear (cheap)　　「高く買う」は 'buy
　　　　dear', 「安く買う」は 'buy cheap'

《　》訳語（句）と密接な名詞・動詞・前置詞などの例を示す。

 例 **結論** 《come to a》 conclusion

  切り抜ける tide over 《difficulties; crisis》

→「その項目を見よ」の表示。

 例 **罷業**【*higyō*】→スト

/　見出し語に対する例文が複数のときの区切りを示す。

‖　見出し語を構成要素とした複合語を並べるときの区切りで，かならずしも50音順ではない。

反　反対語を示す。

注　注意事項を示す。

【あ】

あいかわらず【*aikawarazu*】 ((remain)) unchanged; as usual　例
市況はあいかわらず変動がない．The market *remains unchang-ed.* / 商売はあいもかわらずだ．The business is *as usual.*

愛顧【*aiko*】 patronage; favor　例 不変の愛顧をいただく receive
impartial　*favor*　from ～ / 今後ともよろしく御愛顧のほど願い
上げます．We solicit your further [continued] *patronage*
[*favors*]. / 倍旧御愛顧の ほど願い上げます．We solicit your
redoubled *patronage.*

あいさつ【*aisatsu*】 greeting; best wishes　例 新年の御あいさつ
を申し上げます．We wish to tender you the *greeting* of the
New year．Please accept our *best wishes* for a Happy New
Year. / 時候のあいさつを申し上げます．I wish you the season's
greetings. / 丁寧にあいさつして彼は～と言った．With a polite
greeting, he said ～.

間がら【*aidagara*】 terms　例 ～とは懇意な間がらである　keep
on friendly *terms* with ～ / 貴社とは親しい間がらだ．We are
on good [cordial] *terms* with you.

相手【*aite*】 rival; match　例 電気製品では当社にかなう相手はな
い．In electric appliances, there is no *match* for us. ‖ 相談—
an adviser; a counselor　例 問題が解決したのは相談相手のお
かげ．It was through the help of an *adviser* that the problem
was solved. ‖ を—どる　bring　an　action　against ‖ 競争の—
rival; competitor ‖ 商売などする— one's partner; companion

相手口銭込みシフ値段【*aite kōsenkomi shifu nedan*】 C.I.F. & C.
(CIF plus Commission)

あいにく【*ainiku*】 unfortunately; unluckily; by ill luck; I am
sorry ～　例 あいにくその日に限って便船がなかった．*Unfor-tunately* [*Unluckily*; *By ill luck*] the ship did not sail on that
particular day. / あいにくその品を切らせました．*I am sorry*
we are out of the article．The article is out of stock.

亜鉛板張り箱【*aen itabaribako*】 tinned wooden case　例 商品は亜

鉛板張り箱で包装します．The goods are packed in *tinned wooden case.*

赤字【*akaji*】: —を出す show a loss; go into red figure 例 この商売は赤字だ．This business *shows a loss* [*red figure*]. ‖ —財政 deficit finance ‖ —予算 unbalanced budget

上がる【*agaru*】 advance; go up; rise; be on the advance 例 価格は上がる見込みだ．Prices are expected to *advance* [*go up*; *rise*]. / 価格は上がる一方です．The prices are *rising* steadily. / 物価が上がった．The prices have *risen.* / 物価は20％上がった．The prices have *risen* by twenty percent. / 物価は上がっている．Prices *are on the advance* [*advancing*].

明らか【*akiraka*】 (に) clear(ly); evident(ly); certain(ly) 例 彼が間違っていることはその事実から明らかだ．It is *clear* [*evident*] from the fact that he is mistaken. / 彼が来ることは明らかだ．It is *certain* that he will come. / まずその点を明らかにしなければならない．We must make it *clear* [*clarify* it]. / 明らかに荷造不良のためだ．This is *evidently* due to poor packing.

アクリル繊維【*akuriru sen-i*】 acrylonitric fiber 例 新しいシャツはアクリルと綿の混紡である．The new shirts are a blend of *acrylonitric fiber* and cotton.

悪条件【*akujōken*】 unfavorable conditions [terms] 例 悪条件のために契約は締結に至らなかった．An agreement was not reached due to the *unfavorable conditions.*

揚げ地【*agechi*】 port of discharge; discharging port; landing port 例 東京は日本の主要な揚げ地である．Tokyo is the major *port of discharge* in Japan. / 積み荷は分配のため揚げ地におろされた．The goods were unloaded at the *landing port* for further distribution. ‖ —変更 change of destination ‖ —変更料 diversion charge

揚げる【*ageru*】 land 例 積み荷は神戸で揚げた．We *landed* the cargo at Kobe.

上げる【*ageru*】 (値) advance; raise; increase (a price) 例 値段を10％上げることに決定した．We have decided to *raise* the *price* by 10 percent. ‖ 能率を— enhance efficiency

預かる 【*azukaru*】 (物) keep; receive in trust; be entrusted with 例 その店から見本帳を預かっている. We *are entrusted* by the store *with* a sample [pattern] book. ‖ (金) hold at disposal; be deposited; receive on deposit 例 手取金はお預かり乞う. We ask you kindly to *hold* the net proceeds *at* our *disposal*. / 銀行は金を預かる. The bank *receives* money *on deposit*.

預ける 【*azukeru*】 (物) place [leave] in one's care [charge]; leave in trust; deposit 例 品物を彼に預けよう. We shall *leave* this article *in his care* [*charge*]. / 品物は倉庫に預けた. We *deposited* the goods in a warehouse. / 担保として有価証券を債権者に預けた. We *deposited* bonds with a creditor as security. ‖ (荷物) check one's luggage ‖ (金) deposit [put] 《money in a bank》 例 信用状金額の30%に相当する証拠金をお預け願います. We have to ask you to *deposit* with us a margin equal to 30% of the amount of the letter of credit.

頭金 【*atamakin*】 down payment; deposit 例 どうぞ頭金400ドルを支払ってください. Please make *down payment* of $ 400. / 新車購入の場合30%の頭金を支払えばよい. When you buy a new car, you may make a 30% *down payment* [*deposit*].

新しい 【*atarashii*】 new; fresh; up-to-date; brand-new 例 当社の在庫品はすべてごく新しい. All our stock is *brand-new*. / この魚は新しい. This fish is *fresh*. / このアイデアは新しい. This idea is *up-to-date*.

扱う 【*atsukau*】 treat; deal; handle; work; accept 例 彼は客を丁寧に扱う. He *treats* the guest politely. / あの店は何を扱っていますか. What do they *deal* in at that store? / 貴国で当社製品を扱う代理店として貴社を任命します. We are pleased to appoint you as an agent to *handle* our products in your country. / 綿製品を扱いたい. We want to *handle* cotton goods. / 君はこの機械を扱えるか. Can you *work* this machine? / 郵便局で電報を扱う. They *accept* telegrams at the post office.

悪化する 【*akka suru*】 make the matter worse; grow worse

例 不況で事態はさらに悪化する． The current recession will *make the matter worse.* / 販売の不振が収益の悪化をもたらす． The recent failure of sales will tend to make profits *grow worse.*

あっせん【*assen*】: ＿する procure 例 弊社は競争できる価格で貴社に商品をあっせんできる． We can *procure* goods for you at competitive prices.‖ ～の＿で through the mediation of ～ 例 労組指導者のあっせんでストは回避された． It was *through the mediation of* the union leader that the strike was avoided.

あて名【*atena*】 address 例 手紙を書くさい，あて名ははっきり書かなくてはならない． When you write a letter, you have to write the *address* clearly.‖ ＿を間違って書く wrongly address 例 この封筒のあて名は違う． This envelope is *wrongly addressed.*‖ ＿略号 cable address

後書き【*atogaki*】 postscript; p.s. 例 追伸は手紙の末尾に書かれる． A *postscript* is written at the bottom of the letter.

後回しにする【*atomawashi ni suru*】 leave behind; defer; postpone 例 超過在庫は据え置きにすることが必要だった． It was necessary to *leave behind* the excess stock. / 経営側は会議を後回しすることを決めた． The management decided to *defer* the meeting.

アピールする【*apiiru suru*】 appeal 例 貴社の優れた品質と現代的なデザインが強くアピールしました． The excellent quality and modern design of your goods have *appealed* to us very much.

歩み寄り【*ayumiyori*】 half way 例 先方に歩み寄りの意志がありません． They have no intention to meet us *half way.*

あらかじめ【*arakajime*】 in advance [anticipation] 例 何時たりとも御返礼したいと存じます．まずはあらかじめ御礼申し述べます． We shall always be glad to reciprocate, and thank you *in advance.*

あらゆる努力【*arayuru doryoku*】 one's utmost [best] 例 このようなことが再び起らぬようあらゆる努力をします． We shall do *our utmost* to prevent the recurrence of such an event.

有り難く思う【*arigatakuomou*】be appreciated; be obliged; be grateful [thankful; appreciative] 例 貴社のすぐの御報告有り難く存じます. Your immediate information will *be appreciated.* / その機械の価格をお知らせくだされば有り難く思います. We *are* much *obliged* if you would inform us of the price of the machines. / 1,000ドルの小切手をお送りくだされば まことに有り難く存じます. We shall *be very grateful* to you if you will send us your check for $ 1,000. / 詳しい見本を送っていただき有り難うございました. We *are obliged* to you for sending us the particular samples.

暗号【*angō*】: 公刊—帳 public code book 例 公刊暗号帳はだれでも利用できる. A *public code book* is available to everyone. ‖ 私用—帳 private code book ‖ —で電報を打つ telegraph in [by] code

暗号書【*angōsho*】code book 例 ロンドン発貴電拝見しましたが OSMIJ の暗号は, 当方の暗号書に記載されておりません. Referring to your telegram of London, OSMIJ word is not in our *code book.*

暗号電報【*angō denpō*】code language telegram 例 商品取引の秘密を守るため暗号電報が利用される. *Code language telegram* is utilized to keep a secret of goods trade.

安心する【*anshin suru*】rest assured; assure; be assured; rely on 例 発注くださるいかなる御注文も最善の注意を払いますから御安心ください. You may *rest assured* that order you may place with us will receive our best attention. / 当社の信用状態は東京銀行によって保証されていますから御安心ください. We *assure* you that our credit standing is guaranteed by the Bank of Tokyo. / 本件お指図どおり手配しますから御安心ください. Please *be assured* that the matter will be attended to as instructed.

安着する【*anchaku suru*】arrive safe [safely]; reach in good condition 例 積送品の安着を祈る. We hope that the goods will *arrive safe.*

安定【*antei*】: —させる stabilize 例 政府は, 国の経済成長を安

定させた. The government *stabilized* the nation's economic growth. ‖ —する become stable; be settled **例** 彼は生活が安定している. His life *is settled.*

案内【*an-nai*】: —する advise; inform **例** 下記のとおり船積みの御案内を申し上げます. We will *advise* [*inform*] you of the following shipment. / この商品をさらに供給できることを御案内申し上げます. You *will be interested* to hear that we can offer a further supply of this line. ‖ 出荷— advice of shipment; shipping advice

【い】

遺憾ながら【*ikan-nagara*】 we regret; much to our regret; to our great regret; we express our regret **例** 遺憾ながらお申込条件では注文をお引き受けできません. *Much to our regret,* we are unable to accept your order on the terms offered. / これはまことに遺憾の次第であります. This *we* certainly *regret.* / 遺憾ながらその価格では取り引きは完結できません. *We regret* that the business can't be completed at your prices. / 当方の不完全な包装によって起こった損害に対し深く遺憾の意を表します. *We express our* deep *regret* for the damage caused by our imperfect packing. / 遺憾ながら品物は見本どおりではなかったことがわかりました. *We regret* that we found the goods were not according to the sample. / 悪天候のため遺憾ながら本日商品をお送りすることはできません. *We regret* that we cannot send you the goods today, owing to the bad weather. ‖ —〜をお知らせいたします We are sorry to say that 〜; We inform you with regret that 〜; Much to our regret [To our great regret], we inform you that 〜

異議【*igi*】 objection **例** 船積みに御異議がなければ契約書を送ってください. If you have no *objection* to making shipment, please send us our agreement forms. / 当社の提案に御異議なければ協定書に署名をお願いします. If you have no *objection* to our proposal, please put your signature to the Agreement

on Terms and Conditions. ‖ —なく unanimously **例** その案
は満場異議なく採択された. The proposal was adopted *unani-mously*. ‖ —を唱える object to; protest against; lodge a complaint against

いくぶん 【*ikubun*】 rather; to some extent; to a certain degree;
somewhat **例** 貴社の価格はいくぶん高い. Your prices are
rather high.

意見 【*iken*】 advice; view; opinion **例** 御意見に従いましょう.
We shall follow your *advice*. / この件に関し御意見を承りたい
と存じます. We shall be pleased to learn your *views* on this
matter. / 佐藤氏の信用に関し内密の御意見は貴行に問い合わせ
るよう申し出がありました. We have been referred to your
Bank for confidential *opinion* of the trustworthiness of Mr.
Sato. / 貴社と意見が違う. We have a different *opinion* from
yours. We are not of your *opinion*. / 意見が一致する. We
are of the same *opinion*. We *agree with* you about the
matter. / 見本について十分なテストをしていただいた上で, 御
意見をお聞かせください. Kindly make a thorough test of the
sample and let us have your *opinion*. / 同社の信用状態につ
いて貴社の率直な御意見をお聞かせください. We wish to have
your frank *opinion* on the credit standing of the firm referred to.

意向 【*ikō*】 intention; idea **例** 彼の意向をただした方がよい.
You had better ask his *intention* [*idea*] about it. ‖ —がある
feel inclined to **例** 貴市場において当方製品の販売を引き受け
その販路を拡張してくださる御意向はないかお伺い申し上げま
す. We are writing to inquire whether you would *feel in-clined to* take up and push the sale of our manufactures in
your market. ‖ —にそう meet a person

以上 【*ijō*】 upwards **例** 100ダース以上の注文には, 1ダース当た
りロス建運賃保険料込み価格で45ドルにできます. For an order
of 100 doz., and *upwards*, we could quote you $45 per doz.
C.I.F. Los Angeles.

居座り 【*isuwari*】 unchanged; stationary **例** 市況は居座りであ

る. The market remains *uhchanged*.

急いで 【*isoide*】 in haste; in a hurry; hastily; hurriedly; without delay

急ぐ 【*isogu*】 hasten; hurry; make a hurry; make haste; be in a hurry 例 ～の件取り急ぎ申し上げます. We *hasten* to state you that ～.

委託 【*itaku*】 consignment 例 目下貴殿御委託の品種の引き合いが多くきています. At the moment we have many inquiries for the line of your *consignment*. ‖ ―する consign; entrust something to a person; entrust a person with something 例 その品の販売を当店に委託した. They *consigned* the goods to us. ‖ ―(販売) 品 consignment 例 相当額の委託品を送る. We send you the *consignments* of our goods to a considerable amount. / 貴社の委託販売品は貴社の指し値で売られた. Your *consignments* have been realized at your limits. ‖ ―販売 commission sale; sale on commission [consignment] ‖ ―(販売) で on consignment 例 委託でその品を発送した. They forwarded the goods *on consignment*. / 委託販売で下記商品を送った. We have shipped to you the following goods *on consignment* ‖ ―取引 consignment business ‖ ―加工貿易 processing deal [trade]

いただく 【*itadaku*】 supply 例 その件について何らかの情報をもっておられましたら早急にいただきたく存じます. If you have any information regarding the matter, please *supply* it to us immediately.

著しい 【*ichijirushii*】 remarkable; rapid 例 科学は著しい進歩を遂げた. Science has recently made *remarkable* progress. / 日産トヨタのアメリカへの進出は著しい速度で伸びている. The U.S. imports of Japan's Nissan and Toyota are increasing at a *rapid* rate.

一部 【*ichibu*】 a copy 例 当社のカタログを一部お送りします. We send you *a copy* of our catalog.

一覧 【*ichiran*】: ―後～日払い d/s; D/S; d.s.; D.S.; ～ days after sight 例 貴殿に一覧後60日払いの手形を振り出します.

We shall draw a draft on you at 60 *days after sight*. / 金〜円の
手形一覧後 60 日払いとしてお送りください. Kindly send us the
draft for ¥ 〜 making it payable 60 *days after sight*. ‖ —払
い payable at sight ‖ —払いの手形 draft at sight; sight draft;
S/D; sight bill; demand draft **例** 一覧払いの手形を振り出し
た. We have drawn *a draft at sight*. / 積送品に対し本日送り状
価格〜円, ほか一覧払い手形を取り組みました. なにとぞ提示の
際お引き受け願います. Against this shipment, we have drawn
on you this day a *draft at sight* for the invoice amount of
¥ 〜, which you will please protect on presentation. / 一覧
払い手形の条件で貴方名義信用状 が 開設されるでしょう. They
will open in your favor a letter of credit, providing for a
sight draft.

—律【ichiritsu】: —の(に) flat **例** 手数料として一律に 1 カ月に
つき 1 ドルいただきます. We make it a rule to levy a *flat*
monthly service charge of $ 1. / この町では水の使用量に関係
なく一律料金が課されている. In this town a *flat* rate is charged
for water regardless of the actual quantity used.

—流【ichiryū】: —の leading **例** 当地一流店舗とは全部連絡があ
ります. We are in touch with all the *leading* business houses
here. / 当地一流の輸出商 です. They are *leading* exporters
here. ‖ —商店 reliable dealers **例** 貴社は綿製品を取り扱う一
流商店です. You are one of the *reliable dealers* of cotton
goods. ‖ —商社 leading [first-class] firm; best house; reliable
importers ‖ —品 quality goods; first class article

—式【isshiki】 a full [complete] line of; complete set **例** スポ
ーツ用品一式展示中です. *A full line* of sporting goods is on
display. / A社に複写機一式そろっています. Company A has *a
complete set* of photocopying machines.

—致する【itchi suru】 agree with; accord with; correspond
with; be equal to; be in accordance with **例** 貴社の船積品は
契約と一致していないことが分かった. Your shipments have
turned out to *be* not *in accordance with* contract. / 貴方の記
録と一致すれば上記金額御送金願います. If your figure *agrees*

with ours, you are kindly requested to remit the balance to us. / 注文第28号に対して送付された品物は見本と一致しません. The goods sent in execution of our order No. 28 does not *agree with* your sample.

一手販売 【*itte hanbai*】: —代理店 a sole agency; a sole [exclusive] selling agent 　例　貴社の一手販売代理店になりたい. We are interested in handling *a sole agency* for you. / 彼より貴社が背広用防水サージの一手販売代理店をしていることを承りました. He has given us your name as *sole selling agents* for a waterproof serge for suits. ‖ —代理権 exclusive selling agency 　例　S氏は外国の一流ブドウ酒製造会社3社よりわが国における一手販売代理権を獲得している.　Mr. S has already secured *exclusive selling agencies* in our country for three leading wine brewing companies in foreign countries. ‖ —を行う make an exclusive sale of

一般 【*ippan*】: —の usual; general 　例　この資料は一般の筋からは得られない. This information is not available in the *usual* sources [*general* quarters]. / 他社に一般に認めている条件で信用供与を願う. We would like to be favored with your *usual* credit terms extended to other customers of yours.

移転する 【*iten suru*】 remove 　例　当社は本日上記の所に移転しましたことをお知らせいたします. We inform you that we have *removed* today to the above address.

糸 【*ito*】 yarn (織物，編み物用); thread (縫い糸) 　例　貴見本のような糸は持ち合わせがありません. We are out of the *yarn* like your sample.

以内に 【*inaini*】 within; less than; not more than 　例　10日以内に積み出す take delivery *within* 10 days / 30日以内に銀行に支払いをしなければならぬ. They must pay their bills at the bank *within* 30 days.

意にかなう 【*i-nikanau*】 acceptable; agreeable 　例　契約の条件は両者の意にかなった. The terms of the contract were *agreeable* to both parties.

委任 【*i-nin*】: —する entrust (a person with～) 　例　経営を彼に

委任した．We have entrusted the management to him. ‖ ―状 letter of attorney [procuration]

違反 【ihan】 violation; offence; breach 例 契約違反 *breach* of a contract / それは法律違反だ．It is a *violation* of [*against*] the law. ‖ ―する violate; act against; offend 例 交通規則に違反した．He *violated* the traffic rules. / 法律に違反すると罰せられる．Those who *act against* [*offend*] the law will be punished. ‖ ―して in violation of; against

今に 【imani】 shortly; before long (やがて)

今のところ 【imanotokoro】 at present 例 新しい手袋の在庫は今のところない．There is no stock of new gloves *at present*.

今までは 【imamadewa】 so far; up to now 例 今までは利益の伸びがほとんどない．*So far* there is little advancement in profits. / 生産の水準は今までは成果が上がらなかった．The level of production *up to now* has not been efficient.

依頼 【irai】 request 例 ギブソン商会の依頼により本日送荷した．At the *request* of Messrs. Gibson & Sons, we have delivered to your order. ‖ ―する ask [request] one to do; arrange with 例 信用状開設を当社取引銀行に依頼しました．We have *arranged with* our bankers to open a letter of credit. ‖ ―に応じて in reply to a request

色合い 【iroai】 hue; tint 例 ガラスのきわめて多様な色合いは着色剤によるものです．The wide variety of *hues* and *tints* found in glass are due to the coloring agents.

色よい 【iroyoi】 favorable 例 貴社の色よい返事を期待する．We are looking forward to your *favorable* reply.

引見する 【inken suru】 receive 例 田中氏を御引見くだされば有り難い．I wish to request that you will kindly *receive* Mr. Tanaka.

インコタームス 【inkotāmusu】 International Rules for the Interpretation of Trade Terms; INCOTERMS (貿易条件の解釈に関する国際規則)

印刷物 【insatsubutsu】 literature; print 例 コンピュータ技術にかんする印刷物は広汎にある．The *literature* on computer technology is extensive. / 新在庫品のリストは目下印刷中. The list of new stock is now in *print*. ∥ —在中 Printed Matter

印象【*inshō*】 impression ∥ —を与える impress　例 貴商品がよい印象を与えた. Your goods have *impressed* us favorably. / 当社は貴社に関し, 一取引先からの報告でよい印象を受けております. We are favorably *impressed* by our friend's information concerning your firm.

【う】

請け合う【*ukeau*】 assure; warrant; guarantee　例 貴社に最善の配慮をいたすことを請け合います. We *assure* [*warrant*] you that the same shall have our best attention. / 御通報は厳秘に取り扱うことを請け合います. You are *assured* that anything thus communicated to us will be kept strictly confidential. / この品が上等なことを請け合う. We *guarantee* [*assure* you] that this article is good.

請け負う【*ukeou*】 contract　例 同社は百万ドルで船を請け負った. The company *contracted* for the ship at a million dollars.

承る【*uketamawaru*】 be given; be indebted　例 貴社名および御住所はA氏より承りました. Your name and address have *been given* us by Mr. A.　We *are indebted* for your name and address to Mr. A.

受付【*uketsuke*】: —所 information; an information office [desk]　例 そのことは玄関の受付で尋ねてください. Please ask about the matter at the front *information*. ∥ —係 an usher

受け取る【*uketoru*】 be in receipt of; receive; take　例 7月1日付貴状を受け取りました. We *are in receipt of* [have *received*] your letter of the 1st July. / 同社から次の注文を受け取った. We have *taken* the following order from the company. / 8月11日付引合を受け取りました. We have *received* your enquiry of the 11th August. ∥ 受取済 REC'D [received] ∥ 受け取り帳 R.B. [receipt book]

受［請］ける【*ukeru*】 acknowledge; receive; accept; take ((up))

例 注文を受ける. We *acknowledge* an order.

受け渡し【*ukewatashi*】: ―する deliver **例** 毎月どのくらい受け渡しできるか. How much can you *deliver* per month？‖ ―日 delivery day ‖ ―期日 date for delivery ‖ ―場所 point [place] of delivery

疑わしい【*utagawashii*】 questionable **例** 同社が弊社の条件に同意するかどうか疑わしい. It is *questionable* whether the firm will agree to our terms.

打ち合わせ【*uchiawase*】 arrangement **例** 当社は打ち合わせどおりに行動した. We have acted according to the *arrangements*. ‖ ―る arrange **例** 取引銀行と手形の延期について打ち合わせた. We have *arranged* with our banks to extend the draft. / 取引を始める前に取引条件について打ち合わせたい. Before entering into business, we wish to *arrange* the terms and conditions of business with you.

内金【*uchikin*】: ―として on account **例** 内金として50ポンドの小切手を同封する. We have enclosed cheque for £50 *on account*. / 内金として10万円払った. We paid ￥100,000 *on account*. ‖ ―払 partial payment; payment on account

内訳【*uchiwake*】 items; breakdown; classification **例** 新しい内訳書 the list of new *items* / かかる費用の内訳 a *breakdown* of the costs incurred / 新製品は外国の内訳のところにある. The new products are under foreign *classification*.

写し【*utsushi*】 copy; duplicate **例** 譲渡不能の船荷証券の写し a non-negotiable *copy* of B/L / 船荷証券の写し航空便にて送れ. Send a *duplicate* bill of lading by air.

促す【*unagasu*】 invite [call] attention **例** 次の規則に御注意を促します. Your kind *attention* is *invited* to the following rules. / この問題は多くの人の注意を促した. This problem *called the attention* of many people.

有無【*umu*】 presence or absence **例** 品物の有無にかかわらず貴社と取り引きをしない. In spite of the *presence or absence* of the goods, we will not enter into business relations with you. / 電子計算機はカードやテープにあけた穴の有無のかわりに

回路中の電流の有無を利用する. Electronic computers use the *presence or absence* of current in a circuit instead of the *presence or absence* of holes punched in cards or tape.

埋め合わせ【*umeawase*】：＿に in compensation for 例 損害の埋め合わせにつとめます. I will work for you *in compensation for* the loss.‖ ＿をする make up; make good; recover 例 不足を埋め合わす *make up* for the shortage / 赤字を埋め合わす *make up* the deficit / 失われた信用は埋め合わせがつかない. Credit once lost can never be *made good* [*recovered*].

裏書き【*uragaki*】 endorsement‖ ＿する endorse 例 本状裏面に裏書きする *endorse* on the reverse / 鑑定人は当方の見解を裏書きしてくれるものと信ずる. We are sure that the surveyor will *endorse* our view. / 本信用状引き当てに振り出された手形金額および買取日は買取銀行によって必ず本状裏面に裏書きされること. The amount of each draft drawn under this credit and the date of negotiation must be *endorsed* on the reverse by the negotiating bank.‖ 記名式＿ special endorsement‖ 無記名式＿ general endorsement

売り上げ【*uriage*】 proceeds; sales 例 月間売上が1,000ドルを上回る. The monthly *proceeds* [*sales*] exceed $1,000. / 今月は売り上げが上がった(下がった). The *sales* are up (down) this month. / 正味売上金は貴社勘定貸方へ記帳しました. The net *proceeds* have been placed to the credit of your account.‖ 売上勘定書 account sales‖ ＿高 turnover 例 その結果年間大きな売上高となりましょう. A large annual *turnover* would result.‖ ＿の減少 the loss in sales

売り切れる【*urikireru*】 be sold out; be out of stock (品切れ) 例 その品は売り切れた. The goods have *been sold out* [*are out of stock*]. / この型の品は需要が多くて現在全部売り切れだ. There has been such a demand for this model that our *stock is* entirely *cleared* [our *supply is exhausted*] for the moment. / この品は一時品切れ再補充の期日が分らない. We *are* temporarily *out of* these goods [Our stock *is* temporarily *depleted*], and we can't tell exactly when our supply will be replenished.

売り出し【uridashi】 sale; on sale（売り出し中） 例 その品は目下売り出し中. The goods are *on sale*. / 来る1月10日より16日までの1週間靴の1年1回の割引売出を御案内申し上げます. We take pleasure in announcing our Annual Reduction *Sale* of shoes during the week of January 10-16. / 売り出し品の中には季節向きの新輸入品もあります. *The sale* will include our new importations of seasonable goods that have just arrived.

売り出す【uridasu】 offer for sale; put on the market; place on sale 例 5万ドルで売り出されている家屋の購入を考慮中です. I am now considering the purchase of a house that is *offered for sale* at $ 50,000. / このネジ釘は別のメーカーから売り出されているものと断定できる. We are confident that these screws have been *put on the market* [*placed on sale*] by other manufacturers.

売違御免条件 [先売御免条件付]**【urichigai gomen jōken】** subject to prior sale; subject to being unsold 註 同じ offer をよそにも出すから, よそで売れてしまったら御免を被りたいという条件.

売り手【urite】 seller(s); vendor(s) （契約文） 例 売り手はすべて積み荷に単独海損担保の条件で保険をつけなくてはならない. *Sellers* shall effect marine insurance on all shipments on W.A. [with average]. / 果物の売り手はリンゴを売りに出している. The fruit *vendor* has apples on sale.

売り時【uridoki】 favorable time to sell 例 今が売り時と思わないか. Do you think this is a *favorable time to sell*?

売り申し込み【urimōshikomi】 selling offer; offer 例 5日付貴社の売り申し込み電報引き受けました. We accept your cable *offer* of the 5th.

売る【uru】 sell 例 相手方はいくらで売っているか. At what price are competitors *selling*? ‖ 工場渡しで— sell ex factory ‖ 運賃, 保険料込みで— sell c.i.f. ‖ 現物で— sell on spot 例 バレル当たり5万円で現物売り. The oil is to sell *on spot* for ¥50,000 a barrel. ‖ 競売で— sell by auction ‖ 小売で— sell by retail ‖ 卸で— sell by wholesale

売れ口【*urekuchi*】market　**例** 安い商品は当地では大量の売れ口 があります. At present there is a very large *market* for low-price goods here.

売れ行き【*ureyuki*】sale　**例** 相当の売れ行きがあると思う. We can secure a big *sale* in this line.‖—がよい(悪い)　(do not) sell well; have a good [large](poor) sale; be in good(poor) demand; command a good(poor) sale　**例** この品は売れ行きが よい. The goods are *selling* extremely *well*. / 貴信で当社商品 の売れ行きがよいことを承り大変嬉しく存じます. We are very pleased to note from your letter that our goods have met with a *ready sale*.

売れる【*ureru*】sell [be sold]; be sal(e)able　**例** 貴商品は当市場 でよく売れている. Your goods are *selling* well in our market. / それは飛ぶように売れるだろう. It will *sell* like wildfire. / この 品はもう売れない. These goods *are* not *sal(e)able*.

上回る【*uwamawaru*】exceed; be more [higher] than; be ahead of　**例** 月間売上は 10,000 ドルを上回る状態になった. The monthly proceeds *exceed* $ 10,000 now.

上向傾向【*uwamuki keikō*】tendency upward　**例** 市場相場は著 しく上向傾向で活発です. The market is very brisk with marked *tendency upward*.‖—である go up [high]; trend upward; have an upward direction　**例** 値段は上向傾向にあ る. The price is *going up* [*rising*; *advancing*]. The price *trends upward*. The price *has* [*takes*] *an upward direction* [*tendency*]. The price shows an *advancing tendency* [*a sharp rise*].

運送【*unsō*】transit; transportation　**例** 貨物は運送中. The goods are now in *transit*. / 前回の積送品は運送中に破損した. Your last shipment was damaged in *transit*. / 先般貴方あ て発送の荷物, 運送中に破損したよし遺憾に存じます. We are sorry to hear the goods we forwarded to you have been damaged during *transportation*.‖—する freight; transport; carry　**例** 荷物はトラックで運送された. The goods were *freighted* [*transported*] in a truck. / 船荷はその船で運送され

た. The cargo was *carried* by the vessel. ‖ —取扱業者 forwarding [shipping] agent ‖ —保険 transport insurance ‖ —費 forwarding charge; shipping expenses　例 船をチャーターすれば運賃費は20％安くなる. There is 20 percent reduction of *forwarding charge* by chartering a ship.

運賃【*unchin*】fares; carriage; shipping expenses; freight（貨物）　例 アメリカ旅行を計画中なら運賃の予算を立てておかねばならない. If you are planning a trip to the U.S.A., you must know how much to expect to pay in *fares*. / 貴方で運賃を支払う以上運送店は貴方に対し物品を無事配達する義務 が あ る. As you pay *carriage*, the forwarding agents are responsible to you for safe delivery. ‖ 海上— ocean freight; the freight of marine transportation ‖ 航空— airway freight; the freight of the air transportation ‖ —着払い freight payable at destination ‖ —前払い freight prepaid [paid in advance] ‖ —先払い carriage [freight] forward ‖ —後払い freight collect ‖ —支払済 carriage paid ‖ —込値段 C & F [Cost and Freight]　例 価格は米ドルで神戸港運賃込価格または貴港本船渡し価格のいずれでも結構です. You may quote on *C. & F.* Kobe or F.O.B. your port in U.S. dollars. ‖ —保険料込値段 C.I.F. [Cost, Insurance and Freight]　例 値段は御提案どおり C.I.F. & C. 5％ で出してあります. The price is quoted on *C.I.F.* & C. 5％ as you proposed. / 横浜港までの運賃保険料込価格で，貴社の最良の取引条件を見積ってください. Please quote your best terms *C.I.F* Yokohama. / これらの値段は日本の港本船渡し値段ですが貴社からの御通知があれば，運賃保険料込貴港渡し値段を申し上げることもできます. Please note that these prices are quoted on F.O.B. Japanese port, but we can quote on *C.I.F* your port also upon hearing from you. / 値段は運賃保険料込みニューヨーク渡しを基礎としています. The prices are based no *C.I.F.* New York. Our prices are those on the *C.I.F.* New York basis. The prices quoted are *C.I.F.* New York. We quote you our prices on the basis of *C.I.F.* New York.

運賃率【*unchinritsu*】freight rate; rate of freight　例 運賃率に

ついては弊社横浜店に問い合わせください. As to the *freight rate*, please inquire at our office in Yokohama. / 運賃率をお知らせください. We request you to kindly quote us *the rate of freight*. ‖ —表 freight tariff

運転資金 【*unten shikin*】 working capital; (operating) fund 例 運転資金は多大にあります. They command considerable *funds*.

運転中 【*untenchū*】 in operation; in motion 例 同工場ではロボットが全能力をあげて運転中. The robot is *in* full *operation* in the plant. / 販売政策が目下始動中. The sales policy is now *in motion*. / エレベーターは目下運転中. The elevator is now *working*.

運輸施設 【*unyu shisetsu*】 transportation facility 例 能率のよい運輸施設のおかげで当市は貿易の世界的中心となっている. Thanks to efficient *transportation facilities*, this city has become the trading center of the world.

【え】

英貨 【*eika*】 British money; English currency; sterling 例 東京銀行で英貨に換金できる. The Bank of Tokyo can exchange *English currency*. ‖ —手形 sterling bill; a bill drawn in sterling

営業 【*eigyō*】 business; trade 例 営業を始めて1年になる. We have been in *business* just one year. / 当社の営業様式に同意くださると存じます. We trust you will agree to our mode [manner] of (doing) *business*. / 当社の来年の営業方針 が 決まりました. The *trade* policy of next year of our company is decided. / 商号も営業種目も従前のとおり. We shall continue to *trade* under the same style and on exactly the same lines as heretofore. / 十年来営業の店. This is a firm of ten years' *standing*. / 今期の利益は営業費用も補えない. The profits realized at this season can not cover the *working* expenses. ‖ —する trade; work; establish oneself; carry on business 例 当地で20年営業している. We have *established ourselves* here for twenty years. / 本商店は中田の商号で営業して参りました. This firm has hitherto *carried on business* under the title of Nakata. ‖ —所 representative 例 日本の主要都市に支店や営業所を置いています. We have offices or *representatives* in all major cities and towns in Japan.

絵入り【*eiri*】illustrated 例 絵入りカタログを同封します. Enclosed please find [we send you] an *illustrated* catalogue.

営利会社【*eirigaisha*】a commercial concern; a money-making [lucrative] enterprise

エスクロウ勘定【*esukurou kanjō*】Escrow account 例 貴方エスクロウ勘定に十分資金が残る. Sufficient funds will remain in your *Escrow account*.

延期【*enki*】extension 例 1,000 ポンドの勘定支払いを30日間延期願いたい. We ask you to allow us an *extension* for 30 days for the payment of your account £ 1,000. ‖ —する extend; postpone 例 支払いは3週間延期してよい. The payment may be *extended* for three weeks. / 工事を1週間延期することにした. We have decided to *postpone* the construction work for a week. / 弊社は信用状を4月30日まで延期した. We have *extended* L/C to April 30. / 取引銀行と手形の延期につき打ち合わせた. We have arranged with our banks to *extend* the draft.

縁故【*enko*】connection 例 当社はこの業種において優秀な縁故をもっていないわけでもない. We are not without good *connections* in this line.

援助【*enjo*】assistance ‖ —する assist 例 同社のために何かと御援助くだされば有り難い. We should be much obliged if you would *assist* them in any way. Any *assistance* that you may render them will be highly appreciated.

延長【*enchō*】extension 例 2月3日期限の勘定65万円也につき30日間支払いを延長ねがいます. We ask you to allow us an *extension* for 30 days for the payment of our account ¥ 650,000 due February 3. ‖ —する extend 例 期間を延長しても構わない. We can *extend* the term. / このような事情です

から，何とぞ信用状の有効期限を9月末日まで延長してください．Under the circumstances, please *extend* the expiry date of the Letter of Credit until the end of September.

円手形【*en tegata*】 yen bill; a bill drawn in yen　例 米国の会社は負債を円手形で支払った．The American company paid the debt with *a bill drawn in yen.*

円満【*enman*】: ——な（に）perfect(ly); peaceful(ly); amicable(-bly) 例 円満な妥結 *amicable* agreement / 彼は円満な人柄だ．He is a man of *perfect* character. / その問題は円満に解決した．The trouble has been settled *peacefully.* ‖ ——にやる get along well with 例 彼は同僚得意先と円満な関係を続けるだけの社交性をもち合わせている．He has adequate sociability that enables him to *get along well with* his colleagues and customers.

遠慮【*enryo*】 reserve; hesitation　例 遠慮なくお尋ねください．Please ask us *without reserve* [*unreservedly*]. ‖ ——する be reserved; refrain from; hesitate　例 彼の招待を遠慮した．We declined his invitation. / 当店の商品や奉仕振りに関してお心付きの点があれば遠慮なくお申し越しください．Please *feel free* to write us at any time concerning our goods or our service. / さらにお役に立てることがあれば，御遠慮なくお知らせください．If there is anything more we can do for you, please do not *hesitate* to let us know.

【お】

大口【*ōkuchi*】 big; large; considerable　例 貴社の値段が適当なら大口の注文をしましょう．If your prices are reasonable, we shall place *considerable* orders [*big* order; a *large* order] with you. / 当社の主要取扱品は鉄材で，取引はみな大口のものばかりです．Our main line of business is iron material, almost all transactions are *large.* / 貴社が寄せられた引き合いは当社創業以来例のない大口のものです．From your company we have received this time an enquiry for the *largest* quantity throughout our history.

応じる【*ōjiru*】comply with；agree to　**例**　御要求に応じかねます．We cannot *comply with* your request. / 貴社の支払条件に応じられない．We cannot *comply with* your terms of payment. / 貴社がそれに応じるかどうか知りたい．We would like to know if you would *agree to* it. ‖ に応じて in compliance with　**例**　御請求に応じて見本を送ります．*In compliance with* your request, we send you samples.

応用する【*ōyō suru*】apply　**例**　デザインに関する知識と技術面での経験のすべてを当社の新製品に応用しました．We have *applied* all our design knowledge and craftmanship experience to our new lines.

往復【*ōfuku*】：—切符 a return ticket　**例**　同社は東京ニューヨーク間の往復切符の支払いをした．The company paid for a *return ticket* from Tokyo to New York. ‖ —はがき a return postcard ‖ —文書 letters exchanged　**例**　往復文書は生産者と小売商の間で交わされた．The *letters* were *exchanged* between the producer and the retailer. ‖ —運賃 freight out and home　**例**　往復運賃の日数は3日間．The time taken for the *freight out and home* was 3 days.

おかげ【*okage*】：—で by；through；thanks to　**例**　おかげでこんなに元気になりました．*Thanks to* your help, I am now in such good spirits. / 能率のよい運輸施設のおかげでニューヨークは世界の貿易の中心となっている．*Thanks to* efficient transportation facilities, New York has become the trading center of the world. ‖ —を被る be indebted to

送り状【*okurijō*】invoice　**例**　綿花50俵の送り状を同封したからお受け取りください．Enclosed please find an *invoice* of the 50 bales raw cotton. / 送り状金額5,000ドルに対し都合つき次第早く送金ください．For the *invoice* amount, vis., $5,000, we shall be glad to have your remittance at your earliest convenience. Please send us your remittance as early as possible for the *invoice* amount, $5,000. / 送り状価格の110％に対して付保する．Covering for 110％ of *invoice* value. / 鎌倉丸積荷送り状着かない．Have received no *invoice* for shipment on the M/S "Kamakura Maru. ‖ 商業― commercial invoice ‖ 領事― consular invoice ‖ ―を作る (make an) invoice 例 この注文は横浜運賃保険料込みとして送り状を作ってください. This order is to be *invoiced* C.I.F. Yokohama.

送る【*okuru*】 ship; dispatch; send 例 品物を速達便で送った. We *shipped* the goods by express. / 品物は早速鉄道便で貴社あて送った. The goods were at once *dispatched* by rail to your address. / 機械のカタログを送る. We *send* you a catalog of machines. / お送りする品物の値段は現金払いを基準にして算出してあります. We have quoted the price of the goods we *send* you on a cash payment basis.

遅れる【*okureru*】 be late (for); be behind; be delayed 例 支払いが遅れる *be behind* with payment / 船積みに 5 日遅れる *be* five days' *late* for shipment / 航空機は予定より 10 分遅れて成田空港に着いた. The airplane arrived at Narita Airport ten minutes *behind* schedule. / 船は暴風のため 5 時間遅れた. The ship was *delayed* five hours by the storm.

行う【*okonau*】 conduct; handle 例 貿易を行う *engage in* a trading business / 指定の代理店を通じて取り引きを行います. We *conduct* business there through appointed representatives.

納める【*osameru*】 supply 例 品物は速やかに納めることができる. We can *supply* the goods within a reasonable time.

汚損【*oson*】 contamination 例 汚損のないよう注意. Take care to avoid *contamination*.

お互いのため【*otagai no tame*】 to one's mutual benefit 例 それはお互いのために有利な商売になりますから御安心ください. You may rest assured that it will turn out a profitable business *to our mutual benefit*.

落ち込む【*ochikomu*】 slump 例 フォルクスワーゲンの売れ行きは落ち込みつつある. The sales of Volkswagen are actually *slumping*.

乙仲【*otsunaka*】(乙種海運仲立人) shipping broker; forwarding agent 例 直積みが御希望なので早速乙仲に当たりました. As prompt shipment is required, we immediately contacted the *forwarding agent.*

劣る【*otoru*】 be inferior; do not come up　**例** 現品は見本より劣ります. The goods *do not come up* to the sample. / これはあれより質が劣る. This *is inferior* to that in quality. / 品質がまったく見本より劣っていますから商品をお引き受けできません. We can not accept the goods as they *are* altogether *inferior* in quality to the sample. / 標準品より品質が劣る. The goods *are inferior* in quality to the standard.

オファー【*ofā*】 offer　**例** 反対オファーする make a counter *offer* / オファーを更新する renew an *offer* / オファーを撤回する withdraw an *offer* / このオファーを引き受けるのが得策です. We can strongly recommend you to accept this *offer*. / 下記商品に対し4日以内の御回答を条件としてファームオファーします. We make you a firm *offer* on the following goods subject to your reply being received within four days. We *offer* you firm the following goods for reply reaching in four days. / この商品は需要が多いため当社はこのオファーをこのまま有効にしておくことはできません. このオファーは早い者勝ちにします. Since the goods are in great demand, we can't hold this *offer* open; therefore we are obliged to make the *offer* subject to being unsold. / このオファーを受け取り後4日以内に引き受けくださるかどうか電報でお知らせください. Please inform us by cable within 4 days after your receipt of this *offer*, whether you can accept this offer or not. / 万一貴社がこのオファーを引き受けられないなら当分この品は入手できないでしょう. If you fail to accept the present *offer*, you will be unable to get the goods for some time. ‖ ―する offer　**例** 7月12日金曜日正午までにお引き受けを条件として次のとおりファームオファーいたします. We *offer* you firm the following goods for acceptance by noon, Friday, the 12th July. / 多くの競争会社が安値でオファーしている. A number of competitors are *offering* cheaper prices.

覚え書き【*oboegaki*】 memo; memorandum; note; written agreement　**例** 貴社お買い付けに関する覚え書き3部を同封します.

Enclosed are 3 copies of the *memorandum* of your purchases. / 取引覚書を2通同封します．We are enclosing the *memorandum* of Terms and Conditions of Business in duplicate.

思う【omou】 think; consider; regard; suppose; guess; wish; deem　**例** 貴社に御通知することを義務と思います．We *deem* it our duty to inform you. / その申し込みを詳しく考えてみる必要があった．It was necessary to *consider* his application in detail.

折り返し【orikaeshi】 by return　**例** 折返便で有利な御返事をお待ちしています．We are looking forward to having your favorable reply *by return* of mail. / 折返便で送り状金額の送金を願います．Please give us a remittance covering invoice amount *by return* (of mail). / 折り返し注文書をお送りします．We will send you our order *by return*. / 折り返し3,000ドル御送金ください．Please let us have your cheque for $3,000 *per return*. / 折り返し御返事をお待ちしています．Your kind reply *by return* is awaited.

織物【orimono】 fabric; textile　**例** 絹織物の見本をここに同封します．We enclose herewith the patterns of our silk *fabrics*. / 本品は新製品の織物です．This is a new line of *fabrics*. / 一級の保証付き織物に限って納品します．We supply only first-class and guaranteed *fabrics*. ‖ —業 drapery ‖ —工業 textile industry ‖ 織地 texture ‖ 織糸 yarn

卸し売り【oroshiuri】 (商) wholesale(r)　**例** 当社は欧州各国の卸商によく知られています．We are well known by all the *wholesalers* of all the states in Europe. / 会計主任として卸商店に5年雇われていた．I was employed for five years by a *wholesale* house as an accountant. ‖ 卸相場 wholesale price ‖ —業者 wholesaler; wholesale dealer

【か】

買い上げ【*kaiage*】(る) purchase　例 買上品 the goods *purchased* by you; your *purchase* / 御高覧のほどお願い申し上げます. お買い上げは御随意です. Your inspection is respectfully invited. *Purchase* is not compulsory. / 買上代金支払いのため小切手を送ります. We will send a cheque to you for the *purchase*.

外貨【*gaika*】foreign currency [funds]　例 イランの外貨はほとんど石油でまかなわれる. Most of Iran's *foreign funds* are provided by petroleum. ‖ —予算 foreign exchange budget ‖ —割当 foreign exchange allocation

海外【*kaigai*】overseas　例 海外通信 *overseas* correspondence / A社の佐藤さんは海外勤務に決まった. Mr. Sato of A Company has been concluded the *overseas* service.

開業［店；設］する【*kaigyō suru*】establish; open; found　例 本日上記の所に一般輸出入業を開店しました. We take pleasure in announcing that we have this day *established* ourselves as General Importers and Exporters at the above address. / 本日各種綿製品の委託販売を目的とする商社を開設いたしました. We wish you to know that today we have *opened* [*founded*] a trading firm for the sale and purchase on commission of all classes of Cotton Goods. / スイス製タイプライターの輸入商として開業いたしました. We have been *established* as Importers of Swiss Typewriter. / 当社は日本製商品の輸入出商として開業いたしました. We have *established* as Importers and Exporters of Japanese Goods.

会計【*kaikei*】account　例 その会計係が会計監査をした. The *accountant* made an audit of the *accounts*. / 会計が合わない. *Accounts* do not balance. ‖ —監査役 auditor ‖ —係 accountant　例 今朝の新聞に御広告の会計係の地位に申し込みをいたします. I wish to apply for the position of *accountant* which you advertised in this morning's paper.

解決【*kaiketsu*】settlement　例 この解決を受諾されるのがお得な

ことを分かっていただけると信じます. We trust that you will see the advantage in accepting this *settlement*. ‖ —する solve; settle 例 問題を円満に解決する *solve* a problem [*settle a matter*] peacefully / 貴社が懸案のクレームを解決するのを望む. We hope you will *settle* the pending claim. / 裁判で解決するよりほかない. We have no other way but to *submit* this matter to the court.

外国【*gaikoku*】: —為替手形 foreign bill of exchange 例 輸入品を入手する前に外国為替手形を必要とした. A *foreign bill of exchange* was necessary before the imported goods could be picked up. ‖ —為替相場 foreign exchange rate 例 アメリカの為替相場が上がってきている. There has been a rise in the American *foreign exchange rate*. ‖ —為替資金 foreign exchange fund ‖ —債 foreign loan

解雇する【*kaiko suru*】 dismiss; discharge 例 彼は解雇された. He was *dismissed* from our service. / 少々不都合のかどがあったので解雇しました. We have *discharged* him from our service owing to his unsatisfactory conduct.

外資 【*gaishi*】 foreign capital [funds] 例 外資事情 position of *foreign capital* / 豪州における米外資の額は非常に高い. The amount of American *foreign capital* in Australia is very high. / 第2次大戦後日本に外資が導入された. After World War II there was an introduction of *foreign capital* into Japan.

開始する 【*kaishi suru*】 begin; enter into ((business)); open; start; commence 例 交渉は来週始まる. Negotiations will *begin* next week. / A社は政府と取り引きを始めなかった. Company 'A' did not *enter into business* with the government.

概して 【*gaishite*】 on the whole; generally 例 貴社の条件は概して寛容である. Your terms are very generous *on the whole*. / 概して物価は最近下がった. *Generally* speaking, prices have fallen of late.

会社 【*kaisha*】 company; firm 例 当社は歴史の古い大きな日本の貿易会社です. We are an old and large trading *company* in Japan. / 同社は産業に対する特筆されるべき奉仕に対して有

名な賞をもらった．The *firm* has received a well-known award for its distinguished services to the industry.

回収【*kaishū*】 recovery; collection 例 貸し金の回収 *collection of loans* / 回収のため法的手続を取らねばならない．We must have recourse to legal proceedings for the *recovery*. ‖ ―する withdraw; collect

解除【*kaijo*】 cancellation 例 メーカーは解除のおそれがあるので信用状到着まで注文に取り掛からない．Makers will not proceed with any order until the arrival of the L/C for fear of possible *cancellation*. ‖ ―する cancel; rescind 例 契約を解除するかどうか至急電報でお知らせください．Let us know by cable immediately whether you will *cancel* the contract or not. / 弊社は契約を解除する権利を留保する．We reserve the right to *rescind* the contract.

回状【*kaijō*】 circular 例 貴回状拝受．We are in receipt of your *circular*. ‖ ―を回す circulate

海上保険【*kaijō hoken*】 marine insurance 例 貴社と海上保険契約を結ぶ．We effect *marine insurance* with you. ‖ ―証券 marine insurance policy; M.I.P. ‖ ―業者 underwriter

開設【*kaisetsu*】 establishment; opening 例 開設銀行 *opening bank* / 当地東京銀行を通じて，貴社を受益者とする金額 36,000 ドルの信用状を開設いたしました．We have *opened* a Letter of Credit in your favor for $ 36,000 through The Bank of Tokyo here. / 当方注文品に対する信用状が届かないので至急開設されたい．We have not received the letter of credit covering our order and we request you to *establish* it without delay. ‖ ―する open; establish 例 貴社あてに信用状を開設した．We have *opened* a letter of credit in your favor. / 陶磁器製作所を開設しました．We have *established* a porcelain factory.

改善【*kaizen*】 improvement 例 それは大いに改善の余地がある．It leaves much room for *improvement* [*amelioration*]. ‖ ―する improve 例 市況は改善された．The market condition has been *improved*.

回送する【*kaisō suru*】 pass on; transport 例 貴社の製品が回

送されてきた. Your goods have been *passed on* [*transported*] to us.

回漕【*kaisō*】 shipping; forwarding 　例 回漕業 *shipping* business / 当店は回漕および通関代理店として御用命を承ります. We offer you our services as *forwarding* and customs agents. ‖ ─業者 (問屋) forwarding agent; freight forwarder / コンテナは回漕会社を通じて送られた. The containers were sent through a *shipping agent*.

海損【*kaison*】 average; sea damage 　例 共同海損 general *average* / A会社に単独海損不担保にて付保願います. Effect insurance with A Company free of particular *average*.

買い付け【*kaitsuke*】 indent; purchase 　例 買付契約書 *purchase* agreement / いくらの手数料で買い付けを受諾願えますか. At what commission do you accept the *indent*? / 当地にてお買い付けの御用がありましたら御下命願います. We offer you our services for any *purchase* you may have to make here. / 我社は700トンの買い付けの条件を記載した8月5日付の貴社の手紙を受け取った. We have received your letter dated August 5, covering terms of *purchase* of 700 tons. ‖ ─書 purchase note 　例 当社買付書第58号を同封で御送付申し上げます. We send you herewith our *Purchase Note* No. 58. / 買付書第12号ならびに関係電文の写しをここに同封します. We are sending you herewith our *Purchase Note* No. 12 together with the copies of relative cables. ‖ ─る purchase 　例 お求めの数量をオファー値段で買い付けることは無理です. It would not be possible for us to *purchase* the quantity at the price you offer.

買い手【*kaite*】 buyer; purchaser 　例 買い手を確保しようと努力した. We tried to secure a *buyer*.

書いてある【*kaite aru*】 write 　例 15日付貴状の中に書いてあることは3日付貴状といくぶん異なっています. What you *write* in your letter of the 15th is rather different from your letter of the 3rd. / 貴状に書いてあることをまったく理解できません. We cannot understand the argument *employed* [*explained*; *expressed*; *given*] in your letter.

改訂 [定]【*kaitei*】（する）revise 囫 改訂されたカタログを送ります．We send you our *revised* catalog. / この本は最近改訂された．This book has recently been *revised*. / 当社は商品の価格を改定した．We *revised* the prices of our lines. / 手紙の中のすべての締めくくりの文節が改訂された．All of the closing paragraphs in the letters were *revised*. / 貴社が値段を改定しなければ，当社はよそへ注文しなければならない．Unless you *revise* prices, we shall have to place our order elsewhere.

回転【*kaiten*】turnover 囫 資金の回転 *turnover* of funds / 在庫の回転を増大することが必要だ．It is necessary to increase the *turnover* of the stock. ‖ —信用状 revolving L/C

解読する【*kaidoku suru*】decode 囫 貴社の暗号電信を下記のごとく解読しました．We *decoded* your cypher code as below.

買い取り【*kaitori*】negotiation ‖ 買い取る negotiate 囫 買い取り銀行が保証する be a warranty by the *negotiating* bank / この手形を買い取ってください．Please *negotiate* this draft. / 当方振出手形を東京銀行で買い取ってもらった．We *negotiated* our draft with The Bank of Tokyo. / 東京銀行によって手形が買い取られた．Our draft was *negotiated* with The Bank of Tokyo.

海難【*kainan*】peril of the sea 囫 保険証券は海上で起こる全危険をてん補するのでなく実際の海難の直接の結果だけをてん補する．The policy does not cover all perils on the sea but only those which are the direct result of actual *perils of the sea*. ‖ —に会う meet with a disaster at sea

買い控える【*kaihikaeru*】buy sparingly 囫 茶の値段はまだ底を突いておらずむしろ買い控え気味です．The price of tea has not reached the bottom, so they *are buying sparingly*.

回復【*kaifuku*】（相場）rally；recovery ‖ —する rally 囫 市場は本年後半来回復し始めたように思われる．Market seems to have begun to *rally* since the middle of the year.

解約【*kaiyaku*】（する）cancel 囫 同品が6月末までに入手できなければ，本注文を解約する権利を留保します．Unless the goods are in our hands by the end of June, we reserve the right to *cancel* this order.

改良【*kairyō*】improvement **例** 目立った改良 distinctive *improvement* / 新しい機械やその改良あるいは新しい方法を発明した人は出願してその特許を受けることができる. A person who has invented a new machine, *improvement* thereof, or a new process, may make an application and obtain a patent. / これ以上改良の余地がない. There is no room for further *improvement* on it. / 新発売の機械の種々の改良点はカタログに記してある. The various *improvements* which we have introduced in our new machines are described in our catalog. ‖ —する improve **例** 改良型 improved model / 車はたえず改良が加えられている. Cars are constantly being *improved*. / 製造方法の改良によって卓上電算機を今までより安い値段で提供できるようになりました. *Improved* production methods have allowed us to offer you our Electronic Calculators at lower prices than before.

買う【*kau*】buy; purchase **例** 下記商品をお買い付けください. Please *purchase* the undernoted goods. / 彼はその品を千円で買った. He *bought* the article for 1,000 yen. / 彼はそれを1ダースあたり500円で買った. He *bought* them at 500 yen a dozen. ‖ 高 (安) く— buy dear (cheap); buy at a high (low) price ‖ 買い過ぎる overbuy **例** 買い過ぎが当社の陥りやすい欠点です. *Overbuying* seems to be a liable fault in our firm.

価格【*kakaku*】price; quotation **例** 価格は米ドルをもって保険料, 運賃込みで見積ること. *Prices* are to be quoted in U.S. dollars on the basis of C.I.F. / 弊社の価格は貴市場のいかなる競争にも対抗できます. Our *price* can meet any competition in your market. / 貴社の価格を検討しました. We have investigated your *quotation*. / 価格は据え置いたままです. We have not yet raised our *prices*. / 今までどおりの条件で婦人用スカーフを貴社の最低値[価格]で供給ください. Please furnish us with your lowest *quotations* for the Ladies' Scarfs on usual terms and conditions. / 学童用靴下の最低価格を知らせください. Please quote lowest *prices* on Children's School

Stockings. / 至急価格表の写しを送ってください。 Please send us a copy of *price* list immediately. / 価格表を同封しました。 Enclosed is our *price* list. / 同封の価格表から当社の価格は他社と比較してはるかに安いことが分かるでしょう。 The *price* list enclosed will show you that our *prices* are far more competitive than those of other firms. / 元の価格で売ることは難しい。 It is difficult to sell our goods at the original *price*. / 業者が価格引き上げの形で税を消費者に転稼していることは確実だ。 It is certain that the traders will pass the tax on the consumer in the form of higher *prices*. ‖ 購入— purchasing price ‖ 卸売— wholesale price ‖ 小売— retail price ‖ 現在の— present [current; ruling] price ‖ 従来の— the old prices; prices previously quoted ‖ —協定 price cartel ‖ 見積— estimated price ‖ 査定— appraised value [price] ‖ 公定— official price ‖ 最低輸出— check price; floor price

係員【kakari-in】 clerk 　**例** 調査したところ発送課の新任係員が数字を読み違えたことが判明した。 Our investigation has disclosed that a figure was misread by a new *clerk* in the forwarding section. / 調査の結果当方出荷係員が数を読み違えたことが分かりました。 On investigation we find that our shipping *clerk* misread the number.

書留【kakitome】 registered mail 　**例** 貴下の親展を願うためこの手紙を書留郵便で送ります。 To make sure this is brought to your personal attention, we take the trouble to send this letter by *registered mail*. / この手紙を書留にしていただきたい。 I want to have this letter *registered*. / 弊社注文書は書留にて送ります。 Our order sheet will be sent *registered*. ‖ 別封—で under separate and registered cover 　**例** 別封書留で株券百枚送りました。 *Under separate and registered cover*, we have sent you 100 share certificates.

下記【kaki】: —の following; undermentioned 　**例** 下記の品を提供ねがいます。 Please supply us with the *following* goods. / 下記商品に対し，5日以内の御回答を条件としてファーム・オファーいたします。 We offer you firm the *following* goods for reply

reaching within 5 days. / 下記の者は事務所に出頭されたい.
Those *undermentioned* shall appear in the office in person. ‖
―のとおり as follows　**例** 詳細は下記のとおりです. The details
are *as follows*.

確信する【*kakushin suru*】trust; be [become; feel] confident
例 価格切り下げに努力くださるものと確信します. We *trust*
you will make every effort to revise your prices. / 値打ちも
のであることを確信なさると存じます. You will *become confident* of its value. / 商品は特に貴市場向輸出用に作ったので
貴社の御賛成を得ることを確信しております. The goods are
specially manufactured for export to your market, and we
are confident that they will meet with [win] your approval. /
貴社がこのオファーをお受けくださることを確信していま す.
We *trust* that you will accept this offer. / 大量注文があるこ
とを確信します. We *feel confident* that large orders will be
followed. / その商品に満足なさるものと確信します. We *are
confident* that you will be satisfied with the goods.

拡張する【*kakuchō suru*】extend　**例** ヨーロッパ全域に販売を拡
張したいと存じます. We wish to *extend* sales over the whole
Europe.

確定売り申し込み【*kakutei uri mōshikomi*】firm offer　**例** 月
曜終日有効の確定売り申し込みあれ. Make *firm offer*, holding
good all day Monday. ‖ ―する offer firm　**例** 貴社の即時引受
条件で確定売り申し込みをする. We *offer firm* subject to your
immediate acceptance.

確定保険証券【*kakutei hoken shōken*】valued policy

確定申し込み【*kakutei mōshikomi*】firm offer　**例** 下記商品を確
定申し込みします. We make you *firm offer* on the following
goods.

確認【*kakunin*】acknowledgment; confirmation　**例** 注文確認書
をお送りください. Kindly let us have the *confirmation* of
this order. / 上記条件の確認は4月末までとなっています. Your
confirmation of the above conditions is required not later
than the end of April. ‖ ―する acknowledge (他人の書面を確

認する）; confirm（自己の書面を確認する）　**例**　その条件を確認
しました. We *confirmed* the condition. / 1 月 15 日付貴社の電
報注文を確認します. We *confirm* your cable order of January
15. / 7 月 2 日付弊電 および 7 月 3 日付貴電を 確認します.　We
are glad to *confirm* our cable of July 2 and *acknowledge* your
cable of July 3. / 当社 3 月 1 日付電信注文を受諾された旨の 3
月 10 日付貴信を拝受. We *acknowledge* your telegram of March
1, accepting our cable order of March 10. / これが受諾できる
か御確認ください. Please *confirm* if this is acceptable to you.

確認銀行【*kakunin ginkō*】confirming bank　**例**　東京銀行がロー
ンの確認銀行. The Bank of Tokyo is the *confirming bank* in
the loan.

確認信用状【*kakunin shinyōjō*】confirmed letter of credit　**例**
銀行確認信用状による一覧後 60 日払為替手形.　Draft at 60 d/s
under *confirmed letter of credit*.

確保する【*kakuho suru*】reserve; secure; lay aside; earmark　**例**
貴社の分を確保します. We shall *reserve* the goods for you. /
輸入を確保することが当社にとって最重要である. It is now
most important for us to *secure* imports. / お申し出の値段で
この取り引きを確保することは困難です. It is difficult for us
to *secure* this business at the price you proposed.

確約【*kakuyaku*】assurance　**例**　貴商品を他社に販売しないという
確約を貴社にしていただきたい. We want your *assurance* that
you will not sell your products to other firms. ‖ —する assure
例　この件につき貴社に確約できます. We can *assure* you of
this fact.

格安品【*kakuyasuhin*】an exceptional bargain; a very low-priced
article

掛け【*kake*】credit　**例**　それを掛けで買った. We bought them
on *credit*. / それを掛けで売った. We sold them on *credit*. ‖ —
売り credit sales ‖ —勘定にする charge the amount to one's
account　**例**　それはわたしの掛けにしておいてください. Please
charge it *to my account*.

火災保険【*kasai hoken*】fire insurance ‖ 家屋に—をつける insure

a house against fire; a house is insured for fire ～

貸方【kashikata】 credit side 例 小切手は，貸借対照表の貸方に
入れられた．The cheque was entered into the *credit side* of
the balance sheet. ‖ ―勘定 credit account 例 貸方勘定が銀
行で開かれた．A *credit account* was opened at the bank.

過失【kashitsu】 blame 例 過失がいずれにあるか早速調査します．
We shall ascertain where the *blame* and responsibility should
rest.

貸し付け【kashitsuke】 loan 例 銀行は保証がある場合のみ貸し付
けを行う．The bank will make *loans* only when they carry
a guarantee.

貨車渡し【kashawatashi】 free on rail (way)；F.O.R. 例 その商
品は貨車渡し．The goods are only *free on rail*.

課する【kasuru】 levy tax against～；levy；charge；assess 例
品物または取引に対して課税する *levy* a duty on an article or
a transaction / ～に輸入税を課す *assess* import duty upon ～

課税【kazei】 taxation；levy (tax) 例 輸入車に対する課税 *levy*
tax against imported cars / 最近ホームローンに対する課税の
増加がみられる．There has been a recent *levy* increase in
housing loans. ‖ ―品 taxable [dutiable] article

型【kata】 model 例 貴社の商品の各種の型について御一報くださ
い．Please let us know about the various *models* of your
goods.

カタログ【katarogu】 catalog 例 全カタログを一部送ります．We
are sending a copy of our complete *catalog*. / 御依頼によりカ
タログを航空便で送りました．According to your request, we
have sent *catalogs* by air. / 貴社の広告を拝見，カタログそのほ
か参考資料ならびに貴社の取引条件をお知らせください． Your
advertisement interests us, and we would appreciate your
sending us the related *catalog*, or any other literature
treating of the product, together with your full terms. / カタ
ログを同封します．Enclosed please [you will] find a *catalog*. /
7月1日付お手紙にて御請求（御希望，お指図）のとおりカタロ
グ一部同封します．As requested (desired；instructed) in your

letter of July 1, we are inclosing a copy of our *catalog*. / 貴
社最近のカタログ 1 部および定価表をお送りください．We ask
you to send us a copy of your latest *catalog* and a price
list. / カタログに示された図解説明に満足している．We are
satisfied with the illustration in your *catalog*. 国 小冊子
leaflet(s); pamphlet(s); literature

価値【*kachi*】value 例 この品は価値がない．This article is of
no *value* [useless]. ‖ ─のある valuable; worth ‖ 非常に─のあ
る invaluable; priceless 例 1,000 円の価値のある品 article
worth 1,000 yen / その価値を確信できるでしょう．You will
become confident of its being *valuable*.

がっかりする【*gakkari suru*】be disheartened; be disappointed;
be discouraged; lose heart 例 御返事がないのでがっかりして
います．We *are disheartened* by silence. / それを聞いてがっか
りしました．I *was disappointed* [*disheartened*] to hear it. / が
っかりするにはまだ早い．It is still too early to *lose heart*
[*be discouraged*].

勝手ながら【*kattenagara*】: ─～する take the liberty of [in; to]
例 見本を御点検願うため勝手ながらここに同封いたします．
We *take the liberty to* enclose the patterns herewith for your
inspection. / 勝手ながらお手紙を差し上げます．We *take the
liberty of* [*in*] writing to you. / テキサス産小麦の見本を勝手な
がらお送りします．We *take the liberty to* send you the sample
of wheat produced in Texas. / 勝手ながら貴地 A 商会の財務状
態をお尋ねします．We *take the liberty of* asking your views
on the financial standing of A Co. of your city.

活動地域【*katsudō chiiki*】business territory 例 当代理店の活動
地域は太平洋沿岸からロッキー山脈までです．This agent has
business territories from the Pacific Coast to the Rocky
Mountains.

活発【*kappatsu*】briskness; animation 例 漁網の輸出は昨年の後
半以来引き続き活発である．The Netting's export continued
animation since the latter part of last year. ‖ ─な active;
brisk; firm 反 dull 例 市況は活発である．The market is

active. / 本商品に対して南米で活発な需要が あ る．There is a *brisk* demand for this line in South America.

合併【*gappei*】(会社) amalgamation ‖ ─する unite; amalgamate; be incorporated with; absorb; merge ((into)); affiliate ((to)) 例 それは新設の会社に合併された．It has been *absorbed* in the recently formed company. / 従来後藤商店および太田商会の名義で営業を続けてきた2商社は本日合併，後藤商会の商号を用います．The two firms which have carried on business hitherto under the titles of Goto and Ota & Co, will be *united* from this date under the style of Goto & Co. / 2社は6月1日以後山田商会の名義の下に合併します．On and after the 1st June two firms will *amalgamate* under the style of Yamada & Co.

家庭【*katei*】family; household 例 今回家庭の都合で貴市に移ることになりました．Now I am forced by *family* needs to move to your town. / 当社は家庭用電気製品の輸出に17年の経験があ る．We have 17 years' experience in the export of *household* electric appliances. / 家庭用電気器具の小型のものに需要は活発です．There is a lively demand for the smaller type of *household* electric appliances.

架電する【*kaden suru*】cable; dispatch [send] telegram [cable] 例 本日架電した弊店値段は最低値です．Our price *cabled* today is the lowest. / 本日貴社あて下記の架電をした旨確認申し上げます．We confirm having *dispatched* to you the following *telegram.* We wish to confirm having *cabled* you today as follows. We confirm our *cable dispatched* today reading ～. We have pleasure in confirming our *cable dispatched* to you today as specified below.

過当な【*katōna*】excessive 例 国内市場における過当 競 争 は 海外市場においても同じように繰り返されてい る．The *excessive* competition in the domestic market is duplicated in foreign markets. / 航空会社の利益は大幅に落ちています．その主な原因は航空会社間の過当競争にあるといわれてい る．The airlines are suffering from a serious decline in profits. The main

cause is said to be the *excessive* competition in this industry. /
玩具の価格の低さは玩具製造に従事する中小企業間の過当競争に
よる面が大きい. The lower prices of toys have been largely
caused by *excessive* competition among medium and small-
sized businesses [minor enterprises] engaged in toy manufacture.

かなり【*kanari*】fairly; pretty; substantial; considerable　囫 ブ
ラジルではかなりの数の車を自国で製造している. Brazil makes
a *substantial* [*considerable*] number of its own vehicles. / 生
産を続けていさえすれば, かなりの利益が得られる状態です.
They can make *considerable* profits only if they keep manufacturing. / 彼は毎月かなりの金を本に使う. He spends a *considerable* sum of money on books every month.

加入する【*kanyū suru*】admit; join　囫 林氏を組合員に加入させ
た. We have *admitted* to partnership Mr. Hayashi. / 彼はそ
の旅行団体に加入した. He *joined* the tourist party.

株【*kabu*】share; stock　囫 弊社は株式会社に変更します. We
are turned into a *joint-stock* company. / その会社は20万株で
組織された. The company was formed with 200,000 *shares*. ‖
—主 stockholder　囫 株主は株主総会で投票する権利をもつ.
Stockholders have the right to vote at the general meeting. ‖
—価の変動 fluctuation in the price of stocks ‖ —価 stock price
‖ —式仲買店 stock broker ‖ —式取引所 stock exchange ‖ —の
名義を書き換える transfer stock certificate ‖ —式市場 stock
market　囫 会社は株式市場の変動に神経をつかう. The firm
are nervous of the fluctuations of the *stock market*.

過不足【*kafusoku*】more or less　囫 5％の過不足は売り手の任意
5％ *more or less* at seller's option / 過不足認容条件 *more or
less* terms

貨物【*kamotsu*】cargo; freight　囫 貨物は好天の日に積み込ん
だ. The *cargo* [*freight*] was loaded on a fine day. / 御注文
品を貨物便に託す. We take the liberty of forwarding your
goods by *freight*. ‖ —船 cargo boat; freighter　囫 岸壁では
工場の製品が毎日貨物船に積み込まれている. Everyday at the

pier products of the plant are loaded on *freighters.* ‖ —取扱所 forwarding agency ‖ —取扱業者 freight forwarder ‖ —運送状 way bill; W/B ‖ —引渡保証状 Letter of Guarantee ‖ —の可 載トン数 cargo loading capacity ‖ 付保— insured cargo ‖ — 引換証 waybill

柄 【gara】 design; pattern (柄合または生地質，織物などの見 本)；**例** 布地の柄見本を取りそろえてお送りします. We have pleasure in sending you herewith a good collection of *patterns* of cloth. / 貴店商品の代表的柄見本を至急送ってくださ い. We shall be glad if you will forward us by dispatch your representative range of *patterns.* / 貴社が広告された黒ウ ーステッドの柄見本をお送りください. We should be much obliged if you would kindly send us *patterns* of Black Wor-steds advertised by you.

空売り 【karauri】 short selling [sale] ‖ —する（品物が手元にな いのに売る）sell short

空積み 【karazumi】 broken space

空荷運賃 【karani unchin】 dead freight **例** 空荷運賃が在庫の蓄 積をもたらした. The *dead freight* created an accumulation of stock.

借方 【karikata】 debit **例** 新しい家具の購入は同社の勘定の 借方 に記載された. The purchase of the new furniture created a *debit* on the company's accounts. ‖ —票 debit note ‖ —に記入 する debit **例** この金額は，貴下勘定の借方に記入しました. This amount has been *debited* to your account. / 送り状を同 封，200 ドルは貴方借方勘定に記入しました. We enclose the invoice, amounting to $ 200, with which we have *debited* you.

仮保険証券 【karihoken shōken】 covering note **例** 至急仮保険証 券をお送りください. Kindly let us have a *covering note* as soon as possible.

借りる 【kariru】 borrow; debt; loan; due; rent **例** 彼から金を 借りた. I *borrowed* money from him. / 彼は海岸に小さな別荘 を借りた. He *rented* a cottage by the seaside. ‖ 借りがある be in debt; have a debt; owe a person much money **例**

彼に千円借りがある. I owe him 1,000 yen.

為替【*kawase*】 exchange; draft [a bill of exchange] (為替手形, formal な書式の中では a bill of exchange が多い) **例** 為替は当方に有利である. The *exchange* is favorable to us. / 貴社あてに為替手形を振り出す. We draw a *draft* upon you. / 価格は為替相場で上がり下がりがある. Prices are liable to alternative in accordance with the fluctuation of *exchange*. 本為替手形は6月30日に満期となる. This *bill of exchange* will become due on the 30th June. / 送り状金額に対して東京銀行横浜支店を通じ, D/P条件90日払いの為替手形を貴社あて振り出しましたので, 呈示あり次第手形のお引き受けを願います. For the invoice amount, we have drawn on you a *draft* at 90 d/s, D/P, through The Bank of Tokyo, Yokohama Branch, which accept on presentation. / 為替率はほとんど変動がなかった. Scarcely any variation occurred in the rate of *exchange*. / 送り状金額に対し一覧後60日払いの為替手形を振り出してください. Please draw a *draft* on us at 60 d/s for the amount of the invoice. ‖ 電報—送金する remit by telegraphic transfer (T.T.) ‖ 荷—手形 documentary bill ‖ —手形を買い取る negotiate a draft ‖ —手形を買い戻す refund a draft

代わり【*kawari*】: —に in place of; instead of; in exchange for **例** オートマチックタイプライターに代わって新しいテレプリンターが購入された. A new teleprinter was purchased *instead of* an automatic typewriter. / 労賃の代償として1万円が支払われた. *In exchange for* his labour the worker was paid ¥ 10,000. ‖ —の品 replacement **例** 代わりの品を送る手配をしました. We have made arrangements for a *replacement*.

考える【*kangaeru*】 consider; view **例** 同品はまことに安いと考えます. We *consider* them very competitive. / わが社の業績は不安定だった金融情勢という背景を考えると自負に値するものと思われる. The record of our achievement seems to be all the more creditable when *viewed* against the background of the disturbed monetary conditions.

かんがみて【*kangamite*】 in view of; judging from; considering;

according to 例 この点にかんがみて市況は上向くと思われる. *In view of* this, we are of opinion that the market should tend upwards. / この点にかんがみてこの品は貴市場で好評を得るでしょう. *In view of* this, this item will have good reputation in your market.

関係 【*kankei*】 relation; connection 例 同商会とは特別の関係にある. We have exceptional *relations* with the company. / その国と貿易関係がある. We have trade *relations* with the country. / 当社はメーカーと密接な関係をもっている. We have close *connection* with the manufacturers. ‖ ―会社 affiliated company ‖ ―書類 relevant [relative] documents; related papers 例 関係書類同封します. We enclose herewith the *relative documents*. ‖ ―当局 authorities concerned

歓迎 【*kangei*】 reception 例 新製品が世界で熱狂的歓迎を受けていることがお分かりいただけると思います. You will see what an enthusiastic *reception* our new product has all over the world.

監査 【*kansa*】 auditing 例 監査に当たって幾つかの困難にぶつかった. We have encountered several difficulties in *auditing*.

閑散 【*kansan*】: ―な slack; dull; inactive; quiet 例 いま時分は商売は閑散だ. Business is *slack* during this season. / 市況が閑散である. The market is *dull*.

関して 【*kanshite*】 regarding; concerning; respecting; with [in] regard to; with respect to; in respect of; as regards; as to 例 取引条件に関しては *as regards* the terms of business / この件に関して弊社は貴社から何も聞いていません. We have not heard from you *with respect to* this. / この問題に関し率直な御意見をお聞かせくださされば有り難く存じます. We shall be most grateful if you will give us your frank opinion *on* this matter.

感謝する 【*kansha suru*】 thank for; appreciate; be thoughtful of 例 貴社のお骨折りに感謝します. We *thank* you *for* your trouble. / 4月10日付貴社の引き合いに感謝します. We *thank* you *for* your inquiry of April 10. / この要求を実行くださるなら感謝します. We shall *appreciate* it if you will promptly act upon this request. / 御好意を感謝します. We shall greatly *appreciate* the favor. Your assistance will be greatly *appreciated.* / 御協力を深く感謝します. We highly *appreciate* your best cooperation. / 貴社の寛大さに感謝します. We will *appreciate* your kind indulgence. / 魅力ある品を送っていただき感謝します. It *was* most *thoughtful of* you to send these attractive goods.

願書【gansho】 application 例 願書を提出したい. I wish to present my *application.*

干渉【kanshō】 interference 例 彼は他人の干渉を嫌う. He does not like other people's *interference.* ‖ ―する interfere 例 この仕事に干渉してはいけない. Don't *interfere* in this business. / 先方の商談に干渉するのは不適当だと思う. We think it inopportune for you to *interfere* with their negotiation.

勘定【kanjō】 (会計) accounts (計算) calculation; computation; counting; reckoning (支払) payment of bill; settlement of accounts (勘定書) bill 例 同商会は勘定を常に滞りなく支払う. They have always paid their *accounts* regularly. / 1トンにつき50ドルの割り引きをし, 3,000ドルを当勘定に貸記します. We will allow you a discount of $ 50 per ton, and will credit your *account* with $ 3,000. / 貴勘定決済として50,000ドルの小切手を同封いたします. We are enclosing a cheque for $ 50,000 in payment of your *account.* / 本船渡しの諸掛かりは当方勘定とする. F.O.B. charges are to our *a/c.* / この問い合わせに関する費用は弊社勘定に振り替えください. Any expenses connected with this inquiry, please charge to our *account.* / 経費全部を合算し弊社勘定口に記入願います. You will debit our *account* for all the expenses involved. / 本調査に関してお立て替えいただいた経費は, 弊社勘定にお振り替えください. Any expense to be incurred in connection with this inquiry please charge to our *account.* / 諸掛かりを弊（貴）社勘定の貸し（借り）方に記入乞う. Please credit (debit) charges to our (your) *account.* / 勘定書の金額125万円也. *The amount of the bill* is ¥ 1,250,000. / 御請求の勘定書をお渡しします. We hand you a statement of *account* as requested. / 貴勘定〔口座〕では残額はほんの 10 ドルです. On your *account* there is a little balance of $10. (囲 on one's account の場合, account は勘定口座を意味することが多い.) / 弊社の勘定書の半額だけ即刻御送金ください. Please remit to us half the amount of our statement of *account*. / 未決済を全部払ってくださるよう要求します. We insist upon full payment of your *account* outstanding. / 時期経過勘定の支払いとして小切手を差し上げます. We would like to give you this cheque in lieu of the payment of our pastdue *account*. / 期限済勘定の決済はしばらくお待ちください. Please give us a little more time to settle the *account* due. ‖ —日 pay-day; settlement day ‖ —係 accountant ‖ 現金— cash account ‖ 当座— current account ‖ シャドウ— shadow account ‖ オープン— open account ‖ —をする make up an account ‖ —を精算する settle [liquidate; square] an account 未払—を精算する ask [demand] an account ‖ 〜の—につける charge the amount to one's account ‖ 〜の—および危険で on [for] one's account and risk ‖ 〜の—に組み入れる pass [place] to the account of

関心【*kanshin*】interest 囲 御関心のおしるしを賜わりたくお待ち申します. We await your evidences of *interest*. ‖ —がある be interested in 囲 これらの商品に関心をもっておられるか否か伺いたい. We would like to know if you *are interested in* these goods. / 当社は貴社の家庭用ミシンに関心がありますから最近のカタログを1部お送りください. As we *are interested in* your household sewing machines, please send a copy of your latest catalog. / 御通知あり次第貴社の関心をひく商品見本を喜んでお送りします. Upon hearing from you, we shall be glad to send you samples of the items you *are interested in*. / 当社は貴国製食料品を輸入することに関心があります. We are *interested in* importing provisions produced in your country.

関税【*kanzei*】customs; (custom) duties 囲 電気製品の輸入に対し税関は課税する. *Customs* often *impose duties on* the import of electrical goods. ‖ —率 custom tariff; tariff rates ‖ —済み

の貨物 goods duty paid ‖ —をかける impose duties on ‖ ~特恵— preferential duties ‖ 互恵— reciprocal duties ‖ —障壁 tariff barrier　例　日本は米車の輸入に対し高い関税障壁を設けている．Japan has a high *tariff barrier* on the import of American cars.

完全【*kanzen*】: —な(に) perfect(ly); exact(ly); full(y)　例　貴社積み荷を完全な状態で受け取りました．We have received your shipments in *perfect* condition. / 船積品は完全に見本に合致していることを保証します．We guarantee our shipments to be *exactly* up to the samples. ‖ —雇用 full employment ‖ —操業 full operation

乾燥【*kansō*】: —した dry　例　貴積み荷を乾燥状態で入手した．We have received your shipments in *dry* condition.

缶詰【*kanzume*】 canned food　例　当社は日本製缶詰食料品の輸出商です．We are large exporters of Japanese *Canned Provisions.* / 桃缶 500 箱の横浜船積期日と C.I.F. 値段を 8 月 3 日までに打電してください．Please let us know by cable by August 3 your price C.I.F. Yokohama for 500 cases *canned* peaches besides the date of shipment.

鑑定書【*kanteisho*】 survey note; surveyor's report (商品)　例　鑑定書はその土地が適当であると指摘した．The *surveyor's report* pointed out the suitability of the land.

甲板【*kanpan*】: —積荷 deck cargo; goods on deck　例　コンテナは格好の甲板積荷．Containers are suitable *deck cargo.* / 甲板積荷は天候の被害を受けやすい．*Goods on deck* are subject to weather hazards.

岸壁【*ganpeki*】 pier; quay; wharf　例　工場の敷地内にある岸壁でこの工場の製品が毎日上記の地域に向けて貨物船に積み込まれています．Everyday at the *pier* within the compounds, products of the plant are loaded on freighters bound for the above-mentioned region.

寛容【*kanyō*】: —な generous　例　貴社の条件は非常に寛容である．Your terms are very *generous* on the whole.

管理【*kanri*】 (する) control; administrate　例　株主は株主総会

で投票する権利をもち，会社を管理運営する最終権限をもっている．The stockholders, who have the right to vote at the general meeting, *control* and run the corporation with the final authority. ‖ —の administrative **例** A氏は1950年以降弊社の管理部で働いています．Mr. A has been working in the *Administrative* Department of our company since 1950.

完了する【*kanryō suru*】 complete; settle **例** 送電線鉄塔建設工事を完了した．We have *completed* construction of transmission line towers. / 問い合わせが完了次第，注文品をお送りします．As soon as these inquiries have been *settled*, we shall be pleased to send you an order.

慣例【*kanrei*】 practice; custom; rule **例** 銀行の慣例では利息期間の全体にわたって預金されていた金額に対してのみ利息が支払われることになっている．It is the *practice* of many banks to pay interest on only the amount that has been on deposit for the entire interest period. / 当社は取消不能信用状基礎で取り引きする慣例です．We make it our *custom* [*rule*] to trade on an Irrevocable L/C.

関連【*kanren*】: —して referring to; with (in) reference to **例** 5月10日付お手紙に関連して 当社はお問い合わせの 商品を手持ちしていることを申し上げます．*Referring to* your letter of May 10, we are glad to say we have in stock the goods asked for. / 5月20日付のお手紙に関連して申し上げます．当社は貴店注文品を日本郵船会社によって，積み出す手配をしました．*Referring to* your letter of May 20, we have arranged to ship your order through The Nippon Yusen Kaisha, Ltd. ‖ —する relate to; connect with ‖ —商品 related items ‖ —産業 relative industry.

【き】

起因する [左右される；帰する]【*kiin suru*】 be caused by; be due to; be attributable to **例** 綿製品市場は二つの大きな促進条件に左右される．The cotton products market *is attributable* *to* two major accelerators.

機械 【*kikai*】 machine; machinery 例 弊社の機械は最新式であ
る. Our *machinery* is the most modern of its kind. ‖ —化
mechanized 例 弊社工場は大きくなり，機械化の程度も高くな
る傾向にある. Our plants tend to be larger in size and more
highly *mechanized*.

機会 【*kikai*】 chance; opportunity 例 貴社を訪問する機会がな
い. We have no *chance* to visit your office. / 当社はこの機会
を利用して，貴社と取り引きを開きたい目的で手紙を差し上げま
す. We take this *opportunity* of writing you with a view to
opening an account with you. / 近い将来貴社のお役に立つ機
会があることをお待ち申し上げております. We look forward
to the *opportunity* of being of service to you soon. / 近日中
に再び貴社の御注文に応じる機会が得られるよう期待します.
We look forward to the *opportunity* of filling your order
again in the near future. / 取引における失敗を訂正する機会を
与えてくださったことを深謝します. We deeply thank you for
your having given us the *opportunity* to correct our fault in
this business. / もしこの機会を逃せば，もっと高い価格でもこの
品を入手できないかもしれません. If you miss this *opportunity*,
you may be unable to obtain the item even at a higher
price.

企画 【*kikaku*】 planning; plan 例 新しいオフィスブロックはな
お計画段階である. The new office block is still the *planning*
stage. ‖ —する form [set up] a plan; wrap out a program

規格 【*kikaku*】 standard; gauge; norm; specification 例 弊社
同封の規格を御覧になれば品質の良さを認めていただけると思い
ます. You will understand our good quality after you read
the *specifications* we enclosed. ‖ 日本工業— JIS [Japanese Industrial Standards] 例 機械は JIS 規格です. The machine is
up to *JIS*.

期間 【*kikan*】 period; term 例 船積期間は延長する予定です.
The *period* of shipment is to be extended. / 昨年の同期間に
比べて輸出金額は3割減少している. Compared with the cor-

responding *period* last year, the exports show a decrease of 30 per cent in value.

危機【*kiki*】 crisis; emergency　例 会社は重大な危機を突破した. The company has overcome [tide over] the serious *crisis*. ‖ ―に備える provide against emergency

聞き漏らす【*kikimorasu*】 fail to catch [hear]　例 彼の言ったことを聞き漏らした. I *failed to catch* [*hear*] what he said.

企業【*kigyō*】 enterprise; undertaking; company; corporation　例 この企業は成功の見通しがほとんどない. This *undertaking* has little chance of success. ‖ ―形態 a type of business enterprise ‖ ―合同 a trust ‖ ―連合 a cartel ‖ ―再編成 business reorganization ‖ ―の合理化 rationalization of enterprises

危険【*kiken*】 risk; danger　例 先方と取り引きしても別に危険なことはないと思う. We are of opinion there is no *risk* in dealing with them. / この商売を取り逃がす危険がある. You will run the *risk* of losing this business. / 貴社が取引関係を結ぶに当たって少しの危険もないだろう. You would not run the least *risk* in opening connections with the firm. / この保険証券は貨物が神戸到着後 7 日間の火災危険を含む. This policy includes the *risk* of fire until expiration of seven days after arrival of the goods in Kobe. ‖ ―を担保する take [cover] the risk ‖ ―を伴う involve a risk ‖ ―を少なくする reduce the danger

棄権する【*kiken suru*】 renounce (one's right)

期限【*kigen*】 term　例 支払期限は 6 カ月. The *term* of payment is six months. / 期限が切れる. The *term* expires [runs out]. ‖ 支払―の来た due　例 手形はいつ支払期限になるか. When does the note fall *due*? / 来月が支払期限. The note is *due* next month. ‖ ―経過 overdue　例 期限経過の同封勘定に注意を払われ至急御送金くださいますようお願い申し上げます. We would call your attention to the enclosed account, which is now *overdue*, and ask you, therefore, kindly to favour us with a prompt remittance.

寄港【*kikō*】: ―する call at port　例 その船は途中横浜港に寄港

した. The ship *called at Port* Yokohama on her way. ‖ —地 port of call 例 この汽船は第2の寄港地神戸に向かって航行している. This steamer makes for Kobe as the 2nd *port of call.*

機構 【*kikō*】 structure; organization ‖ 経済— economic structure 例 この国の経済機構はしっかりしている. The *econonic structure* of this country is sound.

技巧 【*gikō*】 art; technic; skill ‖ —を凝らす use one's technical skill 例 問題解決のため彼は技巧を凝らすだろう. He will *use his technical skill* to solve the problem.

帰国する 【*kikoku suru*】 come home 例 輸出部長は来月アメリカから帰国します. The export manager will *come home* from America next month.

記載する 【*kisai suru*】 note; write down; specify 例 商品の番号を記載してください。 Please *note* the number of the goods. / 別紙の通り注文を差し上げます. We have the pleasure in placing the order with you *specified* at [as per] enclosure.

期日 【*kijitsu*】 due date; term (期限 a time limit) ‖ —が切れる expire; fall due 例 この契約は2月10日で期日が切れる. This contract *expires* [*falls due*] on February 10. / 期日に必ず返済ください。 Pay back the loan without fail when it *falls due* [*at due date*].

技術 【*gijutsu*】 technic; technology; technical skill 例 この仕事には技術を要する. This work requires *technical skill.* / 当製品は最新の技術を取り入れた最上品です. Our goods are the best quality goods incorporating the latest *engineering technology.* ‖ —者 technician; engineer ‖ —のある skilled 例 この工場の従業員は他と比較して技術が劣っている. The working force of this factory is less *skilled* than workers in other plants.

基準 【*kijun*】 basis; standard 例 どんな基準でその価格を決めたか. On what *basis* did you fix its price?

希少 【*kishō*】 rarity 例 絹は希少のために珍重された. Silk was esteemed because of its *rarity.*

規制【*kisei*】regulation; control ‖ —を設ける establish a regulation

犠牲【*gisei*】sacrifice; victim 例 何百軒もの家が台風の犠牲となった. Hundreds of houses fell *victims* to the typhoon [were made *victims* of the typhoon]. ‖ —にする sacrifice 例 品質を犠牲にしてはならない. Quality must not be *sacrificed*. ‖ いかなる—を払っても at any sacrifice; at all costs

季節【*kisetsu*】season 例 休暇シーズン前にはもう手に入れられないだろう。We shall not be able to get any more before the holiday *season*.

汽船【*kisen*】steamer; boat; vessel 例 貨物積込の汽船名次の通り. Following is the name of the *steamer* on which the goods are shipped.

基礎【*kiso*】foundation; basis 例 この会社は基礎がしっかりしている. This company is built on a firm *foundation*. ‖ —をおく be based [founded] (on) 例 値段は運賃保険料込ニューヨーク渡しを基礎としております. The prices *are based on* C.I.F. New York. / 同店は最も基礎確実な店です. We are pleased to say that this firm is a highly respectable and *well-founded* concern.

規則【*kisoku*】rule; regulation ‖ —を改正する revise the rules 例 女性会員に関してはその規則を改正します. We will *revise the rules* regarding women members.

期待【*kitai*】expectation; hope 例 貴社の御期待に添えなくて残念です. We are sorry we can not answer your *expectation*. ‖ —する expect; look forward to 例 当社は貴社のよい御返答をお待ち申し上げています. We *look foward to* your favorable reply.

記帳する【*kichō suru*】book 例 有り難く記帳いたしました. We have *booked* with thanks.

貴重【*kichō*】: —な valuable; precious 例 その事故で貴重な積み荷を失った. The *valuable* cargoes were lost in the accident. / 貴重な御提案に感謝します. Many thanks for your *valuable* suggestion.

気付【*kitsuke*】care of; C/O 例 ～気付で手紙を出す address a letter in *care of* ～ / その文書は部長あてで秘書気付. The letter is addressed to the manager, *care of* his secretary.

規定【*kitei*】provisions 例 法律の規定では株主が会社を管理し経営することになっている. According to the *provision* of the law, the stockholders are supposed to control and run the corporation with final authority. ‖ ─する stipulate; prescribe 例 問題の品物は規定された期間内に船積みされるだろう. The goods in question will be shipped within the *stipulated* period. / 計画の中身とその手配は規定された様式に従う必要はない. The content and arrangement of the plan need not follow any *prescribed* pattern.

既定【*kitei*】: ─の prearranged; established; fixed ‖ ─の方針に従い according to prearranged program; as decided [designed; provided; arranged] 例 既定のとおり納品日は6月6日. *As arranged*, the delivery date will be June 6.

軌道に乗る【*kidō ni noru*】set a matter on its way; get under way 例 仕事は軌道に乗った. The work *got under way.*

絹物【*kinumono*】silk goods 例 私は十年以上絹物卸店に雇われていました. I have been in the employment of a firm of *silk goods* wholesaler for over ten years.

規模【*kibo*】scope; scale 例 彼は規模の大きな輸入商を経営している. He runs importers [His import business is run] on a large *scale.*

希望【*kibō*】desire 例 綿織機の販路拡大を希望している. We have the *desire* of expanding the sale of our cotton loom. ‖ ─する wish to; hope; desire 例 弊社はこれらの品物を輸入したい. We *wish to* import these goods. / 御注文品が無事お手元に到着し御満足を与え，さらに御注文くださるよう希望します. We *hope* that the goods will reach you in good condition and give you complete satisfaction so that you may place further orders with us. / 5月13日付お手紙で御希望のとおり新定価表を同封します. As *desired* in your letter of May 13, we enclose a new price list. ‖ ─値段 idea of price ‖ —にそう comply with request ‖ —者 applicant

基本【kihon】 basis; foundation; standard ‖ —的に basically 例 この取り引きは基本的に有望な見通しである. This business *basically* has good prospects for success.

気前の良い【kimae no yoi】 generous 例 貴社の条件は大体において気前が良い. Your terms are very *generous* on the whole.

義務【gimu】 obligation; duty 例 貴社は義務を遂行すべきです. You should fulfil your *obligation*. / 何も義務は生じません. You incur no *obligation*. / 他人の借金まで返す義務はない. We are under no *obligation* to pay another's debts. / 貴社は義務を果たして当社に十分な満足を与えてくれました. You have faithfully discharged your *duties* and given us every satisfaction.

偽名【gimei】 false name ‖ —を使う use a false name ‖ —にて under the false name of 例 彼は偽名を使って旅行中. He is travelling *under a false name*.

疑問【gimon】 doubt; question; problem 例 疑問があれば弊社の代理店にお問い合わせください. Please enquire [ask] our agent if you have any *questions*. ‖ —がある have some doubt about

規約【kiyaku】 agreement; compact; contract 例 それに関して弊社は貴社との間に規約を作った. We made an *agreement* with you about it. ‖ —を守る keep to an agreement

逆【gyaku】 reverse; contrary 例 事実はその逆です. The *contrary* is the case.

逆行する【gyakkō suru】 go against 例 当方には貴意に逆らう気持は毛頭ありません. We have no intention of *going against* your wishes. / その商品は加工されると逆輸入される. We *reimport* the goods once they have been processed.

逆[再]輸出【gyakuyushutsu】 reexport

逆[再]輸入【gyakuyunyū】 reimport

救援物資【kyūen busshi】 relief goods

休業【kyūgyō】 holiday; closing 例 明日は銀行休業日です. It is a bank *holiday* tomorrow. ‖ —する close an office; absence from work 例 当日弊店は休業します. Our store will be *closed on* the day.

急激【*kyūgeki*】: ＿な(に) sudden(ly); radical(ly); rapid(ly)　例
あまり急激なやり方はしない方がよかろう. It would be better
not to proceed too *suddenly.* / 価格は急激な速さで上がってい
ます. Prices rise *exceptionally* fast.

旧式【*kyūshiki*】(の) old fashion(ed); old style　例 デザインが
旧式のため売り上げが低い. As the design is *old fashioned,*
our sales are low.

急送する【*kyūsō suru*】despatch; send by express　例 御注文品
は当地から保証期日の二日前に急送しました. Your order was
despatched from here 2 days ahead of the guaranteed time.

急騰【*kyūtō*】jump; sudden [rapid] rise ‖ ＿する rise rapidly;
jump　例 値段は急騰中である. The prices are *rising rapidly.* /
市場相場は急騰した. The market *had a smart rise* [has
jumped in price; has *made a sudden rise*; has *suddenly gone
up high*; has *advanced suddenly*].

急用【*kyūyō*】urgent business　例 彼は急用でニューヨークへ行
った. He went to New York on *urgent business.*

給料【*kyūryō*】salary; wage　例 給料は1ヶ月20万円希望です.
Salary required would be two hundred thousand yen per
month.

協会【*kyōkai*】society; association　例 協会員は月1回会合す
る. The members of the *association* meet once a month.

業界【*gyōkai*】business circles; industry　例 弊社の商品は業界
から良い評判で迎えられています. Our goods have met with
a good reception from *business circles.* / 当社の値段は業界他
社の値段に比して有利です. Our prices compare favorably with
those of our *competitors.* / 業界中一流会社である. We are a
leader of [a leading company in the] *industry.*

協議【*kyōgi*】discussion　例 一件協議中につき返答できません.
The matter being under *discussion,* we cannot give you any
definite answer. ‖ ＿する discuss, consult　例 生産開発部は2
人の有名なプロとしばしば協議した. Our Product Development
consulted frequently with two famous professionals.

供給【_kyōkyū_**】**（する）supply　例　世界市場でこの品物は供給が需要をはるかに上回っている. _Supplies_ of this commodity in the world markets greatly exceed the demand. / 材木の供給可能数量および価格を返電乞う. What quantity and at what price can you _supply_ wood？/ 勉強値で供給［提供］していただけると期待している. We expect you to _supply_ us with your best prices. / 約 30 の製造業者が当社にこの商品を供給している. Some 30 manufacturers are _supplying_ us with this article.

強硬【_kyōkō_**】**: ＿な drastic; firm　例　〜に強硬な態度をとる take a firm attitude against 〜 / 売り上げが低下を続けるなら強硬手段を取ることになろう. If sales continue to decline, the company will _take drastic measures_.

恐慌【_kyōkō_**】**panic　例　一般的恐慌が到来し, 市場は崩壊して正確な相場は出せません. There is a general _panic_.　The market is going to pieces. It is impossible to give accurate quotations.

共産圏【_kyōsanken_**】**communist bloc　例　共産圏は小麦の 50％を輸入する. The _communist bloc_ imports 50％ of its wheat.

業績【_gyōseki_**】**performance; earnings; results　例　業績は当方の予想を上回るものと思われる. _Results_ seem to exceed our expectations.

競争【_kyōsō_**】**competition　例　この種の商品に対する競争は激しい. The _competition_ in this line is keen. ‖ ＿相手 competitor　例　貴社の競争相手が市場の最安値で売り申し込みをしてきています. Your _competitors_ are offering the lowest prices in this market. ‖ と＿して in competition with〜　例　アメリカ商品と競争して売ることができる. We can sell these goods _in competition with_ American goods. ‖ ＿的な(に) competitive(ly)　例　わが社が競争できるのは, それがあるからだ. It enables us to operate _competitively_. / 日本の玩具は国際市場において品質価格の両面で競争力がある. Japanese toys are _competitive_ in the international market in both quality and price. / この価格は当市場では競争力がありません. These prices are not _competitive_ enough for the market here.

強調する【_kyōchō suru_**】**emphasize　例　弊社はこの点を強調しま

す．We emphasize this point.

協定【*kyōtei*】arrangement; agreement　**例** 支払条件に関して今少し有利な協定をできないか．Regarding terms of payment, can you not make a better *arrangement*? / 目下協定は結びかねます．We are not in a position to enter into an *agreement* at this time. ‖ 取引条件—書 agreement on terms and conditions of business ‖ 貿易— trade agreement

共同【*kyōdō*】cooperation; partnership ‖ —経営 joint management ‖ —事業 joint enterprise ‖ —で事業をする enter into partnership; do business together　**例** この問題が解決できれば共同事業ができる．If we can solve this problem, we can *do business together*.

共同海損【*kyōdō kaison*】general average; G.A. ‖ —分担金 general average contribution

興味【*kyōmi*】interest　**例** トランジスターの記事を読み大いに興味を感じました．We read the article about transistors with much *interest*. ‖ —がある be interested in　**例** 御社の業種には深く興味を持っています．We *are* deeply *interested in* your line of business. ‖ —を起こさせる arouse interest in

業務【*gyōmu*】business　**例** 業務を拡大するために貴国消費者の間に高級品の市場を開拓したいと念じています．In order to expand *business*, we are desirous of opening a market for our high-grade articles in your country. ‖ —担当者 person in charge of the affairs [business]　**例** この度山田三郎氏が当商会業務担当社員として入社いたしました．We have received Mr. S. Yamada in *charge of business* into our firm.

協力【*kyōryoku*】cooperation　**例** 御協力を深く感謝します．We highly appreciate your *cooperation*. / 販売の減少は貴社の御協力をいただけなかったためです．The fall in the sales is due to the absence of your *cooperation* with us. ‖ —して in cooperation with ‖ —する cooperate　**例** 貴製品を売ることについてはいつでも御協力できます．We shall always be ready to *cooperate* with you in marketing of your products.

許可【*kyoka*】permission　**例** それについて貴社の許可が欲しい．

We want your *permission* for it.

局面 【*kyokumen*】 aspect; situation ‖ —転換 a development in the situation **例** 局面の展開が見られた. There has been *a development in the situation.*

極力 【*kyokuryoku*】 as much as possible; to the utmost; to the best of one's power [ability] **例** 貴社は極力弊社を援助するため努力した. You did your *best* to help us.

拒絶 [否] する 【*kyozetsu suru*】 refuse; reject; decline; deny; protest **例** 手形の引き受けを拒絶する protest a bill / A会社は弊社の弁償要求を拒絶した. A company *rejected* our claim. / 値引きをされても買い手は引き取りを拒絶するでしょう. Our buyer will *refuse* to take delivery of the goods even if you may make an allowance. / 船積みが6月10日を過ぎれば, 品物の受け取りは拒否します. We shall have to *decline* to accept the goods if they are shipped after June 10.

漁網 【*gyomō*】 fishing net **例** 貴社は信頼できる漁網輸入商です. You are one of the reliable importers of *fishing nets.*

切り下げる 【*kirisageru*】 revise; devaluate **例** ポンドを5％切り下げる *devaluate* the pound by 5 per cent / 価格切り下げに御努力くださるものと信じます. We trust you will make every effort to *revise* your prices.

切り抜ける 【*kirinukeru*】 tide over [recover] 《difficulties; crisis》 **例** 社長はこの難局を切り抜ける決意をした. The president determined to *tide over* this crisis. / 早く窮状を切り抜けられることを望みます. We wish you a speedy *recovery* from your difficulties.

記録 【*kiroku*】 a record; a document **例** 当社の製品は例年にない記録破りの売れ行きです. Our goods have unusual *record-breaking* sales. ‖ —する record; register; write down; keep on record **例** 砂糖は新安値を記録した. The sugar *registered* a new low. ‖ —に残す put on record ‖ —をとる keep a record of ‖ —破りの record-breaking

議論 【*giron*】 discussion; opinion; argument **例** それについては議論がまちまちだ. *Opinions* are divided on it. / 種々の議論

がある．There is much *argument* about it.‖ —の余地なし leaves no room for discussion

疑惑 【*giwaku*】 suspicion 例 疑惑を解く clear one's suspicion / 彼の行動には疑惑を覚える．His actions arouse my *suspicion*.

金額 【*kingaku*】 amount 例 金額10万円の小切手有り難く存じます．We thank you for your cheque in the *amount* of a hundred thousand yen.

緊急 【*kinkyū*】: —の urgent; immediate 例 緊急手配をする make *immediate* arrangements for / この問題は非常に緊急を要します．This matter is very *urgent*.

均衡 【*kinkō*】 balance 例 需給のバランスを維持できれば利益の増加が望める．If we can maintain the *balance* of supply and demand, we will maximize our profits.‖ —を保つ keep the balance

銀行 【*ginkō*】 bank‖ —手形 bank draft; B/D‖ —売レート bank selling rate‖ 信用状発行— establishing (issuing) bank‖ 通知— advising bank‖ 買取— negotiating (issuing) bank‖ 引受— accepting bank‖ —口座 banking account 例 この金は現金で払う必要はないが，銀行口座に振込まねばならない．The money must not be paid in cash but credited to a *banking account*.‖ —信用 bank credit 例 すべての金融業者は銀行信用が得がたいことを知っている．All financiers know that *bank credit* is unobtainable.‖ —割引率 bank's discount rate 例 銀行割引率は上がりました．There has been an advance in the *bank's discount rate*.‖ —信用照会先 bank reference 例 当社の銀行信用照会先は東京銀行です．Our *bank reference* is The Bank of Tokyo.

緊縮政策 【*kinshuku seisaku*】 retrenchment policy 例 緊縮政策は取らない．We have no *retrenchment policy*.

近代化 【*kindaika*】 modernization‖ —する modernize 例 当工場は拡大され近代化された．Our plant has been enlarged and *modernized*.

緊迫 【*kinpaku*】: —した imminent 例 南アジアでは輸入統制が緊迫状態にある．An import control is *imminent* in South Asia.

勤務する 【*kinmu suru*】 serve; work; be employed 　例 私は5年以上三井貿易に勤務しており，英語，ドイツ語および速記術の知識を相当持っています．I have *been with* the Mitsui Trading Co., Ltd. for more than five years and moreover possess a good knowledge of English, German and shorthand.

金利 【*kinri*】 interest 　例 銀行は未払金につき普通1.5％の金利を取る．The banks usually collect 1.5% *interest* on the balance.

【く】

空港 【*kūkō*】 airport 　例 空港まで貴社の輸出部長を出迎えます．We meet your Export Manager at the *airport*.

偶然 【*gūzen*】 (by) chance [accident] ‖ ―～する happen (to) 　例 弊社はロンドン商業会議所から貴社の名前を偶然に知りました．We *happen to* know your name from the London Chamber of Commerce.

空輸する 【*kūyu suru*】 transport by air 　例 そのパルプ材はカナダから空輸された．The pulp wood was *transported by air* from Canada.

苦情 【*kujō*】 complaint 　例 苦情を受け入れる accept one's *complaint* / 苦情を訴える address [make] a *complaint* / ～から～についての苦情の申し入れを受ける receive a *complaint* from ～ of ～ / この商品に関しては一度も苦情を受けたことがない． No *complaints* have so far been made against us concerning this article. / 船会社に厳重な苦情を申し入れています．We are making a strong *complaint* to the shipping company. / 顧客から苦情が出なければよいがと思います．We hope that we do not encounter *difficulties* from our customers. ‖ ―を言う complain (about; against) 　例 積荷米の品質について苦情を申し立てることを遺憾に存じます．We are sorry to have to *complain* of the quality of the shipment of rice.

崩す 【*kuzusu*】 reduce (price) (価格); tumble down (the market) (市場) 　例 需要を維持するため値を崩すことが必要．It is necessary to *reduce prices* to maintain demand.

具体【*gutai*】: —的 (に) concrete(ly); definite(ly) 例 取引条件をもっと具体的に説明してください. Please explain the trade terms 'more *concretely*. / 御要望は具体的に書いていただいた方が，御満足のゆくような御援助ができます. The more *specific* your request is, the more satisfactorily we can help you. ‖ —案 definite plan ‖ —策 concrete measure

口約束【*kuchiyakusoku*】oral agreement 例 この点に関し口約束があった. There was an *oral agreement* made on this point. ‖ —する make a verbal promise

屈辱的【*kutsujokuteki*】: —な face-losing; humiliating 例 それは当社にとって屈辱的な体験でした. It was a *humiliating* experience for us.

工夫する【*kufū suru*】devise; contrive; elaborate 例 弊社の電気器具は特別の 工夫 が凝らされてい る. Our Electric Appliances are specially *elaborated*.

組合【*kumiai*】association; society; league; guild; union 例 組合を組織した. We formed [organized] a *partnership* [an *association*].

組み立てる【*kumitateru*】assemble; construct 例 この自動車は部品を西ドイツから輸入して日本で組み立てた. This car was *assembled* in Japan out of the parts imported from West Germany.

組手形【*kumitegata*】a set of bills

組む【*kumu*】(仕事を一緒に) tie up with; get with; cooperate (為替手形) draw (a draft on); draw (a bill in favor of some one) 例 銀行で手形を組む [振り出す]. We will *draw a draft on* our bank. ‖ と組んで in partnership with ～ 例 弊社は貴社と組んで事業を計画する. We do business *in partnership with* you.

倉【*kura*】a warehouse ‖ —入れする put in storage 例 余剰製品は倉入れされる. The surplus products will be *put in storage*. ‖ —荷証券 warehouse warrant; W/W

比べる【*kuraberu*】compare 例 当社の値段は業界他社の値段に比べて有利です. Our prices *compare* favorably with those of our competitors. ‖ ―と比べて in comparison with 例 他と比べて5分高いので being 5 % higher *in comparison with* others / 日本は昨年1,000万台以上の自動車を生産したが，これは10年前に比べて4.6倍にあたる．Last year Japan turned out more than 10,000,000 automobiles—a number which is 4.6 times *as large as* [a 460% increase *over*] 10 years ago. / アメリカにおける陶磁器類の輸入は昨年8,175万ドルで一昨年に比べて10%増になっています．The U.S. imports of chinaware last year amounted to $81,750,000, an increase of 10% *over* the preceding year. ‖ 比べものにならない out of comparison

繰り上げる【*kuriageru*】 advance 例 A社に送る自動車の船積みを一週間繰り上げる．The date of shipment of cars to send A company is *advanced* by a week.

繰り越す【*kurikosu*】 (次期へ) carry forward; (前期より) bring forward 例 その金額は翌月へ繰り越された．The amount was *carried forward* to the next month.

苦しい【*kurushii*】: ―事情 *difficulties* 例 苦しい事情はよく分ります．We fully understand your *difficulties*. / どんな苦しみにも堪えよ．Endure whatever *difficulties* [you may have]. ‖ ―立場に追い込まれる be driven into an awkward position; be put into difficulty

クレーム【*kureimu*】 claim 例 懸案のクレームを解決願いたい．We hope you will settle the pending *claim*. / 目減りの件については運送業者に対し求償されるようお勧めします．With regard to the loss in weight, we would suggest that you make your *claim* on the forwarding agent. / 貴クレームに応じられない理由を御理解くださることを望みます．We hope you will understand why we cannot accept your *claim*. / 数日中に発見されない場合はクレーム金額の清算を期待します．If they cannot be found within a few days, we shall expect a settlement in full for our *claim*. / 輸送中の破損に対するクレームには応じられません．We cannot accept *claims* for breakages in transit. ‖ 求償権 claim for indemnity ‖ 指図債権 claim to order ‖ ―する claim; file a claim against [with] one for;

claim on a person for ～ ‖ ～に対し―がある have a claim on ‖ ―に応ずる entertain [accept] one's claim; meet a claim ‖ ―を受け容れる grant [honor] one's claim ‖ ～に対して損害の―を提起する institute a claim for damages against (人) ‖ ―を拒絶する reject a claim ‖ ―を解決する settle a claim ‖ ―を取り下げる withdraw one's claim ‖ ある事柄，商品に対して―が発生する a claim takes place over ～

加えるに 【kuwaeruni】 in addition to 例 通常の商品に加えるに，日用品も製造しています. *In addition to* our usual goods, we also manufacture daily necessities.

詳しい 【kuwashii】 specific; detailed 例 もっと詳しいことは弊社代理店にお聞きください. For further *detailed* information, please ask our agent.

【け】

敬意 【keii】 respect 例 弊社は喜んで貴社の御親切に対し敬意を表します. We are glad to pay our *respects* to your kindness.

経営 【keiei】 management 例 会社の経営は変わりなし. The *management* of the firm remains unaltered. ‖ ―する manage; run; operate; carry on; conduct 例 商業を営む *conduct* a mercantile business / 事業を経営する *run* one's business / この会社は雑貨品卸商を営んでいます. The company has been *carrying on* general goods wholesale business. ‖ ―者 the management; manager; executive 例 価格政策は経営陣にとって重大な関心事である. Price policy is a prime concern of *the management*. / 経営者は絶対の権威がある. The *manager* has absolute authority.

経過 【keika】 progress; development; course 例 貴社との商談の経過において in the *course* of our negotiation with you / この商品の価格の経過について特別の注意を払ってください. Please pay special attention to the *development* of the market price of these goods. ‖ ―報告 a report on progress

警戒 【keikai】 precaution; caution 例 この商社と取り引きの際

は特に警戒してすべて現金取引にされることをお勧めします. In case you enter into business relations with this firm, we should advise you to exercise extreme *caution* and to do business only on cash terms. ‖ —の precautionary 例 同店と取り引きする場合には，警戒の上処置される方がよいと思います. You will do well to take *precautionary* measures when dealing with the firm.

計画【keikaku】 plan; scheme; program 例 長期計画 a long-range *plan* / 財政計画 financial *program* / 5 カ年計画 a five-year *plan* / この計画は有利に展開するでしょう. This *plan* will turn to advantage. ‖ —を立てる make a plan; form a scheme

景気【keiki】 business; prosperity; boom 例 この国は今工業が好景気を示している. The country is having a great *boom* in industry. / 不景気だ. *Business* is dull. / 日本の景気は外国貿易による. Japan's *prosperity* depends upon foreign trade. ‖ —上昇 business upswing; uptrend of business activities ‖ —下降 business decline

経験【keiken】 experience 例 私は実務に若干の経験があります. I have some *experience* in business. / 私の業務経験は次のとおりです. My business *experience* is as follows. / 小生の教育と経験に関する詳細は別紙に記載のとおりです. The details of my education and *experience* are given on the enclosed [attached] sheet.

傾向【keikō】 tendency 例 物価は下降の傾向を示している. Prices are showing a *tendncy* to reduce. / 東京の人口は増加の傾向を示している. The population of Tokyo shows a *tendency* to increase. ‖ —がある tend to; be liable to 例 物価は為替の変動で変わる傾向にある. Prices *are liable to* make alteration in accordance with the fluctuation of exchange rates. / 日本の家庭はますます電化される傾向がある. Households in Japan *tend to* be electrified more and more [as years go by]. / 値段は上昇傾向にある. The price *tends* upward. The price has an upward *tendency*. The price shows an advancing *tendency*.

経済【keizai】 economy 例 先進国は発展途上国に対し経済の安定

を助長する必要がある．An advanced nation needs to develop a stable *economy* of underdeveloping countries. / 国民の経済活動は現在健全な歩みを続けている．The people are now enjoying a robust *economy*. / 一般に日本車が好まれているのはその経済性，実用性，取り扱いの容易さにある．In general, Japanese cars are liked for their *economy*, practicality, and ease of handling. / 価格の割りには値打ちもので経済的な買い物に関心があります．We are interested in *economy* buys and value for money. ‖ ―の economic　例　その国の 2,500 万の国民の経済活動は健全な進展を遂げています．The *economic* activity of her 25 million people is now making healthy progress. / 今日まで政府は経済界と株式市場をきわめてうまく指導してきました．The government has so far managed the *economic* circles and the stock market with great ability.

計算【keisan】calculation; computation　例　先ごろの計算によると according to recent *computation* / 上記のデータに基づく計算 the *calculation* based on the above data / 最近の計算によると年間アメリカはヨーロッパの特許に対して 4,500 万ドルを支払っている．The latest *calculation* shows that the U.S. paid $45 million a year for European patents. ‖ ―書　statement　例　貴社の当座勘定の計算書を同封してお送りします．We take pleasure in sending you herewith a *statement* of your current account with us. / 計算書は 50 ドルの貴社受取残高を示しています．The *statement* shows a balance in your favour of $50.

計算器【keisanki】calculator; computer　例　計算器は小さくなってきている．The *calculators* have been getting smaller in size.

係争【keisō】dispute　例　その問題は係争に発展した．The matter has developed into a *dispute*.

軽卒【keisotsu】: ―な imprudent　例　同商会と取り引きを開始することは軽卒のそしりを免れないと存じます．It would be *imprudent* to enter into any connection with them.

経費【keihi】expenses　例　経費はすべて書き出した価格に含まれている．All *expenses* are included in the price quoted. / 本調査に関してお立て替えいただいた経費は，弊社勘定にお振り替え

ください. Any *expense* incurred in connection with this inquiry please charge to our account. / この問い合わせに関連する経費はすべて貴請求書受取次第喜んでお支払いいたします. Any *expenses* connected with this inquiry will be gladly paid by us upon receipt of your bill.

契約【keiyaku】 contract; agreement 例 本覚書は契約後3カ年間有効とする. This memorandum is to be effective for three years after the *contract*. / まだなんら契約が成立していない. No *contract* has yet been concluded. / 契約を変更することに同意した. We have agreed with them in amending the *contract*. / 船積みは各契約において定められた期日内になされること. Shipment is to be made within the time stipulated in each *contract*. / 貴方の承認を条件に契約しました. We have already closed the *contract* subject to your approval. / 契約に反する船積み. Shipment (effected) against a *contract*. / 契約金は十分安い. The *contract* price is low enough. / 謹んで二通の契約書をお渡しします. We respectfully hand you our *agreement* forms in duplicate. / 契約期間を延ばすよう勧めます. We recommend you to extend the *contract* period. ‖ ―する contract; enter into [make] an agreement; conclude a contract 例 貴注文品を契約どおり積めるよう，信用状をただちに開設いただければ有り難い. We shall be glad if you will open an L/C without delay so that we may ship your goods as *contracted*. / いかなる値段で契約できるか. At what price can you *contract*? ‖ ―条項 stipulations; provisions; article; contract clauses 例 契約条項に従い商品を包装しました. We packed the goods in accordance with the *stipulations*. ‖ ―履行 fulfilment [carrying out] of a contract ‖ ―数量 contract quantity ‖ ―違反 breach of contract ‖ ―解除 cancellation of contract ‖ ―変更 renewal of contract ‖ ―条件 terms of contract ‖ ―率 contracted rate

経由【keiyu】 via; by way of 例 貴社注文品はホノルル経由パシフィック号に船積されました. Your orders were shipped per M.S. "Pacific" *via* Honolulu.

経歴【keireki】 career　囲 彼は輸出部長の経歴がある. He has a *career* as an export manager. / これは当社の商売上の経歴中始めての経験です. This is our first experience in our business *careers*.

系列【keiretsu】: ―に入る be affiliated into the combination ‖ ―会社 members of the allied enterprises; the group of companies; the associates; an affiliated company　囲 この系列会社は非常に成績がよい. *This group of companies* is extremely successful.

毛織物【keorimono】 woolen fabrics　囲 当社は毛織物の販売代理店を求めています. We are looking for an agent for the sale of our *woolen fabrics*.

激化する【gekika suru】 intensify　囲 この種商品の競争は激化しました. The competition of the goods was greatly *intensified*.

激増する【gekizō suru】 increase suddenly [markedly]　囲 この商品の需要は激増しています. The demand of these goods *increases suddenly.* / 当社には注文が激増しています. We *have a rush* of orders.

下旬【gejun】 late in a month　囲 10月下旬 *at the end of* [*late in*] October

決意する【ketsui suru】 decide　囲 政府はこの計画の断行を決意した. The government *decided* to put this program into realization.

欠航する【kekkō suru】 suspend voyage　囲 東京大阪間の定期船は冬には欠航しがちです. The liners between Tokyo and Osaka are liable to be *suspended* in winter.

決済[算]【kessai】 settlement　囲 すぐ決済くださるよう催促申し上げます. We urge that you make this *settlement* without delay. / 遺憾ながら弊店は目下のところ決済できかねます. We much regret to say that we are unable to make you a *settlement* for the present. / 当社は半期決算を行った. We did a half-yearly *settlement.* ‖ ―報告 a statement of account ‖ ―期間 settlement [accounting] period ‖ ―する settle an account　囲 当社では毎月末に決算する. We *settle accounts* at the end of every month.

欠損【*kesson*】loss; deficit 例 この取り引きは1万円の欠損となる. This business results in a *loss* of 10,000 yen. / その結果100万円の欠損となった. This caused deficit of one million yen.

決定【*kettei*】decision 例 当社はこの価格の決定権はない. We have no *decision* over this price. / 至急貴方の確定的決定電請う. Telegraph us your definite *decision* as soon as possible. / これ以上本オファーにしておくこと不可能につき至急貴方の決定を待つ(電). Must have your *decision* at once as it is impossible to keep offer open any longer. / それは委員会の決定に従って販売されることになっている. It is to be sold in accordance with the *decision* of the committee [as the committee determines]. / この件につき貴社の早急な決定をお願いします. We ask for your immediate *decision* on the matter.

欠点【*ketten*】defect; fault; weak point 例 わが社の欠点は従業員の不足である. We have a weak point for lack of hands.

月賦【*geppu*】monthly instalments 例 当社はこの商品代金を5万円ずつ月賦で支払う. We pay the price for the goods by *monthly instalments* of 50,000 yen each.

月末【*getsumatsu*】the end of the month 例 この商品は月末渡しです. These goods are delivered at *the end of the month.*

結論【*ketsuron*】《come to a》conclusion 例 この交渉は結論に達した. This negotiation *came to a conclusion.* / これまでに集めることのできた業務上の報告からは現在まだ決定的な結論が出せない. The business reports which we have been able to accumulate so far do not allow us to draw a definite *conclusion* right now.

懸念【*kenen*】(する) fear; worry; be anxious 例 懸念が高まる. A *fear* grows. / 当社は結果について懸念しています. We *are anxious* about the result.

気配【*kehai*】tendency 例 市場は上昇傾向の気配です. The market has had an upward *tendency.*

下落【*geraku*】(する) fall; decline 例 外国為替相場の総下落 a

general *decline* in the rate of foreign exchange / 目下のとこ
ろ早期下落の兆しはない模様です. There is no indication of
an early decline at present. / 物価は下落しつつある. The
prices are *declining*. / 価格は下落する見込み. Prices are expected to *decline*. / 全積荷の約半分の市場面値が相当下落してい
ます. The market value of about 50 per cent of the total
shipment is considerably *reduced*.

懸案【*ken-an*】 a pending [an outstanding] question 囲 懸案の
クレームを解決してほしい. We hope that you will settle the
pending claim.

原案【*gen-an*】 original plan 囲 当社は貴社の原案に賛成いたし
ます. We support your *original plan*.

原因【*gen-in*】 cause; origin; reason 囲 米企業の欧州企業に対
する優位性の原因は沢山ある. There are many *causes* of the
superiority of American business over European enterprises
[businesses; counterparts]. / 原因は能率の低い農法と肥料の不
足にある. The *reason* is found in insufficient farming techni-
que and shortage of fertilizers. || に—する cause; be due to;
be attributable to 囲 これが原因で貴社に大変面倒を掛けた.
This *caused* you a great deal of trouble. / 物価の高騰は農
産物を放出しないのが主な原因である. The rise in price *is
attributable* mainly *to* the farmers' holding of their stocks.

原価【*genka*】 cost 囲 原価が少し下がった. There is a little
decrease in the *cost*. / これらの価格はかろうじて生産原価をカ
バーする. These prices barely cover the *cost* of production.
|| —を切って at a loss; below cost 囲 原価を切っても売り続
けなければならない. They may even have to keep selling
at a loss.

減価【*genka*】 allowance; discount; reduction in price 囲 1
個につき少なくとも 900 円の減価を御請求申し上げねばなりませ
ん. We must claim an *allowance* [*discount*] at least ￥900
per case. / それに対しては相当な減価をしていただけると信じて
います. We trust that you will be able to give us a reason-
able *allowance* for them. || —償却 depreciation

見解【*kenkai*】view; opinion **囫** その問題については当社は別の見解を持っている. We have a different *view* about the matter. / それは見解の相違である. It's a matter of *opinion*.

減額【*gengaku*】reduction; cut; reduced price **囫** 値下げがあるにちがいない. There must be a *cut* in prices.

研究【*kenkyū*】(する) study; research **囫** 目下, 方法手段を研究中です. We are *discussing* [*studying*] ways and means. / 弊社の研究センターでは研究員たちが鋼の物性に対する高圧の効果を研究しています. Scientists are *studying* the effects of high pressures on the behavior of steel in our *research* center. ‖ ―室[科] seminary **囫** 私は大阪商大研究科を修了しました. I have got through the *seminary* of the Osaka Commercial College. ‖ ―心 scholastic ambition; thirst for knowledge **囫** 彼は研究心が旺盛である. He has a real *thirst for knowledge*.

言及する【*genkyū suru*】refer (to) **囫** 当社はこの問題に言及しないように気を付けた. We took care not to *refer to* this matter.

現金【*genkin*】cash **囫** それは現金で支払われた. It was paid in *cash*. / 支払いが現金でなされるのはまれだ. Payments are rarely made in *cash*. / 現金取引のみをお勧めいたします. We would advise *cash* transactions only. / 品物は注文と同時に現金払いで送付されました. The order was forwarded to us with the *cash*. / 現金預金がなくては取引できません. We cannot do business without a *cash* deposit. ‖ ―出納器 cash register ‖ ―にする cash; realize **囫** 約半分は容易に現金化できる. About half of the order is readily *realizable*.

厳禁する【*genkin suru*】forbid [prohibit] strictly **囫** この商品は輸入することを厳禁されている. These goods are *strictly prohibited* from being imported.

権限【*kengen*】authority **囫** 当社はこの商品に関して輸出の権限を与えられた. We were given *authority* to export these products. ‖ ―を与える empower; authorize **囫** IFC は世界銀行から4億ドルを限度として借り入れをする権限を与えられている. The IFC is *authorized* [*empowered*] to borrow up to $ 400 million from the World Bank.

検査 【kensa】 inspection 例 商品は厳重な検査を通っております.
The goods passed rigorous *inspections*. / 検査の結果，800 ヤー
ドに織りむらが見つかりました. As a result of *inspection*, we
found stripes on 800 yards. ‖ 一証明書 inspection certificate

現在 【genzai】 at present; for the moment ‖ 一の current;
existing

現在高 【genzaidaka】 the amount in [on] hand; stock in [on]
hand 例 9 月 30 日現在の残高 the *balance* as of September
30 / 現在高はいつもの額を上回っている. *Stock on hand* is
above the usual amount.

原産地 【gensanchi】 the country of origin 例 原産地は各包装の
上に明記すること. *The country of origin* should be clearly
stamped on each package.

現市況 【genshikyō】 the present position of the market; the
present market conditions 例 同商品における現市況いかがで
すか. What is *the present position of the market* in the
products?

厳守する 【genshu suru】 observe [keep] strictly 例 当社は秘密
を厳守します. We *keep* a secret *strictly*. / 企業は規則を厳守し
なければならない. The firm must *observe* the rules.

減少 【genshō】 decrease; reduction 例 わが国の輸入は年々減少
しつつある. Imports to our country are on the *decrease* year
by year. ‖ 一する diminish; be reduced; decline; go down

現状 【genjō】 present situation [condition]; existing circumstances; status quo 例 当社の電子計算機の生産は現状を維持
しています. The production of electronic computers maintains
its *present situation*. / 現状においてはこれが当社のなし得る最
善のオファーです. This is the very best offer we can make
under the *existing* [*present*] *circumstances*. / 現状を維持した方
がよい. The *status quo* had better be maintained. / それは現状
ではちょっと無理だ. You can hardly do it under the *present
conditions*.

原子力 【genshiryoku】 atomic power [energy] 例 航空機用原
子力エンジンも，もう少しで実現されそうなところに来ている.

Atomic powered aircraft engines now seem to be a reality.

減じる 【*genjiru*】 deduct 例 当社はこの品物については5％の減額をいたします. We *deduct* 5% from the price of the goods.

減税 【*genzei*】 tax reduction; reduction of taxes ‖ —する reduce taxes 例 この品は3％減税された. These goods *taxes were reduced* by 3%.

原則 【*gensoku*】: —として as a rule 例 原則として当社の取り引きは信用状にて行っています. *As a rule*, we do business on the Letter of Credit.

舷側 【*gensoku*】 ship's side ‖ —渡し free alongside; f.a.s.

見地 【*kenchi*】 point of view; standpoint 例 購入者の見地からみて，この製品の価格は高い. From purchaser's *point of view* [standpoint], the price of this article is rather high.

現地 【*genchi*】 field; spot 例 当社のプラント輸出前に現地視察のため社員が赴きます. Before the exportation of our plants, the staff of our company will go into *the field* for investigation. ‖ —の[で] in the region; on the scene [spot] 例 現地の食糧品市場は大変競争が激しい状態だ. The food market *in the region* is in a very competitive condition.

顕著 【*kencho*】: —な notable; remarkable; conspicuous; outstanding 例 下落傾向は特に国際商品において顕著であった. The downward tendency was especially *conspicuous* in the international trade article. / ナイロンの性質のうちで最も顕著なものは絹にまさる弾力性です. Of the excellent qualities of nylon, the most *outstanding* is its elasticity, which exceeds even that of silk.

限度 【*gendo*】 limit; bounds ‖ —がある there is a limit in; be limited to ‖ —として within the limits ((of)); up to 例 当社は1千万円を限度として借り入れをする権能を与えられた. We were empowered to borrow *up to* ￥10,000,000 from the bank.

検討 【*kentō*】: —中 under study; under review ‖ —の結果 upon examination; after a thorough study 例 ～の値段を御検討次第，電報の引き合いを求めます. *Upon examination* of our

quotations on ~, please send us your inquiries by cable. ‖ ＿
する examine; review; study; consider; discuss 囫 あらゆ
る角度から検討した. *We considered* the matter in all its
bearings. We *studied* the matter from all angles. / 貴社から
書簡をいただいたらすぐそれらについて検討したい. We would
like to *discuss* them upon hearing from you. / この会社に関
する貴社の報告書をよく検討しました. We have *reviewed* all
the reports you have given us on this company.

見当【*kentō*】: ＿が外れる misdirect; direct wrongly; make a
wrong guess ‖ ＿の worth of 囫 わが社には常時 200 万円見当
の在庫があります. We usually stock about 2 million yen
worth of merchandise.

現場【*genba*】spot 囫 ロンドンでは綿花現場渡し 1 ポンドにつき
17.8 セントで底値を突いた. The price of raw cotton touched
the lowest point at 17.80 cents per pound for the *spot* delivery in London. / 自由に現場を御覧ください. We shall welcome
the survey of the *spot* by your representative. ‖ ＿渡し条件
loco terms ‖ ＿監督 foreman

現品【*genpin*】goods in stock; stock on hand 囫 現品はい
つもの額を上回っている. *Stock on hand* is above the usual
amount. ‖ ＿先渡し goods promptly delivered ‖ ＿引換払 cash
on delivery; C.O.D. 囫 現品引換払で配送ください. Please
deliver *C.O.D.*

絹布商【*kenpushō*】silk mercer 囫 絹布商を開業しました. We
have established ourselves as *silk mercers*.

現物【*genbutsu*】spot goods; spots 囫 現物を見てから買うこと
にしている. We make it our custom to buy an article after
seeing *spot goods*. ‖ ＿取引 spot trading ‖ ＿市場 spot market
‖ ＿値段 spot price

原本【*genpon*】original (work [copy]) 囫 信用状原本を至急当
方に送付いただきたい. Please send us the L/C *original* immediately.

権利【*kenri*】right; claim; privilege ‖ ＿の行使 exercise of the
right ‖ ＿を獲得する acquire the rights ‖ ＿金 key money; a

premium ‖ —落ち値段（株式の）ex rights; ex new; ex warrants ‖ —を行使する exercise the rights　例　最初の選択をする権利を行使する．We will *exercise the right* to make first choice.

原料【*genryō*】raw material　例　原料高 high cost of *raw materials* / 原料払底 shortage of *raw materials* / 原料品の価格が上昇したことを御存知と思います．You are probably aware of the rise in *raw material* prices.

【こ】

故意【*koi*】: —の（に）intentional(ly); deliberate(ly); (on purpose)　例　遅延は故意の怠慢による．The delay is due to *intentional* neglect. / 彼は故意にそれをやった．He did it *on purpose* [*intentionally*].

請う【*kou*】ask for; request; beg; appeal　例　彼の援助を請いなさい．*Ask for* his assistance.

好意【*kōi*】favor; courtesy　例　少なくとも御返事くださるくらいの御好意は願います．At least, please grant us the *favor* of a reply. / 将来機会があれば，御好意に報いることをお約束します．If there is a chance [Should there be an opportunity] in the future, we shall be only too glad to reciprocate your *courtesy*. / 商工会議所の御好意により貴社が信頼のおける輸出商だと知りました．By *courtesy* of Chamber of Commerce and Industry, we have come to know that you are a large and reliable exporter. / 御好意に対しあらかじめお礼申し上げます．We thank you in advance [request you to accept our thanks] for the anticipated *favor*. / 御好意深謝いたします．Thank you very much for your *courtesy*.

合意【*gōi*】: —の上で by mutual agreement [consent]　例　この約束は双方の合意によってなされた．This promise was made *by mutual consent*.

後援【*kōen*】（者）support(er); (sponsor)　例　政府後援の government-*sponsored* / 彼には森という後援者がある．He has a *supporter* in the person of Mori. / 彼を後援してあげなさい．Give him *support*.

高価【kōka】: —な expensive; costly; dear; valuable **例** 高価品 valuable goods / 貴社の価格は少し高価です． Your prices are rather *high*.

硬貨【kōka】 hard money; hard currency; metallic currency; coin **例** ソ連は硬貨で支払う． The Soviet Union pays us in *hard currency*.

効果【kōka】 effect; result **例** 効果をもたらす bring an immediate *result* / 効果はただちに生じた． The *effect* was immediate． / その方法は効果が薄い． The means will have little *effect*.

硬化する【kōka suru】 stiffen [harden] ((one's attitude)) **例** 何年もの経験が彼の態度を硬化させた． Years of experince has *hardened his attitude*.

梗概【kōgai】 outline **例** 会合の梗概を述べてください． Please *give an outline of* the meeting.

航海中【kōkaichū】 at sea; on [during] a voyage **例** 今では航海中の船に電話ができる． We can telephone to a man on board a ship *at sea* today． / 航海中われわれの船は数度暴風雨にあった． Our ship was overtaken by a storm several times *during our voyage*.

合格【gōkaku】: —する pass [succeed in] an examination **例** 受験者の2割が検定試験に合格した． Twenty per cent of the applicants *passed* [*succeeded in*] the certificate examination. ‖ —しない fail to pass

交換【kōkan】 exchange; replacement **例** 電信の交換により同封注文のごとく商談の締結をみた． The *exchange* of telegrams has resulted in business as per the enclosed order． / 欠陥品の代わりにすぐに36の交換品を送ってください． Will you send us right away 36 *replacements* for the defective units？‖ —条件 bargaining point; counter proposition ‖ 手形—所 clearing house

好機【kōki】 chance; favorable opportunity **例** 弊社は好機を逸した． We missed the *chance*． / この好機を逃がしてはならな

い. You must not lose this *good chance*. / 好機到来. A *favorable opportunity* now presents itself.

後期【*kōki*】latter period; later term 囫 後期には2割生産をふやす. We will increase production by 20% for the *latter period*.

抗議【*kōgi*】: ―する protest to a person; make a protest against 囫 部長に抗議した. He *protested* to his manager. ‖ ―を申し込む enter a protest (with a person)

合議【*gōgi*】: ―の上で after consultation; by mutual consent 囫 部長と合議のうえその問題を解決した. We solved the problem *after consultation* with our manager.

高級【*kōkyū*】: ―(の) high-grade [-class]; high quality 囫 高級品を廉価にお求めになれます. You may rely on receiving a *high-grade* articles at low prices. / 弊社は高級品を輸出してきました. We have been exporting *high quality* goods.

公共【*kōkyō*】: ―の public; common 囫 彼は公共の福祉に貢献した. He contributed to the *public* welfare. ‖ ―事業 a public enterprise; a public project ‖ ―の利益 public good; public benefit

工業【*kōgyō*】(the manufacturing) industry (製造工業); the industries (総称) 囫 最近, 工業は著しく進歩した. Recently *industry* has developed remarkably. / 東京は日本の工業の中心地です. Tokyo is the *manufacturing* center of Japan. / エレクトロニクス産業は各種工業中うらやむべき地位にある. The electronic *industry* is placed in an enviable position among the *manufacturing industries*. / 国民の経済活動は健全な歩みを続けており昨年17%の成長を示した工業部門もある. The economic activity of the people is making healthy progress with an *industrial* sector that grew by as much as 17% last year. ‖ ―部門 industrial sector ‖ ―簿記 industrial bookkeeping ‖ ―技術 industrial technology ‖ ―用化学薬品 industrial chemicals

航空【*kōkū*】aviation; flight; flying 囫 乗客は今年かなり増えているが, 各航空会社の利益は大幅に落ちている. Despite impressive [fair] passenger gains this year, the *airline* com-

panies are suffering from a serious decline in profits. ‖ —便
で送る airmail; send by airmail 囫 弊社は貴社に新しい見本
を航空便で送ることに決めました. We have decided to *airmail*
a new sample to you. / 取り急ぎ当社見本を航空便で送ります.
We hasten to *send* you our samples *by airmail*. ‖ —運送受託
書 Air Consignment Note ‖ —貨物運送状 Air Transportation
Waybill ‖ —貨物受領書 Air Receipt ‖ —証券 Airway Bill ‖ —荷
物 airfreight ‖ —郵便小包受領書 Airmail receipt

合計 【*gōkei*】 total 囫 彼の出費は合計 200 ドルに達した. His
expenses reached a *total* of 200 dollars. ‖ —で~になる come
[amount] to 囫 それは合計数百万ポンドに達した. It *amounted
to* millions of pounds. ‖ —して in the aggregate; in total

好景気 【*kōkeiki*】 prosperity; boom ‖ 景気付く boom 囫 株式界
は好景気だ. The stock market is *booming*.

貢献する 【*kōken suru*】 make a contribution; contribute (to);
render services (to) 囫 国家に貢献する *render services* to the
state / 弊社は両国の友好関係樹立に大いに貢献した. We con-
tributed a lot towards establishing peace between the two
countries. / 弊社は貿易の発展のために大いに貢献した. We
made a great *contribution* toward the development of trade.

航行 【*kōkō*】 sailing 囫 海岸近くでは航行 [船の進み] は悪かった.
Sailing was bad near the coast.

広告 【*kōkoku*】 advertisement 囫 今朝の新聞紙上で若い 会計助
手入用との広告を偶然見つけました. I happened to see your
advertisement for a young assistant accountant in this
morning's paper. / タイムズ紙上の広告を見ましたので, 私はタ
イピストとして就職を申し込みます. In reply to your *advertisement* in Times, I wish to offer my services as a typist. ‖ —
する advertise 囫 本日のタイムズ紙上に御広告の電気器具の絵
入目録一冊御送付願います. Please send us a copy of your
illustrated booklet of Electric Appliances as *advertised* in
the Times. / 今朝の新聞に広告した. We *advertised* in this
morning's paper. ‖ —ビラ handbill ‖ —欄 an advertisement
column

交互計算 【*kōgokeisan*】 account current **例** 当行は御希望の通り貴店をお得意先として交互計算勘定を開きます．We number you among our clients by opening you an *account current* as desired. ‖ ―書 statement of account current

口座 【*kōza*】 account **例** 当行は貴下名義の口座を開いたことを通知申し上げます．We are pleased to inform you that we have opened an *account* in your name. ‖ 振替― a postal transfer account

公債 【*kōsai*】 (a public) loan; bond (証書) **例** 4分利付き公債 4 per cent *bonds* ‖ ―を募集する raise a loan ‖ ―を償還する redeem a loan

工作 【*kōsaku*】 operation; working; construction ‖ ―場 a work shop

公算 【*kōsan*】 probability **例** 弊社は好機を逸したという公算が大である．There is a strong *probability* that we missed the chance.

公使 【*kōshi*】 a minister **例** 朝公使と会談する．We have a meeting with the *minister* in the morning. ‖ 特命全権― an envoy extraordinary and minister plenipotentiary ‖ ―館 legation

行使する 【*kōshi suru*】 exercise **例** 判事は任務を遂行し職権を行使する．The judge *exercises* the duties and powers of his offices.

合資会社 【*gōshi gaisha*】 limited partnership **例** 合資会社がこういう状況では適当でしょう．A *limited partnership* would be appropriate in these circumstances.

口実 【*kōjitsu*】 excuse; pretext ‖ を―に on the pretext of **例** 彼は病気を口実に事務所を休んだ．He kept away from office *on the pretext of* being ill.

控除 【*kōjo*】 deduction ‖ 基礎― basic deduction; personal exemption ‖ ―する deduct ‖ ―額 the amount deducted **例** その額から1万円を控除される have 10,000 yen *deducted* from the amount / 控除額は個人費用に充当するものでした．*The amount deducted* was to cover private expenses.

交渉 【kōshō】 negotiation 例 直接交渉に入る enter into direct negotiations / オランダ造船会社との交渉は不調に終った. *Negotiations* with a Dutch shipbuilding company have resulted in failure. ‖ —する negotiate; get in touch with 例 A社はまだ現地輸入業者と交渉中です. The A company is still *negotiating with* local importers. / 新丸ビル 400 番の同社と御交渉ください. You *get in touch with* them at 400 Shin-Marunouchi Building.

公証人 【kōshōnin】 notary public; N.P.

工場 【kōjō】 factory; plant; workshop; mill 例 弊社はその工場からすべての商品を買います. We buy all the goods from the *mills*. ‖ —長 factory (plant) manager ‖ —渡し ex factory ‖ —渡値段 ex factory price

更新 【kōshin】 renewal ‖ —する renew 例 商標は 20 年ごとに更新することができる. A trademark may be *renewed* every twenty years.

幸甚 【kōjin】: —である shall be very glad [much obliged]; appreciate 例 多少猶予いただければ幸甚です. We shall *be much obliged* if you will give us a little more time. / 東京貿易会社の貴市場における評判を知らせていただければ幸甚に存じます. We would *appreciate* it if you inform us of the reputation of the Tokyo Trading Co., Ltd. in your market.

後進国 【kōshinkoku】 (発展途上国) developing country 例 これらの製品は後進国ではよく売れる. These prodocts sell well in developing *countries*.

合成樹脂 【gōsei jushi】 plastic 例 レーヨンはセルロースから作られた合成樹脂の一種である. Rayon is a kind of *plastic* made from cellulose.

口銭 【kōsen】 commission 例 いつも多大の口銭を稼ぐ. They always earn a huge *commission*. / 弊社は口銭問屋を開業しました. We have established ourselves as *commission* agent.

構想 【kōsō】 conception; idea; a plan; a plot 例 構想が雄大である be grand in *conception* / 構想を練らなければならない. We shall have to think out *a plan*.

後退【kōtai】retreat; recession **例** ヨーロッパでは景気の後退が心配される. In Europe the business *recession* is feared. / 今日の所得率の後退を重視する必要があろう. You should take seriously the current *recessions* in the earnings rates.

光沢【kōtaku】luster; brilliance **例** 数千年間, 絹は珍品で光沢があるため尊重され高貴の衣服であった. For thousands of years silk was the garment of royalty and nobility because of its rarity and *brilliance*.

公団【kōdan】public corporation **例** 公団は株主に対し責任がある. A *public corporation* is responsible to its shareholders.

こう着【kōchaku】: —状態に at a deadlock **例** 生産はこう着状態にあります. The production is *at a deadlock*.

工賃【kōchin】the cost of labor **例** 弊社は工賃を減らすことに努力した. We tried to reduce *the cost of labor*.

好都合【kōtsugō】: —の convenient; favorable **例** 代理店になると都合のよいことがお分かりになると思います. We hope you will find it *convenient* to be represented. / この方が好都合です. This will be more *convenient* to us.

工程【kōtei】(manufacturing) process; progress (of work) **例** 生産工程は特許を受けている. The *manufacturing process* is patented.

公定【kōtei】: —の official ‖ —割引率 official discount rate ‖ —歩合 official rate **例** 公定歩合よりレートを低くできますか. Can we have a lower rate than the *official rate*? ‖ —価格 official price **例** 公定価格は来週上がりそう. The *official price* is likely to increase next week. ‖ —相場 official quotation ‖ —相場で at official quotations

好転する【kōten suru】improve; (take a) turn for the better **例** 市況は好転しています. The market condition has been *improved* [is *taking a favorable turn*]. / 仕入状況好転により次の商品を提供できます. As a result of the *favorable* supply situation, we are able to offer you the following goods.

高度【kōdo】: —の high; advanced **例** 高度成長 *high* growth / アメリカの活動は少数の高度技術産業に集中している. The

American activity is concentrated in a few *high* technology industries. / それを製作するには高度の技術を要する. An *advanced* technique is required for producing it.

口頭【*kōtō*】: —の（で）oral(ly) **例** 口頭試問 an *oral* examination / 彼はそれを口頭で申し入れた. He proposed it *orally.*

行動【*kōdō*】: —する act **例** 人は行動のいかんによって判断される. We are judged by how we *act.*

合同【*gōdō*】: —の amalgamated **例** 合同の業務を営みます. Our *amalgamated* business will be carried on. ‖ —で in partnership with **例** 彼は父と合同で会社を設立した. He set up a company *in partnership with* his father.

甲仲【*kōnaka*】（甲種海運仲立人）space broker; freight broker **例** この甲仲は信頼できる. This *freight broker* is very reliable.

後任【*kōnin*】 successor **例** 彼の後任は決まっていない. His *successor* has not been decided upon. ‖ 〜の—として in succession to 〜

公認【*kōnin*】: —として officially **例** A氏は日本社会党公認として立候補した. Mr. A ran as an *officially* adopted candidate by the Japan Socialist Party. ‖ —会計士 C.P.A.; certified public accountant ‖ —記録 an official record ‖ 非—の unofficial

購買【*kōbai*】（する）purchase **例** 本品購買時期は冬です. The winter is the season for *purchasing* this article. ‖ —力 purchasing power ‖ —力平価 purchasing power parity

好評【*kōhyō*】 good [great] reputation; (の) favorite **例** この品はアメリカで好評です. This quality is enjoying a *good reputation* in the U.S.A. / 見本には好評の商標のものをすべて盛り込んだ. Our samples comprise all the *favorite* brands. / 卓球用ラケットは高品質のため好評を得た. We have earned *a great reputation* for excellence of quality in our ping-pong rackets.（ピンポン用ラケットを paddle という）/ 当社製品は世界中で好評を博しています. Our products are enjoying a *good reputation* all over the world.

公表【*kōhyō*】 official [public] announcement; publication **例** 書簡を公表します. We will make a letter *open to the public.* ‖

意見を—する make one's opinion known

交付する【*kōfu suru*】grant; deliver **例** 通知書を交付する transfer a slip; serve a notice / どうぞ船積指図書を御交付ください. Please *grant* us a shipping order.

公文書【*kōbunsho*】an official document ‖ —偽造 forgery of an official document **例** 公文書偽造で告発されよう. He will be charged with forgery of *an official document.*

合弁【*gōben*】: —の joint **例** 合弁事業の形で行きたいという提案に興味があります. We are interested in the suggestion to establish some type of *joint* venture. ‖ —会社 joint corporation ‖ —で経営する operate under joint venture

公報【*kōhō*】official report; bulletin **例** 貴社の公報に当社の宣伝を入れてくだされば幸いです. We should be obliged if you would insert our advertisement in your *bulletin.*

合法【*gōhō*】: —的な lawful, legal ‖ —的手段で by lawful means **例** この問題は合法的手段によって解決する必要がある. This problem must be solved *by lawful means.*

合名会社【*gōmei gaisha*】unlimited [general] partnership **例** われわれは合名会社を組織する予定. We intend to organize a general partnership. / 彼は父と一緒に合名会社を設立した. He set up an *unlimited partnership* with his father.

被る【*kōmuru*】suffer; sustain **例** 小売値は変動を被った. Retail prices *suffered* fluctuations. / 当方は大変な損失を被る. We *sustain* a great loss. / 当社は貴船積みが遅れただけ売り損じを被った. We *sustained* a loss of sales as a result of the delay of your shipment.

項目【*kōmoku*】clause; item **例** 社則は10項目から成る. The company regulations consist of ten *clauses.* / それはどの項目に入りますか. Under what *item* does it come?

公約する【*kōyaku suru*】pledge oneself (publicly) **例** 首相は減税を公約した. The Prime Minister *pledged himself* to give a tax reduction.

小売り【*kouri*】retail (sale; selling) **例** 販売店への義理上，当社では直接小売りをいたしません. In justice to our dealers, we do no *retail selling* ourselves. / 小売業を開店しました. We have opened a *retail* trade. / 私儀これまで薬品小売商店に勤務いたしました. I have been employed with a *retail* drug store. ‖ ―価格 retail price ‖ ―商 retailer

高利【kōri】 high interest **例** 高利で金借りができる. We can only borrow money *at a high rate of interest.* ‖ ―をむさぼる charge high interest ‖ ―貸しをする practice usury

合理【gōri】: ―的な(に) rational(ly) **例** それは合理的な考えだ. It is a *rational* idea. / それをもっと合理的に説明してもらいたい. We want to have it explained more *logically.* ‖ ―化する rationalize **例** わたしたちの生活は著しく合理化した. Our life has been remarkably *rationalized.*

高率【kōritsu】 high rate **例** ビールの高率課税が続くことはほとんど間違いありません. It is almost certain that beer will continue to be taxed *heavily* in the future.

効率【kōritsu】 efficiency **例** 最大限の効率のためにはこの方法で操作されなければならない. It must be operated in this way for maximum *efficiency.*

考慮【kōryo】 consideration **例** このことは当分考慮しないことに決定した. It is decided that we should leave this out of *consideration.* / 諸掛りの点では相当御考慮願えると思う. We are entitled to your careful *consideration* in receipt of charges. / その件は考慮中である. The matter is under *consideration.* ‖ 特別な― special regard ‖ ―する consider **例** 会計係の候補として考慮していただきたいと思います. I should like to have you *consider* me as an applicant for the position of accountant.

効力【kōryoku】 effect **例** その法律は5月1日から効力が発生する. The law takes *effect* on May 1. ‖ ―のある effective **例** この契約はもう効力がない. This contract is no longer *effective.*

航路【kōro】 route; line **例** われわれはヨーロッパ航路を選ぶ. We prefer the European *line.* ‖ 定期― regular line ‖ ―変更 deviation; change course

港湾【kōwan】 harbor ‖ ―荷役 stevedore ‖ ―施設 harbor facilities　**例** 港湾施設はここでは十分整っている. *Harbor facilities* are quite adequate here.

誤解 【*gokai*】 misunderstanding　**例** それは誤解です. That is a *misunderstanding*.

子株 【*kokabu*】 new stocks; new shares　**例** 子株が来週発行になる. *New shares* will be issued next week.

誤記 【*goki*】 clerical error; error in writing; misentry　**例** このミスは誤記によるものでした. This mistake was due to *clerical error*.

小切手 【*kogitte*】 check　**例** 100 ドルの小切手を同封しました. We are enclosing our *check* for \$ 100. / 小切手も手紙に同封することになる. A *check* will also be enclosed in the letter. / 金額 27 万円也小切手お送り願いたい. Your *check* for the full amount of ¥270,000 will be greatly appreciated. / 5,000 ドルの小切手をお送りくだされればまことに有り難く存じます. We shall be very appreciative to you if you will send us your *check* for \$ 5,000. ‖ 横線― crossed check ‖ 不渡り― dishonored check ‖ ―を現金に替える cash a check ‖ ―を振り出す issue a check ‖ ―で支払う pay by check

顧客 【*kokyaku*】 buyer; customer; client　**例** 我々は顧客の関心を誘うことができた. We have been able to interest our *buyers*. / 当店の製品が顧客に最善のサービスとなりうるように常に注意しています. We make it a practice to see that our *customers* get the best of service from our product. / 新しい顧客を増やすために努力しました. We made efforts to develop new *clients*. / 顧客はちょっとの高値にも我慢できないという. *Customers* say that they can not put up with slightest higher prices.

語句 【*goku*】 phrase; words and phrases　**例** 問題の語句は削除された. The problematic *phrase* has been deleted.

国際 【*kokusai*】 ―加入電信 Telex Teleprinter Exchange ‖ ―金融会社 I.F.C.=International Finance Corporation ‖ ―通貨基金 I.M.F.=International Monetary Fund ‖ ―収支 the balance of international payment　**例** 国際収支の型は一般に経済が発展す

るに従って変化します. The form of *the balance of international payment* generally changes in proportion to the advance of economical development. ‖ —電報 the international telegram 例 貿易取引に緊急を要する場合国際電報 が利用される. In a state of emergency in trade the *international telegram* is used. ‖ —輸送 international transportation 例 国際輸送には定期船による輸送と不定期船による輸送がある. In *international transportation*, there is conveyance by liner and conveyance by tramper.

国債 【*kokusai*】 a national loan [debt] 例 国債を募集する必要がある. It is necessary to *raise a national loan*.

告示 【*kokuji*】 notice 例 このカタログの定価は告示しないで変更することがある. The prices in this catalog are subject to change without *notice*. ‖ —を出す send out a *bulletin*; give notice; notify

国産 【*kokusan*】 (品) home products, domestic goods ‖ —の home-made 例 この品物は国産です. This article is *home-made*.

小口 【*koguchi*】 small [petty] order 例 本注文はごく小口であり, 当方の利益はきわめて薄い. This order is a particularly *petty order* and leaves us but meagre profit. / 貴社に過去3年小口の注文をしてきた. We have been giving you *small orders* for the past 3 years. ‖ —荷物 small lot [cargo]; a parcel ‖ —扱貨物 small lots consignment

国内 【*kokunai*】: —の domestic; internal; home 例 国内需要のため市況は強調です. The market is strong due to *domestic* [*inland*] demands. ‖ —価格 domestic price ‖ —消費 home consumption ‖ —信用状 domestic L/C

極秘 【*gokuhi*】 strict confidence [secrecy]; top secret ‖ —に in strict confidence 例 お知らせいただいたことは極秘に取り扱います. Any information you may give us will be treated *in strict confidence*. We shall treat the matter in strict confidence.

国民所得 【*kokumin shotoku*】 national income [earnings] 例 国

民所得は減少しつつある. *National income* is on the decrease.

国民総生産【*kokumin sōseisan*】gross national product [GNP]
囲 国民総生産は実質 5 ％の年間成長率を示した. *Gross national
product* maintained an increase rate of 5 percent in real
terms.

穀物【*kokumotsu*】cereals (英) corns; grains (米)　囲 主要取扱
商品は穀物. Our main trade is in *grains*.

ココム【*kokomu*】Co-ordinating Committee for Export Control
[COCOM] (対共産圏輸出統制機構　アイスランドを除く NATO
加盟国と日本の 15 カ国で組織されている.)

心当たり【*kokoro atari*】: —がある have something in mind　囲
彼には心当たりがある. He *has something in mind*.

心得【*kokoroe*】knowledge; rules　囲 事務心得 office *rules* / 彼
は商法の心得がある. He has some *knowledge* of commercial
laws.

心掛ける【*kokorogakeru*】keep [bear] in mind　囲 それは心掛け
ておこう. I will *bear* it *in mind*. I will *consider* it.

試み【*kokoromi*】test; (の) trial　囲 これは新しい試みだ. This
is a new *trial*. / これが最初の試みです. This is the first *test*. /
試みの御注文をいただきまして今後も御愛顧をいただき得ること
を確信いたしております. We are confident that a *trial* order
would win your further custom [patronage].

故障【*koshō*】breakdown; accident; mishap; obstacle; trouble
囲 機械の一時故障 a temporary *derangement* of machinery /
途中故障なく着いた. We arrived without any *trouble* [*accident*] on the way. / 当機械は故障がなく運転は簡単です. Our
machine is quite *trouble* free and is easy to operate. ‖ —を
生ずる go wrong with ～; get out of order; have a breakdown　囲 これは時々故障する. This sometimes *goes out of
order*. / 車が故障した. The car had a *breakdown*. The car
broke down. / モーターが故障している. Something is *wrong*
with the motor. / —付船荷証券 foul B/L; dirty bill of lading

個人的【*kojinteki*】: —(に) individual(ly); personal(ly); private
(ly)　囲 貴殿が個人的に尊敬されていることを知って喜びにたえ

ません. It is gratifying to learn of the esteem in which you are held *personally* [to learn that you are *personally* respected]. ‖ ─企業 individual enterprise ‖ ─経営 private management

答えて 【*kotaete*】 replying to; in reply; in response 例 10 日付引き合いに答えて価格表を同封した. *Replying to* [*Answering*] your inquiry of the 10th, we enclosed our price list. / これは 7 月 1 日付信信に答えるものです. This is *in reply* [*answer*; *response*] *to* your letter of July 1.

誇張 【*kochō*】 exaggeration 例 これは決して誇張ではありません. This is by no means an *exaggeration*. ‖ ─する exaggerate 例 A氏は誇張して話す癖がある. Mr. A has a way of *exaggerating*.

小包郵便 【*kozutsumi yūbin*】 parcel post 例 この包を小包郵便で出してください. Please send this package by *parcel post*. / 10 月 1 日付御注文品は早速調達して, 本日小包郵便でお送りします. Your order of October 1 has had our prompt attention, and the goods are being sent to you today by *parcel post*. / 新製品の見本 1 箱小包便で送ります. A box of samples of our new products is being sent to you by *parcel post*.

固定 【*kotei*】: ─資産 fixed assets ‖ ─費 fixed cost ((変動費 variable cost) 例 固定費は減額が必要. Our *fixed costs* must be reduced. ‖ ─している remain stationary

断わる 【*kotowaru*】 decline; refuse; reject; turn down 例 貴社の受注を断わる. We deeply regret having to *decline* your order. We wish you to understand our position of having to *decline* your offer. We hope you will understand the circumstances which compel us to *decline* your order. Production difficulties force us to *decline* further orders for this model for the time being. Supplies of raw materials are becoming difficult to obtain and we have no alternative but to *decline* your order.

この件に関し 【*konoken ni kanshi*】 on this matter 例 貴社の御意見を伺いたい. We want to have your opinion *on this matter*.

この場合【*konobaai*】in this instance 例 この場合は，別のメーカーと話を進める方がよいでしょう．It would be better for you to approach another manufacturer *in this instance.*

このような状態で【*konoyōna jōtai de*】under these circumstances 例 こういう状態ですから会は次の機会まで延ばします．*Under these circumstances,* we will put off the meeting until the next chance.

困らせる【*komaraseru*】annoy; embarrass; trouble 例 彼は当社を困らせるためにそれをやった．He did it just to *annoy* [*bother*; *trouble*] us. / そのため本当に当社は困った．It really *put* us *in trouble.*

困る【*komaru*】be in trouble; be hard up ((for money)); be embarrased; be at a loss ((for an answer)) 例 困っている．It is *embarrasing* [*regrettable*; *deplorable*]. / その店は当方と困ったことになっている．The shop *is in trouble* with us. / 貴商品の品質について苦情を申し上げなければならないことは実に困ったことです．It *is a matter for regret* that we have to complain of the quality of your goods. / 返事に困った．We *were at a loss* how to answer [for an answer]. / 彼は金に困っている．He is *hard up* for money. / 貴社在庫がほとんどないのは困ります．It is *regrettable* that you have little stock. ‖ 困ったことには to our annoyance 例 困ったことには，A社に注文した製品がまだ着かない．*To our annoyance,* the goods on order from A company have not arrived yet.

込み【*komi*】including [incl.]; included; with ‖ 運賃— freight prepaid ‖ 税金— duty paid 例 商品は税込みで送られる．The goods will be sent *duty paid.*

ころ【*koro*】around; about; on or about; toward(s) 例 4月初めごろ *towards* the beginning of April / 初納品は3月第1週ごろの見込み．The initial delivery will be *around* the first week in March.

壊れる【*kowareru*】be broken; break; be damaged ‖ 壊れやすい fragile 例 壊れやすい物 *Fragile* article / 壊れ物注意．*Fragile.* Handle with care. *Fragile—with care.* / ガラスは壊れやすい．

Glass is *fragile.*

懇願する【*kongan suru*】 beg; solicit for 例 御注文を懇願します. We solicit your order. ‖ —の上 at one's solicitation

根拠【*konkyo*】 basis; base; ground; foundation 例 このうわさは根拠がない. This rumor has no *foundation.* This rumor is *groundless.* ‖ —を置く base on; substantiate 例 当社の値段が他社に比して有利だという主張を根拠づける資料を送りました. We have sent you evidence to *support* [*substantiate*] our claim that our prices compare favorably with those of our competitors. ‖ —に基づいて on the basis of; on the ground that

今後【*kongo*】 hereafter; henceforth; hence

懇談【*kondan*】 consultation; discussion; talk ‖ —する have friendly talk with; consult heart to heart on the matter ‖ —の結果 upon [through] discussion; as a result of our unreserved exchange of views 例 懇談の結果問題は解決した. We solved the problem *upon thorough discussion.*

コンテナ輸送【*kontena yusō*】 containership transportation 例 コンテナ輸送が最も効率的. *Containership transportation* is the most efficient.

困難【*kon-nan*】 difficulty; trouble 例 M商会の破産以来同店は困難のもとに努力しています. Since the bankruptcy of M & Co, they are laboring under great *difficulties.*

こん包【*konpō*】 packing; parcel 例 こん包に荷印をお付けください. Please have the *parcels* marked. ‖ —材料 packing materials ‖ —料 packing charge ‖ —する pack 例 製品は, 運送のためしっかりこん包されなければならない. The manufactured goods must be *tightly packed* for transportation.

混乱【*konran*】 confusion; disorder 例 港は相当混乱している. There is considerable *confusion* in the port. / 町中が大混乱だった. The whole town was in a state of great *confusion.* ‖ —する be in [thrown into] confusion; run into confusion; fall into disorder; plunge into turmoil

【さ】

サービス【*sābisu*】service **例** 御愛顧を謝し，できる限りのサービスをさせていただきます．（文尾）We appreciate your patronage and will endeavor to render you every possible *service*. / あの店はサービスがいい．They give good *service* at that store. *Service* is good at that store. / この勘定書きにはサービス料も入っている．*Service* is charged on this bill. / そのメーカーはアフターサービスと部品を保証する．The manufacturer guarantees *service* and parts.

最悪【*saiaku*】the worst **例** 最悪の場合に備えなければならない．We must prepare [be prepared] for *the worst*. / 最悪の事態でも明るく振る舞うべきだ．We must keep cheerful even when things are at *their worst*. / 最悪の事態を切り抜けた．We got over *the worst*. / 最悪の場合には同社の援助を仰ぐ．*In the worst case* [*If the worst comes to the worst*], we will ask for their assistance.

再開【*saikai*】reopening; resumption ‖ —する reopen; resume **例** 貿易を再開する *reopen* foreign trade / 交渉を再開する reopen [resume] negotiations / 久しぶりに営業を再開した．The firm resumed their business after a long period. / その空港は戦後再開された．The airport was *reopened* after the war.

災害【*saigai*】disaster; accident ‖ —補償 accident compensation **例** 同社は災害補償案を有する．The company has an *accident compensation* scheme. ‖ —を被る suffer from a disaster ‖ —救助法 Natural Disaster Relief Law ‖ —地 the stricken district

財界【*zaikai*】economic world **例** 好景気で財界が活気づいた．*The economic world* is heading towards a boom. / 財界の事情が悪化している．*The economic world* is getting worse. ‖ —の大立て者 a leading [big] financier

最近【*saikin*】: —の the latest; up-to-date **例** 貴社最近のカタログ1部および価格表をお送りくださるようお願いします．We ask you to send us a copy of your *latest* catalog and price list.

細工【*saiku*】 workmanship; craftsmanship 囫 同社の細工は優秀. This company's *workmanship* is excellent. ‖ —する manipulate; work; make

最恵国約款【*saikeikoku yakkan*】 the most favored nation clause 囫 わが国は幾つかの契約で最恵国約款を保有. Our country has the *most favored nation clause* in some contracts.

債券【*saiken*】 bond; debenture 囫 債券は株式仲買人から簡単に購入できる. *Bonds* are easily bought through stockbrokers.

債権【*saiken*】 credit; claim ‖ —者 creditor 囫 全債券者に手紙を出し月末に支払いをすると伝えてください. Please send a letter to all of our *creditors* and tell them we will pay them at the end of the month. ‖ —確認 acknowledgement of obligation

再検討【*saikentō*】: —する reexamine; review ‖ —を要する require re-examination [further study] ‖ —の結果 as a result of re-investigation; upon re-examination [re-consideration] 囫 再検討の結果試し注文をすることにしました. *Upon our re-examination* we have decided to make a trial order.

在荷【*zaika*】 stock 囫 在荷はなはだ多く, 買申込少なく, その結果相場はいたって不振です. *Stocks* are very heavy, with few offers; consequently prices are flat. / 在荷がどんどん安くなりつつありますから, 至急注文をくださることをお勧めします. As the *stock* is fast running low, we advise you to lose no time in placing your order. / 在荷が累積していますので, これ以上の委託販売はお勧めしたくない. Because of the very large *stocks* lying here, we would not advise further consignments at present. / 当地市場目下在荷不足. The market here is at present suffering from the shortage of *stocks*.

最後【*saigo*】: —に for the last time; ultimately 囫 最後に月曜までは在庫品の出荷ができません. *For the last time* we cannot deliver the stock until Monday. / 最終的に社長によって決定が下されるでしょう. The decision will *ultimately* be decided by the president. ‖ —の手段として in the last resort; as one's only resource 例 最後の手段として政府から借金する必要があろう. *In the last resort* it will be necessary to borrow the money from the government.

在庫【*zaiko*】 stock; goods on hand 例 在庫が豊富. We have a large *stock* on hand. / 在庫品が不足を告げた. The goods in *stock* have run short. / 在庫がない. We have no *stock* of the goods. We have no goods in *stock*. / 在庫品を調査することを要求した. We called to examine their *stocks*. / 御注文はたいてい在庫品で供給できます. We can execute most orders from *stock*. / 一流メーカー3社は手元ストック増加のため割引をしている. The three leading manufacturers have been reducing the price owing to the increasing *stocks* on their hands. / 現在の在庫が出尽くせば2度と安い値段は出ません. We shall be unable to repeat low prices when our present *stock* is exhausted. / 年末に棚卸しをするので，それまでに在庫を一掃したい. It is our aim to clear this *stock* before the end of the year when we are stocktaking. ‖ —品を売る dispose of a stock ‖ —品目録を作る make an inventory 例 毎月在庫品目録を作る店がいくつかある. Some shops *make an inventory* of their stock every month. ‖ —調整 inventory adjustment 例 新在庫品のために在庫調整をする必要があった. Because of the new stock it was necessary to make an *inventory adjustment*. ‖ —を補充する 例 資材の在庫補充はいつになるか見当がつかない. We have no idea when the material will be *restocked* ‖ —過剰である overstock 例 現在在庫品過多のため，当社は遺憾ながら貴社の申し込みを引き受けることができません. Because we are *overstocked* at present, we regret we are not in a position to accept your offer.

最高【*saikō*】: —級 the highest quality 例 わが国では最高級のあらゆる日用品が安く販売されている. In our country practically all daily necessities of *the highest quality* are sold at low prices. ‖ —速度 top speed ‖ —級 AAA 例 最高級21番手生糸 3 A 21 d Raw Silk ‖ —価格 ceiling price (米); top

price（英）囫 この品は今年の最高値を記録した. This article
recorded the *top price* [*new peaks*] for this year.

再考【*saikō*】 reconsideration; second thoughts 囫 このことにつ
いては再考の余地がない. There is no room for *reconsideration* concerning [about] this matter. / 再考の結果彼は行く決
心をした. On *second thoughts* [Upon *reconsideration*] he
decided to go. ‖ —する reconsider 囫 この問題は再考する必
要がある. This matter needs to be *reconsidered*.

さい先【*saisaki*】 a good start 囫 さい先を祝う wish one *good
luck* / 道中のさい先を祝う wish one *a safe journey* ‖ —のよい
have [make; get] a good [lucky] start [beginning] 囫 さ
い先よく世に出る get a good start in life / 事業のさい先はよ
い. The business has *begun under fair auspices*.

採算【*saisan*】 margin; estimation; calculation 囫 貴指値では
採算がとれない, 値引きの余地ないか. Your limit leaves us
no *margin*. Is there no room for concession? / 輸出取引に
しても輸入取引にしても, 取り引きの成否は売買価格の採算によ
る. In the export or import trade, the issue of the trade
depends on the *estimation* of the sale price. ‖ —がとれない
disregard profit; be below the cost; be unprofitable ‖ —が
とれる be profitable; pay; be remunerative ‖ —圏内 within
paying limit ‖ —限度 level workable 囫 貴値段は当方の採算限
度より1割方高すぎるようです. Your quotation is about 10%
higher than the *level workable* to us.

再三【*saisan*】 again and again; repeatedly; over and over
again; once and again 囫 再三注意した. We warned you
again and again. / まちがった船積について再三注意した. We
have reminded you of the wrong shipment *on several
occasions*.

財産【*zaisan*】 estate; property 囫 死去した人の財産はそれを残
された人の間で分配される. When a person dies, his *estate* is
divided up among those to whom he has left it. / その機械類
は, 当社の資産である. That item of machinery is the *property*
of our company. / 当社取引銀行は株式会社東海銀行東京店であ

り，当社の財産状態は同行に問い合わせください．Our Bankers are The Tokai Bank, Ltd., Tokyo, whom you may please ask for our *credit standing*. ‖ —目録 inventory of property ‖ —を作る make a fortune 例 新製品の売れ行きがこんなによいと同社は一財産作るだろう．If the new range of products keep selling so quickly, the company will *make a fortune.*

最小限【*saishōgen*】the minimum; the least; the smallest 例 従業員に払われる給料の最低は年300万円．The *minimum* salary paid to the workers is 3 million yen a year. / ビルの売却は株主の最少限の危険負担でなされるだろう．The sale of the building will be made with the *minimum* of risk to our share holders. ‖ —にとどめる minimize; maintain at minimum 例 同社は最少限2割の利益幅を維持できる．The company can maintain *at minimum* a 20% profit margin. ‖ 最小引受可能数量 minimum quantity acceptable 例 貴社の最小引受可能数量を調査した．We have investigated with interest your *minimum quantity acceptable.*

最上【*saijō*】the best 例 当社の商品は上等品質であり，また最上の仕上げであることを保証できます．We can assure you that our goods are of the first class quality and of *the best* workmanship. ‖ —級品 top [best; highest] quality goods [products]; goods of best brands

催促する【*saisoku suru*】press; urge; demand; expedite 例 借金返済を催促した．They *urged* [*demanded*] us to pay back our debts. / 返事を催促されてすぐ手紙を書いた．As we were *asked* [*requested*] to answer, we wrote to them at once.

最大限【*saidaigen*】(に) (at one's) maximum; (to) the utmost 例 できる最大限の割引です．This is our *maximum* allowance that we can make. / 最高の製品を作り出すために全員が最大限の努力をする必要がある．To produce the highest quality products it is necessary that everyone works *at his maximum* effort.

財団法人【*zaidan hōjin*】foundation; juridical [incorporated] foundation

再注文する【*saichūmon suru*】repeat orders; place reorders 例 この注文が満足に履行されるなら喜んで再注文しましょう. If this order is executed in a satisfactory manner, we shall be glad to send you *repeat orders*. / 再注文をいただきたい. We hope to receive your repeat orders. / 再注文できる. We are sure to *place reorders* with you.

最低【*saitei*】: ＿値段 lowest price 例 何とぞ最低値段を付けて見本をお送りください. Kindly send us samples with your *lowest prices*. / 下記のとおり最低値段を申し上げます. We quote you our *lowest price(s)* as follows. / この手紙受け取りしだい, 靴500足運賃保険料込みシンガポール渡し最低値段を電報でお知らせください. On receipt of this letter, please cable us your *lowest prices* C.I.F. Singapore for 500 pair of shoes. / 商品の最低値段を御通知ください. Please quote us the *lowest price* for the goods. ‖ ＿価格 floor price（米）; minimum price（英）‖ ＿量注文 minimum order

最適【*saiteki*】: ＿の the most suitable; fittest 例 本人を貴店に最適の人物として推薦申し上げます. We heartily recommend him as *the* person *best fit* for your shop in view of his honesty.

細部【*saibu*】: ＿に関しては as to the particulars; for further details

債務【*saimu*】obligation; debts; indebtedness; liabilities 例 債務はすぐ支払われた. All *obligations* have been paid at once. / いかなる債務も支払能力がある. They are solvent for any *engagement*. / あの会社は一度も債務履行を怠ったことはありません. That firm have never failed to meet their *obligations*. ‖ ＿を果たす perform one's obligation ‖ ＿不履行 default of obligation

財務［政］【*zaimu*】financial affairs 例 財務はすべてA氏の管理下にある. All *financial affairs* are under the control of Mr A. ‖ ＿諸表 financial statements 例 今月の財務諸表は同社の赤字の縮少を示している. This month's *financial statements* show an improvement of the company's deficit. ‖ ＿状態

financial standing [position] **例** 当社の財務状態について銀行にお問い合わせください. You may please ask our bankers for our *financial standing.* / 取り引きしようとする会社の財務状態を調査すべきです. You should inquire into the *financial standing* of a firm with whom you intend to have dealings. / 彼は財務上の援助が必要だ. He needs *financial* help. / 突然ながら貴地A商会の財務状態をお尋ねします. We take the liberty of asking your views on the *financial standing* of A & Co. of your city. / 商社の評判, 信頼性, 財務状態, 取引関係について御高見を承わりたい. We shall be obliged if you will give us your opinion as to their character, trustworthiness, *financial position* and business connections. ‖ 赤字— unbalanced finance ‖ 健全— sound finance ‖ —投融資 treasure loans and investments

最優先 【saiyūsen】 the first preference [choice]; top priority **例** その問題は最優先事項として取り扱われた. The problem was given *the highest* [*top*] *priority.* / 新しい時間表を作成することが最優先の課題. *Top priority* must be *given* to organizing the new time table.

裁量 【sairyō】 discretion; discretionary power **例** この件は貴社の裁量に任せます. We leave this matter to your *discretion.* / 全裁量権を委任します. We give you full *discretionary power.*

材料 【zairyō】 material; factor; element; data ‖ 原— raw materials ‖ —難 short of materials; lack of data

さかのぼる 【sakanoboru】 trace back; go back to the past; be retrospective **例** 新運賃レートは4月1日にさかのぼる. The new rate of freight *is retrospective* from April 1. ‖ さかのぼって retrospectively **例** 新給与ベースは4月1日にさかのぼって支給される. The new basis for salaries is applicable *retrospectively* to April 1.

下がる 【sagaru】 fall; drop; go down; decline; sag (物価) **例** 値段は下がり気味で市場は平静. The market has now gone extremely quiet with prices inclined to *sag.* / 賃金は必ず下がる. Wages will *fall* without fail. / 相場が下がる. Market *de-*

clines [*falls*; *loses*]. / 相場が下がり勝ちになる. Market *droops*. / 値段が下がる. Prices *go down* (*wards*) [*decline*; *fall*]. / 下がり気味. Prices tend *downwards*.

盛ん 【*sakan*】: ＿な (に) prosperous (ly); successful (ly); cordial (ly); vigorous (ly); (in full flourish) 例 盛んな会だった. We had a *successful* meeting. / 盛んに議論した. They argued *vigorously*. / 盛んな歓迎を受けた. I was given a *cordial* reception [a *warm* welcome].

先売【*sakiuri*】 prior sale 例 売申込はすべて先売御免条件です. All offers are subject to *prior sale*.

先払い 【*sakibarai*】 payment in advance; advance payment; prepayment 例 A社はいつも先払いをする. Company A always makes its *payments in advance*. / 当社は購入品すべての先払いを要求する. Our company requires *prepayment* of all purchases. ‖ ＿運賃 carriage forward; freight payable at destination

先日付【*sakihizuke*】 (を付ける) antedate (後日付 postdate) 例 アメリカへの輸出品は入港先での検証を容易にするため後日付にすることが必要. All goods for export to America need to be *postdated* to enable easier identification at the port of entry. / 輸送中の全商品を先日付にすることが必要. It is neceessary to *antedate* all goods in transit.

先物【*sakimono*】 forward [future] deliveries ‖ ＿為替の予約 forward exchange contract ‖ ＿為替取引 (相場) forward exchange dealing or transaction [rate] ‖ ＿で売る sell for future delivery ‖ ＿売買をする deal in futures ‖ ＿買い purchase of futures

先行き 【*sakiyuki*】 prospect ‖ ＿よい prosperous 例 羊毛市場の先行きよく値段はしっかりのようである. It seems that the wool market continues to be *prosperous*, and the price remains firm. ‖ ＿不安 fear of unfavorable development

先渡し【*sakiwatashi*】 forward delivery 例 先渡しの停とんにより商品の販売が制限された. The sale of goods was restricted due to the breakdown of *forward deliveries*. / 先渡しの場所

をはっきり示すべきだ. The location of the *forward delivery* should be cleary indicated. / 配送される商品には先渡しの通知がなされるべきだ. All goods for distribution should be indicated by a *forward delivery* notice.

削除する【*sakujo suru*】 eliminate; cross [out]; remove; omit; cancel　例 昨日の注文の中から下記の品を削除ください. Please *omit* from our order of yesterday the following goods.

下げ【*sage*】 (値段) decline; downswing ‖ ―る decline　例 利益は去年3月始めから下げ始めた. Profits began to *decline* at the beginning of March last year.

下げ足【*sageashi*】 (相場) downward [decline] trend [tendency]

下げ渋る【*sageshiburu*】 ((market)) be steady　例 為替レートはこの2カ月（下げ渋って）安定している. The exchange rate has been *steady* for the last couple of months.

さしあたり【*sashiatari*】 for the time being; for the present; so far　例 さしあたり人を雇い入れる必要はない. It is not necessary to employ any more people *for the time being*. / さしあたり売り上げの上昇は見込めない. *So far* there has been little improvement in sales.

挿絵入り【*sashie-iri*】: ―の illustrated　例 挿絵入りのカタログを送ってください. Please send us a copy of your *illustrated* catalog.

指図【*sashizu*】 instructions; direction; order (書); request　例 詳細はお指図どおりにしますから御安心ください. You can rely on us to carry out your *instructions* in every detail. / その旨お指図ください. Please give us *instructions* to that effect. / お指図に従って注文品を船積みしました. According to [In agreement to] your *instructions* we have shipped your order. / 5月10日付お指図に従い, 貨物は鉄道便で本日送りました. In accordance with [According to] your *instructions* [*request*] of the 10th May, we have today sent the goods by rail. / 同封の船積指図書に基づいて船積準備をしてください. Please make the shipping arrangements in accordance with [as per] our shipping *instructions* [*order*] enclosed. ‖ ―する

direct; instruct (to); order; command; give directions 例 貴社約定品を発送するよう製造業者に指図した. We have *instructed* our manufacturers to forward your contracts. / ただちに見本と値段を添えて貴社に連絡するよう指図した. We have already *instructed* them to contact you immediately with necessary samples and prices. / 指図どおり船積みできない. We are unable to ship as *instructed* [*directed*]. / 6月10日付お手紙にてお指図のカタログ1部を同封します. As *instructed* in your letter of June 10, we are inclosing a copy of our catalog. / この手形支払を支店へ指図されたい. Please *direct* your branch to honor this bill. / 当社は東京銀行にこの注文金額の信用状を開くよう指図しました. We have *instructed* our Bankers, The Bank of Tokyo, Ltd., to open an L/C for the amount of this order. ‖ ―を仰ぐ ask for instructions ‖ ―人 orderer; director ‖ 出庫[荷]―書 (貨物引渡―書) delivery order; D/O ‖ ～に船積みの―をする instruct ～ for shipment ‖ 迫って―あるまで pending further instructions ‖ ～の―によって under one's instructions ‖ ～に対して～の―を与える give instructions to ～ on ～ ‖ ～の―にそむく violate one's instructions

差し迫った 【*sashisematta*】 pressing; impending; imminent; urgent 例 売り上げの減少, 利益の低下, 市場の喪失が倒産の差し迫ったことを知らせる. Poor sales, declining profits and loss of markets show that bankruptcy is *imminent*. / 市場割り当ての新しい開発が差し迫った緊急課題. The new developments in market allocation is a *pressing* issue.

差し支え 【*sashitsukae*】 obstruction; hindrance; obstacle; inconvenience ‖ ―なければ with your permission; by your leave; if agreeable 例 差し支えなければ明日来てください. Please come tomorrow if it is not *inconvenient* to you.

指値 【*sashine*】 bid; offer; limit 例 当方の指値で新規注文を受けるよう努力してください. Do your best to book new orders at our *limit*. / 貴社の指値では利ざやがありません. Your *limit* leaves us no margin. / 指値でファームオファーできます. You may be able to make a firm offer at your *limit price*. / 貴社の指値で引き受けます. We will enter this order according to your *limits*. / 貴社の指値を有効にしておいてください. Please hold your *bid* open. ‖ 買付—値 buying limit ‖ 売却— selling limit ‖ —する bid; limit ‖ —注文 limit order

差し控える【*sashihikaeru*】refrain from; withhold 例 超過支出を差し控えることが必要. It is necessary to *refrain from* excessive spending. / 他社からの全情報を差し控える［制する］必要がある. We should *withhold* all information from other companies.

差し引き【*sashihiki*】deduction 例 御要求の差し引きはまったく不合理です. The *deduction* required by you is entirely unreasonable. ‖ 差し引く deduct; allow for 例 箱代を差し引くのは当方の慣例に反する. It is quite contrary to our usual practice to *allow for* [*deduct*] cases. / 当社は税差引後の年間純利益の 15％を A 氏に支払う義務がある. We are bound to pay Mr. A 15％ of the net profits of the year after *deducting* taxes.

雑貨【*zakka*】sundry goods; sundries; general merchandise (一般); general cargo (貨物) 例 2月1日付御書面で当方と日本雑貨の取引開始御希望の旨お申し越しに接し有り難く存じます. We are grateful (to you) for your letter of February 1, in which you propose to enter into relations with us in Japanese *Sundries*. / 当社は最近当地において雑貨の一般輸出入商として開業しました. We have (been) recently established (ourselves) here as General Exporters and Importers of *Sundry Goods*. / 雑貨業を開店しました. We have established a *general goods* business. ‖ —商 general store [dealer]

殺到【*sattō*】rush; flood 例 アメリカからの注文殺到のため市場は強含みです. Owing to the *rush* [*flood*] of orders from U.S.A., the market is strong. ‖ 注文が—する have a rush of orders ‖ 申し込みが—する be flooded with applications

雑費【*zappi*】miscellaneous expenses; sundry expenses; incidentals 例 雑費の割合はどのくらいですか. What is the per-

centage of *incidentals* [*miscellaneous expenses*]？/修繕費など
の雑費に 1,750 ドル支出しました．We paid $ 1,750 for repairs
and *miscellaneous expenses.*

さばく【*sabaku*】sell; find a market; dispose of; deal with　　例 最
近販売の低下により余剰在庫のさばけ口を見いだす必要がある．
Due to the fall in recent sales it is necessary to *find a market*
that will purchase the excess stocks. / 要望されない商品をさ
ばくことが必要である．It is sometimes necessary to *dispose
of* goods which are now no longer needed. / 経営陣は会社
の経営と生産の問題をさばく．Managers *deal with* matters of
company administration and production.

サブエージェント【*subuējento*】a subagent

サブコン【*sabukon*】subject to (our final) confirmation (売手再
確認条件)

差別【*sabetsu*】：＿をつける make distinction; distinguish between A and B　　例 いずれが良質の商品を作るかを見いだす
ため，甲乙両社の差別が必要．It is necessary to *distinguish
between* company A *and* company B in order to work out
which one produces the better quality goods. ‖ ＿待遇 dis-
criminative treatment　　例 労務者は時として経営側から差別待
遇を受けることがある．Workers sometimes receive *discrimina-
tive treatment* from the management.

妨げる【*samatageru*】disturb; prevent; hinder; obstruct; hold
up　　例 鉄道ストのため積み荷が妨げられた．Shipment of the
merchandise was *held up* by the railroad strike. / 賃上げ
を求める労務者のストで生産の継続が阻害され公衆を妨害する．
Strikes by workers over wage increases *prevent* continued
production and *hinder* the public.

左右する【*sayū suru*】have influence upon; affect upon;
control; influence　　例 工場の立地はその規模と機械化を大きく
左右する．The location of the plant *has* considerable *influence
upon* its size and mechanization. / この要素はその問題を左右
する．The factors *affect upon* the problem.

作用【*sayō*】action; function; effect　　例 これは塩の作用で溶け

る. This melts by the *action* of salt. ‖ ―する act [work]《upon》 **例** この機械はポンプの作用をする. This device acts as a pump. ‖ 化学― (a) chemical action

参加 【sanka】 participation ‖ ―する participate in; take part in; enter; join ‖ ―商社 participant firms; participated trade houses

傘下企業 【sanka kigyō】 affiliated enterprises; subsidiaries **例** 三菱のような大会社は多くの傘下企業を支配下に持っている. A large company like Mitsubishi has many *subsidiaries* under its control.

残額 【zangaku】 《pay》 the remainder; balance **例** 残額を支払ってください. Please pay us *the remainder*. / 残額は船積み後2週間以内に支払うこと. The *balance* should be paid within two weeks after shipment. / 当社受取分の残額を精算ください. Please settle the *balance* due to us. / 残額65,000円は貴社への支払分です. The *balance* of ¥65,000 is due to you. / 残額は年利5分の抵当借りをしている. We receive a mortgage loan [borrow money on mortgage] for *the remainder* at the interest rate of 5% p. a.

産業 【sangyō】 industry **例** 発明を奨励し産業を振興するため文明国の政府は特許を与える権限を持っている. To encourage inventions and promote *industries*, governments of civilized countries are authorized to grant patents. / すぐれた産業技術と豊富な資金を武器としてアメリカの巨大会社は世界の多くの産業を手中に収めつつある. Armed with definitely superior *industrial* technology and abundant funds, giant U.S. companies are winning control over many *industries* in the world. ‖ ―革命 industrial revolution ‖ 根幹― key industries ‖ ―合理化 rationalization of industry ‖ 関連― related industry

参考 【sankō】 reference **例** 会社の参考にするため, この情報資料用紙に書き込んでください. For the companies *reference*, could you please fill out this information form? ‖ ―資料 reference materials; data; information ‖ ―として consulting; following the examples; hinted by ‖ ―までに for your reference [information; guidance] 例 参考までに申し上げると当社は製造に従事しています. *For your information* we have been engaged in manufacturing.

参照【*sanshō*】reference; consultation ‖ —して with reference to; refer to; subsequent to ‖ —する refer ((to)); compare ((with)) 例 詳細については値段表御参照ください. We *refer* you *to* our price-list for further particulars. ‖ —番号 reference number

残高【*zandaka*】balance; remainder 例 残高は月末に支払います. The *balance* due will be paid at the end of the month. ‖ 当方受取勘定— balance in our favor ‖ 貴方勘定— balance of your account

産地【*sanchi*】producing country [district]; producer; production country of origin (原産地); habitat (動植物などの産地) 例 日本は世界一の米の産地だ. Japan is the greatest *producer* [*producing country*] of rice in the world. / 甲府はぶどうの産地として有名だ. Kofu is famous for its *production* of grapes.

桟橋【*sanbashi*】wharf; pier; quay 例 船は桟橋につないである. The ship is moored at the *pier*. ‖ —料 wharfage; pier dues; pierage ‖ —に船が横付けになる come [lie] alongside the pier 例 船は桟橋に横付けになっている. The ship is *lying alongside the pier*. ‖ 船を—に横付けにする bring a ship alongside the pier ‖ 浮— a landing stage; floating pier

サンプル【*sanpuru*】→見本

残余【*zanyo*】remainder; balance ‖ —の remaining 例 弊社の勘定書の30%, 即ち6万円は即時お支払いいただき, 残余の70%, 14万円は7ヶ月にわたる月賦でお支払いください. Please pay now 60,000 yen of the amount of our statement, and pay 140,000 yen, the *remaining* 70%, in seven monthly instalments.

【し】

仕上げ【*shiage*】finish; completion 例 仕事を仕上げるまでここにいます. We shall stay here till the *completion* of the work. /

その品物は非常に素晴らしい仕上げとなっています．The merchandise is of excellent quality with fine *finish*. ‖ —る finish; complete

シーアイエフ【*shiaiefu*】CIF [cost, insurance and freight]; CIF and C [cost, insurance, freight and commission]　例 桃缶詰 500箱の船積期日と横浜 CIF 値段を8月1日までに打電してください．Please let us know by cable by August 1 your price *C.I.F.* Yokohama for 500 cases of canned peaches besides the date of shipment.

仕入れ【*shiire*】purchase; stocking　例 この仕入れは相当の利益をもたらすことと信じます．We trust this *purchase* will bring you a good profit. / 製造元から多量に仕入れたためにこのような破格の安値をつけて売ることができます．Quantity *purchases* from the manufacturers have enabled us to place exceptionally low prices on this merchandise. ‖ —る get in a stock of; lay in; stock goobs ‖ —品を補充する replenish one's stock ‖ —価格 purchasing price ‖ —品 stock ‖ —係 purchase clerk　例 私は東京デパートの仕入係でした．I was with the Tokyo Department Store as a *purchase clerk*. / 貴社仕入係に使っていただけませんか．I beg you to inquire whether you can make use of my services as *a purchase clerk* in your firm.

市価【*shika*】market [current] (price)　例 市価は上向き気配．*Market price*(s) work(s) up. / 市価（市場相場）は変動なし．The *market* shows no change [remains unchanged]. / 市価は著しく上向き傾向で活発です．The *market* is very brisk with a marked tendency upward(s). / 市価は急騰した．The *market* had a smart rise. The *market* has jumped in price. The *market* has made a sudden rise. The *market* has suddenly gone up high. The *market* has advanced suddenly. / 市価が下がる．*Market* declines [falls]. ‖ —を上げる raise [force up] the market ‖ —を下げる reduce [force down] the market

時価【*jika*】current [ruling; prevailing] price　例 この商品は当市場においてもっとも低い時価を示しています．These goods show the lowest *current price* in this market. ‖ —表 p/c (price current)

資格【*shikaku*】(権能) qualification; eligibility (法律上) capacity; capability (権利上) right; title (教員など) licence; certificate 例 彼は資格を備えていると思う. I think he possesses the necessary *qualifications*. / 個人の資格でその会合に出席する. I am to attend the meeting in an individual *capacity*.‖ ～の―で in the capacity of‖ ―がある be entitled to; be qualified; be capable of 例 当店は数年米国の会社の代理店を務め満足に任務を果しておりますからその資格はあると存じます. We have for some years been the agents of a manufacturer in America, giving them complete satisfaction, and *are qualified* to act in this capacity.‖ ―を与える entitle; qualify (for) 例 彼は出席の資格がある. He *is qualified* for attendance.‖ ―を得る obtain qualification (for) 例 彼は輸入商の資格を取った. He *obtained the qualification* to practice an import business.

時間【*jikan*】time 例 時間の経過 passage of time / 御返事には時間節約のため, できる限り完全な情報をお願いします. In replying to us, please give us as complete information as possible in order to save time. / この時計は時間が正確です. This watch *keeps good time*. / 飛行機は時間どおり着いた. The airplane arrived *on time*. / 時間表を見損なって車に乗り遅れた. As I misread the *time table*, I missed the train.‖ ―外手当 overtime (pay [allowance])‖ ―外費 overtime charge

時機【*jiki*】opportunity; chance; occasion 例 時機の来るのを待つとよい. You had better wait for a *chance* (to come). / 時機外れ. It is out of *season*.‖ ―に適した appropriate; opportune; well-timed; timely

磁器【*jiki*】porcelain 例 貴社の磁器類に特別の興味を持っています. We cherish a special interest in your *porcelain*. Your *porcelain* has interested us very much.

直積み【*jikizumi*】immediate [prompt] shipment 例 御注文受け取りしだい直積みします. We can make *immediate* [*prompt*] *shipment* upon receipt of your order.

直渡し【*jikiwatashi*】prompt delivery **例** 御注文受け取りしだい直渡しします. We can make prompt delivery upon receipt of your order.

至急【*shikyū*】: —の(に) urgent(ly); prompt(ly); immediate(ly); early; soon; with dispatch **例** 至急電報 *urgent* telegram / 至急彼に返事を出した. We sent him a *prompt* reply. / 信用状は至急開設します. We will open an L/C *immediately.* / 至急この注文を調達ください. Please execute this order *with dispatch.* / 至急の御返事をお待ちします. We are anxiously waiting for an *early* reply from you. We are looking for your *early* answer [forward to hearing from you *soon*]. We are expecting your reply *at your earliest convenience.* An *early* reply from you will be appreciated. / 貴社商品至急入用ですから引き渡しのできるもっとも早い日時を教えてください. As your goods are *urgently* needed, please state the earliest date you can deliver. / 当社は至急積み出しができるよう電報で信用状を開きましょう. We shall open an L/C by cable to enable you to make *prompt* shipment.

市況【*shikyō*】market (condition [situation]); the state of the market **例** 市況は有利です. *Market conditions* are favorable. / 市況は活発. The *market* is active [brisk]. / 当市況についてお知らせします. We are pleased to advise you of *the states of* our *markets.* / 値段は市況の変動によって変更する. The price is subject to *market* fluctuations. / 市況は非常に不振で買い手を一向に見いだせない. The *market* is so dull [depressed] that we can not find any buyer. / 市況は立ち直っている. The *market* is improving. ‖ 閑散の— quiet market condition ‖ 強調の— strong market condition ‖ 横ばいの— unchanged market condition ‖ —調査 market research [survey] ‖ —調査報告 a market report

仕切る【*shikiru*】invoice **例** 原価の1割増しで仕切れ. *Invoice* [*Make an invoice for*] this article at cost plus 10%. ‖ 仕切値段 invoice price ‖ 仕切書 an invoice

資金【*shikin*】capital; funds **例** この事業には何百万という資金

が必要だ. Millions of *funds* are necessary for the business. / わずかの資金で商売を始めた. We started business with a small *capital*. ‖ 運転— working funds ‖ —難 short of fund [capital]; financial difficulty ‖ —欠乏 lack of funds ‖ —を調達する raise funds for ‖ 建築— a building fund ‖ —の回転 turnover of capital

刺激 【*shigeki*】 stimulus; impulse **例** 競争はしばしば商売の刺激になる. Rivalry is often a *stimulus* to trade. ‖ —する stimulate; incite; excite **例** 地方産業を刺激する *stimulate* local business / 今日人々は刺激のみを求める傾向が強い. People today are apt to seek only something *exciting*.

試験 【*shiken*】 examination; test; trial **例** その機械が動くかどうか見るためにもう一度試験をした. He gave the machine another *trial* to see if it would work. / 彼は試験的に雇われている. He is employed on a *trial* basis. ‖ —中 on trial ‖ —的注文 a trial order ‖ —的に as a trial; by way of trial

事故 【*jiko*】 accident; trouble; incident **例** 重工業の多くの労務者は労災事故に苦しめられる. Many workers in heavy industry suffer due to an industrial *accident*. ‖ 飛行機— an air accident ‖ —が起こる accident happens **例** たいてい事故は警告なしに起きる. Most *accidents* happen without warning.

仕事 【*shigoto*】 work; labor; business; task; occupation; job; duty **例** 仕事は順調に進んでいる. The *work* is well on [goes well]. It's way to completion. ‖ —する work **例** もっと注意深く仕事をしなさい. You must *work* more carefully.

施策 【*shisaku*】 measure **例** 弊社は万全の施策を講じた. Our firm took the best possible *measures*.

資産 【*shisan*】 property; assets; fortune; means; worth **例** 昨年末現在における正味資産は 1,000 万円をこえた. The net *worth* at the end of last year exceeded ￥ 10,000,000. / 本年会社の全資産は 100 万ドルという記録的な増加を示した. Our total *assets* [*property*; *means*; *fortune*] increased during the year by the record sum of $ 1,000,000. ‖ —状態 financial standing ‖ 有形— visible assets ‖ 無形—invisible assets ‖ 有形固定—

tangible fixed assets

持参人【*jisannin*】 bearer 囫 この小切手は持参人払いだ. This cheque is payable to the *bearer*. / 本状持参者に情報を与えてください. Please give your information to the *bearer* of this letter.

指示【*shiji*】 instruction; indication; suggestion 囫 追って何分の御指示をお待ち申します. We await your further *instructions* [*directions*]. / A商会の指示で貴社と取り引きを開きたく, この手紙を差し上げます. At the *suggestion* of Messrs. A & Co., we are writing this with an earnest desire to open an account with you. ‖ —あり次第 upon your advice; on receipt of your instructions; as soon as we are instructed ‖ —に従う follow instructions

支障【*shishō*】 interference; trouble; obstacle; objection; inconvenience 囫 支障を感じなかった. We didn't feel much *inconvenience*. / 新しい重役陣を作るのに何ら障害はなかった. There was no *obstacle* in joining the new board of Directors. / 品物は注文と同時に現金払いで御送付願っておりましたが, それで支障は感じませんでした. Orders used to be forwarded to us C.W.O. *to our satisfaction*.

市場【*shijō*】 market; mart; fair 囫 常に市場を開拓しなければならない. We must always cultivate a *market*. / この分野の市場は今日伸びている. A *market* of this line is spreading these days. / 新市場を開設しています. We are opening up a new *market*. / 貴国に市場を開設したい. We are desirous of opening a *market* in your country. / 市場は沈滞気味です. The *market* is dull. / 市場相場は変動ありません. The *market* shows no change [remains unchanged]. There is no change in the *market*. / 市場相場は著しく上向き傾向で活発です. The *market* is very brisk with marked tendency upwards. / 市場相場は急騰した. The *market* has made a sudden rise [suddenly gone up high; advanced suddenly]. / 当地市場相場は非常に不活発で実際ほとんど取り引きがありません. The *market* here is exceedingly inactive and practically no business is being done [there is very little business doing]. / 商品は特に貴市場向輸出用に作りました。 The goods are specially manufactured for export to your market. / 市場価格がまもなく上がりそうです. As the *market* is likely to rise very soon. / 貴地区に市場があるかどうか御意見を伺いたい. We would welcome your advice as to whether there is a *market* in your district. ‖ —に出す put on the market ‖ —に出ている be on [in] the market

事情【*jijō*】circumstances; reasons 囫 やむを得ざる事情のために for some unavoidable *reasons* / 家庭の事情で辞職しました. I resigned my post *owing to* my family *reasons*. / その事情を大いに遺憾に思う. We much regret the *circumstances*. / その事情に対して心から遺憾の意を表さざるを得ません. We cannot but express our sincere regret at the *circumstances*. / それは事情しだいです. That depends on the *circumstances*. ‖ こういう—ですから under these circumstances; such being the case 囫 こういう事情ですから、会は次の機会まで延ばします. *Under these circumstances* we will put off the meeting till the next chance.

時勢【*jisei*】the times 囫 彼の考えは時勢に遅れている. His thought is behind the *times*. / 時勢に先んぜよ. Go ahead of the *times*. / いま生産中の商品は時勢に遅れている. The goods being produced now are behind *the times*.

時代【*jidai*】the times; the age 囫 現代は原子時代だ. Now is *the* atomic *age*. / 科学は時代と共に進歩する. Science makes progress with *the times*. ‖ —遅れ out of date [fashion]; outdated; antiquated 囫 この車は時代遅れになった. This car has gone *out of fashion*. / それは時代遅れの考えだ. It is an *old-fashioned* idea. / 新しいデザインに関する彼の考えは時代遅れだ. His thoughts about the new design are *out of date*.

従う【*shitagau*】follow; comply 《with a request》; agree to 《a proposal》; be subject to 囫 喜んで御指示に従います. We are glad to *follow* your instructions. / 御忠告に従います. We *follow* [*take*] your advice.

下積み【*shitazumi*】bottom stowage 囫 下積みは腐敗しないきち

んと組み立てられた商品には最良. *Bottom stowage* is best for non-perishable and solidly constructed goods. / 下積無用. Not to be *stowed* below another [*packed* under heavy] cargo.

下値【*shitane*】 lower price ‖ —で売る undersell ‖ —で買う underbuy ‖ —で見積もる(り) underestimate; estimate conservatively; (conservative estimate) 例 会社は3月の売上率を下値（内輪）に見積もって品切れとなった. Due to the *conservative estimate* of the rate of sales for March, the company ran out of stock. ‖ —をつける lower the prices 例 下値によって同業者より安く売れる. By *lowering* its *prices* a company can *undersell* its competitor.

下向き【*shitamuki*】 a downward tendency 例 市況は下向きである. The market has a *downward tendency*.

実業界【*jitsugyōkai*】 the business world 例 貴社お問い合わせの会社はわが国の実業界でトップクラスの会社です. The company which you inquired about is in the top class of *the business world* in our country.

実現【*jitsugen*】 realization; materialization 例 長い間の夢の実現を楽しみに待っていた. We were looking forward to the *realization* of our dream for a long time. ‖ —する realize; materialize; make effective; give effect to 例 希望実現のため最善を尽くす. We shall try our best to *realize* our hope. / この事業計画を実現するのは不可能だと思われます. It seems impossible for us to *realize* this business plan. / 当社の努力にもかかわらずいまのところ取り引きは実現していません. In spite of our effort, no business has *materialized* so far.

実行する【*jikkō suru*】 put into practice; carry out; execute; keep; fulfil 例 その計画を実行に移しなさい. *Put* the plan *into practice*. *Carry out* the plan. / 実行不可能の約束をするな. Never make a promise that you can't *carry out*. / いつも約束を実行します. We will *keep* [*fulfil*] our promise. / 本注文を実行するに当たっては注意を払ってください. Please be careful in *executing* this order.

実施【*jisshi*】 execution; effect 例 この計画の実施は年内は困難

だ. The *execution* of this plan is difficult during this year. / 貴社との契約を実施するため建設する工場を見ていただいたことを感謝します. Please accept our thanks for your visit to the factory to be built in *execution* of our contract with you. ‖ —する carry into [take] effect; enforce; execute; put in(to) force 例 新時間表は4月1日から実施される. The new time-table *takes effect* on April 1. / ぜいたく品に対する統制規則は本月10日に実施される. The regulations for the control over luxurious goods shall be *put in force* on the 10th of this month.

失敗【*shippai*】 failure; mistake; error 例 交渉は失敗に終わった. The negotiation ended in a *failure*. / 努力は失敗に終わった. Our efforts ended in *failure*.

実費【*jippi*】 actual expenses; cost (price) 例 それは実費で売ります. We shall sell it to you at *cost*. ‖ —販売 cost sale

実務【*jitsumu*】 practical business; business practice 例 会社がお互いにスパイするのは企業の普通の業務ではない. It is not common *business practice* for companies to spy on each other.

実用【*jitsuyō*】 practical use; utility; practicality (性) 例 その経済性, 実用性, 取り扱いの容易さが好まれる. They are liked for their economy, *practicality* and easy handling. / この機械は実用にあまり役立たない. This machine is of little *practical use*. ‖ —品 necessaries; a utility article

指定【*shitei*】 appointment; designation ‖ —する appoint; name; designate; specify 例 指定日 *specified* [*designated*; *appointed*] date / 別段の御指示がなければ unless otherwise *specified* / どうか会合の日と場所を指定してください. Please *appoint* us a date and place for the meeting. / 彼は指定の時間に来た. He came at the *appointed* time. / 面会御希望なら御指定どおりいつでも参上します. Should you desire an interview [if you care to see me], I should be most pleased to call on you at any time you may *appoint*. / 指定の値で買ってください. Please buy the goods at the figure *named*. / 当社をロンドンの一手代理店に指定くださる貴状拝受しました. Thank you very much for your letter *appointing* us your sole agents for London. / 御指定の日に商品を船積みしました. We have effected shipment of the goods on the *appointed* day.

支店【*shiten*】 branch (office); B.O. 例 弊社はほとんど全国にわたって広範な支店網を持っています. We have a very wide network of *branches*, covering almost the whole of country. / 神戸に支店開設の予定. We intend to open a *branch office* in Kobe. / 支店を開設しました. We have opened *a branch* establishment. ‖ ―長 branch (office) manager ‖ 東京銀行大阪― the Osaka Branch of the Bank of Tokyo; the Bank of Tokyo, Osaka

自動車【*jidōsha*】 automobile ‖ ―製造業（メーカー）automobile producer [maker] 例 フォードは大きな自動車メーカー. The Ford Motor Company is a large *automobile producer*. ‖ ―業界 the automobile industry ‖ ―購入代金 cost for purchasing the car 例 車のもともとの原価は50万円だったが今は2割減額された. The *original cost of the car* was 500,000 yen, but it has been reduced by 20%.

自動承認制【*jidōshōninsei*】 automatic approval of imports; A.A. (system) 例 日本に入ってくる多くの商品が自動承認制になり自動的に輸入が認められる. Many goods entering Japan are given automatic entry under the *A.A. system*.

品【*shina*】 article; goods; wares; line; merchandise; quality 例 この品は当方では扱っていない. The *ware* is out of our *line* of business. / あの店の品は高い. The *wares* in that store are dear. / この品は春の季節を目当てに特に注文したものです. These *articles* were specially ordered for the spring season. / それは品がいい. It is good in *quality* [of good *quality*]. / 当社の品は品質がよく値段も安い. Our *goods* are of high quality and of low price. / 貴社は品が至急御入用でしょう. You may be in a hurry for the *goods*. / 残念ながら御注文の品は注文殺到のため売り切れとなりました. We are sorry that the *goods* you ordered have been sold out owing to the rush of orders. The recent rush of orders has exhausted our stock of the *article* you ordered. ‖ —切れ out of stock 例 御注文の品は品切れです. The goods you ordered are *out of stock*. Our *stock* is *sold out* [*exhausted*]. To be *no* longer *in stock*. / 引き合いの品は品切れです. The article you inquired for is *out of stock*. / 延引の理由は全く当時持ち合わせがなかったためです. The delay has been caused by *running out of stock* [owing to the fact that we were *out of stock* of the goods]. ‖ —薄となる the stock runs short; be in short supply ‖ —が豊富 have a large stock of ‖ —傷み damage; rotten and damaged ‖ —切れ値段 famine prices ‖ —薄 scarcity of goods [stock]; short of supply 例 市場価格は品薄のため急激に騰貴しました. The market has made a rapid advance owing to the *scarcity of stocks*.

しにせ 【*shinise*】 a shop of long [old] standing; long [old]-established shop 例 創業の古い陶器の輸出商です. We are *long-established* exporters of china.

辞任 【*jinin*】 resignation ‖ —する resign (one's office) 例 同氏は仕方なく辞任した. He has been compelled to *resign* his position [a managership].

支配 【*shihai*】 control; management; direction 例 彼の支配下にある. We are under his *control*. ‖ —する control; dominate; influence 例 彼は感情に支配されやすい. He is apt to be *influenced* by personal feelings. / 何人も世論を支配できない. No one can *dominate* public opinion. / これは当社の運命を支配する重大問題だ. This is a serious problem which will *decide* the fate of our company.

支払い 【*shiharai*】 payment; charge 例 最も簡単な支払方法. It will be the simplest way of *payment*. / 支払条件は送り状金額の 15% 引き現金払い. The terms of *payment* is a 15% discount for cash on the total invoice amount. / 商人は支払請求書で現金に交換する. The merchant exchanges his *charge* slips for cash. / 本手形呈示の節はなにとぞお支払いください. We ask your kind *protection* for this draft on presentation. ‖ 支払う pay; cover 例 至急支払う. We will *pay* you immediately. / 為替手形を支払う. We will *pay* you the bill. / 7月1日付貴送り状支払いのために500ドルの小切手を同封します. We enclose a cheque for $500 to *cover* your invoice of the 1st July. / この注文の支払いに充てるため金額500ドルの信用状を開設した. In order to *cover* this order we have opened an L/C for $500. / 貴社の手形を支払うために必要な準備金を送ってください. Please send us the necessary funds to *meet* [*pay*] your drafts. / 記録をお調べくださるなら船積品に対し支払い済みであることがお分かりいただけるでしょう. If you check your records, you'll see that we *paid* for that shipment. ‖ —期限となる be due; mature; come to maturity ‖ 出金する defray ‖ 決済する settle ‖ 負債を決済する discharge ‖ 皆済する liquidate; pay off; clear off 囫 破産したのでその取り引きの皆済を必要とした. It was necessary to *liquidate* the business because it went bankrupt. ‖ 貸借をなくする balance ‖ 保険料の—条件 payment of the premium ‖ —品物渡 G.A.P. goods against payment); D.A.P. (delivery against payment) ‖ 内金 payment on account ‖ 前納 payment in advance ‖ —能力 financial ability [responsibility]; solvency 囫 貴地富士貿易会社の支払能力を秘密にお知らせくだされればまことに有り難く存じます. We shall be glad if you will let us know in confidence the *solvency* of Fuji Trading & Co. of your city. ‖ —不能 insolvent 囫 支払不能となったので銀行は同社に金を貸すことを拒否した. The bank refused to lend any money to the company because it was *insolvent*. ‖ —拒絶手形 non-payment bill ‖ —延期 postponement of payment ‖ —期限の過ぎた overdue; past due ‖ —為替手形 bill payable

資本 【*shihon*】 capital (金) 囫 弊社の資本金は50万ドル. Our company's *capital* is $500,000. ‖ —過少 be undercapitalized 囫 貴社の資産と負債を検討したら幾分資本過少と存ぜられます. It appears from a study of the assets and liabilities that your firm is somewhat *undercapitalized*.

事務 【*jimu*】 business; office work; deskwork; routine (日常事務) 囫 事務的手腕がある. He has *business* ability. ‖ —的に

in a businesslike manner　圏 事務的に処理せよ. Do it *in a businesslike manner.* ‖ ―機械 office [business] machine [equipment]　圏 事務機器を専門に納入する会社です. These are the firms who specialize in the supply of *office equipment.* ‖ ―員 clerk; an office girl　圏 彼が係員です. He is the *clerk* in charge. / 5月1日ジャパン・タイムズで広告された事務員に応募したく思います. I should like to apply for the position of the *clerk* you advertized in the Japan Times of May 1. ‖ ―用品 office supplies ‖ ―をとる transact [execute] business; be at one's desk　圏 私は銀行で事務を執っている. I *am at my desk* in the bank.

仕向け【*shimuke*】treatment; despatch; destination (地); consignee (先)　圏 仕向港 port of *destination* [*discharge*] / クレームは商品の仕向地陸揚げ後14日内に売り手 あてに打電 すべきこと. The claim is to be cabled within 14 days from the date of final discharge of goods at *destination.* ‖ ～向け destined for　圏 この品はマニラ向けです. These goods are *destined for* Manila.

指名する【*shimei suru*】name; designate; nominate　圏 彼は議長に指名された. He was *named* [*nominated*] for chairman. / 指名船は満載のため 船腹予約できない. We cannot reserve space as the *named* vessel is filled up.

下(半)期【*shimo(han)ki*】the latter half of the year; second half of the year　圏 今年の下期にはインフレも弱まるものと予測される. The inflation rate is expected to decline in *the latter half of the year.* / 下半期は多くの会社に最も忙しい時期となる. *The second half of the year* is often the busiest for many companies.

社員【*shain*】clerk; staff member; employee; personnel　圏 わが社員はよく訓練されている. Our *staff* is thoroughly trained. / 彼は当社社員だ. He is a *member* (of the staff) of this company.

社債【*shasai*】debentures　圏 株主と社債権者はほとんど同じ. Shareholders are hardly different from *debenture* holders. /

成功した会社で社債は貴重な投資である. In a sucessful company *debenture* stock is a valuable investment. ‖ 長期— long-term debenture ‖ 短期— short-term debenture

写真複写【*shashin-fukusha*】a photostat (copy) 例 最近署名された契約書の写真複写を作ることも時として必要だ. It is sometimes necessary to make a *photostat copy* of a recently signed contract.

写本【*shahon*】(コピー) copy 例 写本を戻してくれるよう望みます. We hope you will return to us a *copy*.

社内【*shanai*】: —の internal; inter office 例 社内の騒乱が事業を崩壊させた. *Internal* disturbances ruined the business. / 社内メモは社長秘書によって配られた. The *inter office* memo was delivered by the president's secretary. ‖ ——同 all the staff of a company

社命【*shamei*】order of the company 例 京都支店の閉鎖は社命によるものだった. The closing down of the Kyoto branch was *by order of the company*. / 各従業員は社命で働く. Every employee works *under company orders*.

社用【*shayō*】company business; the business of the company 例 社長は社用でアメリカにいます. The president is in America on *company business*.

従価税【*jūkazei*】ad valorem [ad val.] duty 例 米製靴の値上げは新従価税のためでした. The increase in price of American shoes was due to the new *ad valorem duty*.

集金人【*shūkin-nin*】(money; bill) collector 例 集金人として青木商会に勤務していました. I was with Messrs. Aoki & Co., as a *money* [*bill*] *collector*. / 弊社集金人が金曜日の朝参上いたします. Our *collector* will have the pleasure of calling upon you on Friday morning.

終結する【*shūketsu suru*】conclude 例 終結するには一両日を要する. These will require a day or two to *conclude*.

従事する【*jūji suru*】engage [be engaged] ((in)) 例 輸出業に従事している. We *are engaged in* the exporting business. / 銀行家として実業に従事している. *I am engaged in* business as

a banker. / 製造業者は輸出貿易に従事することを望んでいます.
The manufacturer wishes to *engage* in export trade. / 同社が
どのような商売に従事しているか知りたい. We are particularly
interested to know in what line of business they *are* mainly
engaged. / その商社は 1920 年以来綿製品の輸出に従事していま
す. They have *been engaging in* the export of Cotton Goods
since 1920.

住所【*jūsho***】** dwelling; abode; domicile; address 　例　社長の住
所は極秘です. The president's *address* is confidential. / 全社
員の住所は 302 号室にファイルしてある. All the company employees' *addresses* are on file in Room 302. ‖ 郵便返送— return address 　例　返送住所は封筒裏面に書かれた. The *return
address* was written on the back of the envelope.

自由選択【*jiyū sentaku***】** option 　例　その人はその土地の自由選択
権として 10 万円払った. He paid ¥ 100,000 for an *option* on
the land.

集中【*shūchū***】** concentration 　例　大都市に産業が著しく集中して
いる. In large cities there is a heavy *concentration* of industry. ‖ —する concentrate; center 　例　アメリカの活動は少
数の先端技術産業に集中している. The American activity *is
concentrated in* a few high technology industries. / 工場は
この地方に集中している. Factories are *centered* in this part
of the country. / この仕事に集中なさい. *Concentrate* all your
energies upon this task. ‖ —排除 decentralization 　例　産業の
集中排除は政府の計画中優先課題である. The *decentralization*
of industry is a major priority in many government programs.

重点【*jūten***】:** —を置く place emphasis on; emphasize; give
priority to; lay [put] stress ((on)) 　例　電気器具の高級品に重
点を置いています. We *lay a stress* [A *stress is laid*] on high
qualities of electric appliances.

重役【*jūyaku***】** director 　例　そのローンが認可されたのは重役の助
言による. It was on the advice of a *director* that the loan
was approved. ‖ —会 board of directors 　例　重役会が会社経
営の責任を負う. The *board of directors* are directly respon-

sible for the management of a company.

重要 【*jūyō*】 importance 囫 この問題の重要さを知っています
か. Do you know the *importance* of this problem? ‖ —商品
staple commodities ‖ —な important 囫 彼は重要人物だ. He
is a very *important* person [a man of *importance*]. ‖ —視す
る regard it as important; take a matter seriously

従来 【*jūrai*】: —の conventional; former 囫 この品は従来の品
にとって代わるでしょう. The goods will take the place of
conventional goods. / 従来どおりの信用を回復することは容易で
はあるまい. They will by no means find it an easy matter to
recover their *former* credit. ‖ —は hitherto; up to this time;
so far; thus far; heretofore ‖ —通り as usual; as in the past

修理 【*shūri*】 repair; mending 囫 修理費を御負担ください. We
request you to pay the charge for the *repair*.

重量 【*jūryō*】 weight ‖ —トン weight ton ‖ —不足 short weight ‖
総— gross weight ‖ —容積証明書 Certificate of Weight &
Measurement

従量税 【*jūryōzei*】 specific duty 囫 この商品の従量税は総額の
5%. The *specific duty* on this article is 5% of its total price.
‖ —率 specific tariff

受益者 【*juekisha*】: —として in one's favor 囫 貴社を受益者と
して信用状を開設した. We opened [established] an L/C *in
your favor*. / 東京銀行に貴社を受益者として 15,000 ドルの取消
不能信用状を発行するよう指図しました. We have instructed
The Bank of Tokyo to issue [open] an Irrevocable L/C *in
your favor* for (the amount of) $15,000.

祝詞 【*shukushi*】 cordial [sincere] congratulation 囫 この初注
文に対し, 祝詞を申し上げます. Please accept our *cordial*
[*sincere*] *congratulation* on this initial order.

授権資本 【*jukenshihon*】 an authorized capital 囫 同社の授権資
本は 2,000 万円. The company has an *authorized capital* of
20 million Yen.

受信 【*jushin*】: —人 recipient; addressee ‖ —する receive
《message; letter; telegram》 囫 ニューヨークから 5 時に受信

した. We *received* the telegram message at five from New York. ‖ —機 a receiver; a receiving set

受注 【*juchū*】 acceptance of order 例 受注が生産増強を促した. The *acceptance of the order* required an increase in production. ‖ —する accept an order 例 この新しいコンピュータの注文を引き受けますか. Will you *accept an order* for this new computer.

出荷 【*shukka*】 shipment; forwarding 例 受注後 30 日以内に出荷のこと. *Shipment* should be made within thirty days from receipt of order. / 空輸代金は高い. The cost of *shipment* by air is usually high. ‖ —案内 shipping advice ‖ —する ship forward ‖ —指図書 delivery order; D/O

出願 【*shutsugan*】 application ‖ —人 applicant; person making the application 例 その考えは出願人に知られていた. The idea has been known to the *applicants*. ‖ —する make an application for; apply for

出港 【*shukkō*】 departure; clearance; sailing 例 出港の正確な時間が知らされるだろう. Exact time of the ship's *departure* will be informed. / 出港日取および時刻は保証できない. Cannot guarantee the date and time of *sailing*. ‖ —する leave port; set sail from; clear a port 例 東京丸は本日ここを出港した. M.S. Tokyo Maru *left* here today. ‖ —停止 embargo ‖ —日 date for sailing

出資 【*shusshi*】 investment; financing ‖ —する invest; contribute; finance 例 他社に出資している. Our company *invests* in another company.

出帆 【*shuppan*】 sailing; departure 例 出帆日と到着日を打電してください. Please cable us your *sailing* and arriving date. ‖ —する sail; set sail ((for)) 例 いつ出帆し到着する予定ですか. When do you *sail* and expect to arrive here ? / 2 週間以内にサンフランシスコに向け出帆予定. The ship is to *set sail* for San Francisco within two weeks.

主要 【*shuyō*】: —な principal; leading; main; staple 例 当社主要商品の値段表を同封します. Enclosed is a quotation on the staple products our company produces.

需要 【*juyō*】 demand; requirement 例 輸出需要のため市況は強調. The market is strong due to export *demands*. / 需要期が近づいている. The season of *demand* is approaching. / この種の商品に対する当社の需要はかなり大. Our *requirements* for this line are fairly large [considerably heavy]. / 綿花の需要はない. There is no *demand* for cotton. / 需要は増加の傾向を示している. *Demands* are showing a tendency to increase. / 需要に応じるため現在フル操業している. To meet the *demand*, we are now running at full capacity. / 需要期が近づいているため御注文に応じられないことになるかもしれません. We might not be able to comply with your order because the season of *demand* is approaching. / この品物に対する需要が多いので至急注文を勧めます. In view of the heavy *demand* for this line, we advise you to order at once. / このような品物には当地では需要がありません. There is no *demand* here for such goods. / この品は需要が多い. This article is in great *demand*. / それに対する一般の需要が減った. The general *demand* for it has decreased. / 供給が需要に追いつかない. Supply can't keep up with *demand*. / 当市場において貴製品に対しかなりの需要がありますから，貴社と相当取り引きができることを期待しております. As there is a good *demand* for your products in this market, we expect to be able to do a good business with you. / 海外にも潜在需要があるかもしれないと思った. We thought there might be latent *demands* abroad.

受領する 【*juryō suru*】 receive; accept; be in receipt of 例 本月 9 日付書留正に受領. We have received your letter dated the 9th of this month.

種類 【*shurui*】 kind; sort; class; type 例 取り引きしている商品の種類を知って驚くだろう. You will be surprised to know how many *varieties* of goods we are doing business in [dealing with]. / これは全部同じ種類. These are all of the same *kind*. / どんな品が欲しいのか. What *sort* of goods do you want？

順 【jun】 order; turn **例** 順が狂っている. They are in the wrong *order*. ‖ —に in turn [order] **例** イロハ順に *in* alphabetical *order* / 順に入りなさい. Come *in turn*. / 注文は順番に遂行します. Orders will be executed *in turn*.

準備 【junbi】 preparation; arrangement; (準備資金) fund **例** 手形の支払いに必要な準備金を間に合うよう送ってほしい. Please send us in due time the necessary *funds* to meet your drafts. ‖ 船積— preparations for shipment ‖ —する prepare oneself ((for)); be ready ((for)); arrange **例** 約定品は船積準備ができていますが, 配船が全くありません. Contracts *are ready for* shipment, but no steamer is available. / 最悪の事態に備えなければならない. We must *be prepared for* the worst. / 6月30日満期の引受済み手形代金支払の準備乞う. Please *be prepared* to meet your acceptance falling due on the 30th June. / 貴社商品はちょうどよい時機に準備されるよう製造業者から引き渡されるでしょう. Your goods will be delivered to us from the manufacturers as *arranged* in time.

純量 【junryō】 net weight **例** その商品の純量は 20 kg であった. The *net weight* of the goods was calculated to be 20 kg.

使用 【shiyō】 use; employment ‖ —する use; make use of; employ **例** この品は広く使用されている. This article is in general use. / 同封のカタログにより, この鉄鋼は米国では主要な製造業者によってかなり広く使用されていることをお認めいただけるでしょう. From the catalogs inclosed you will note that this Steel is being extensively *used* by the leading manufacturers in U.S.A. ‖ —料 charge for dues **例** この上またドック使用料が課される. There is also a further *charge* made *for* dock *dues*.

照会 【shōkai】 inquiry; reference (先) **例** 9月20日付御照会を感謝します. We thank you for [appreciate] your *inquiry* of September 20. / 信用照会がよかったら先方と契約してよいか. If their *references* are good, may we enter into an agreement with them? ‖ —する inquire ((of a person for a thing)); refer ((to a person for a thing)) **例** 東京銀行へ御照会くださ

い. Please *refer* [We *refer you*] *to* The Bank of Tokyo. / もっと詳しいことはシティーバンクへ御照会ください. We may *refer* you to the City Bank for further information. / 当社の信用状態に関しては，Aに御照会ください. As regards our standing, please *refer* to A.

商会【*shōkai*】firm; company　例　当商会は綿の輸入業です. Our *firm* is a cotton importer. / 同商会は船積みの遅延に不平を言った. The *company* have complained about the delay in shipments.　囲　firm, company, bank は集合体全体を1つと考えるときは単数扱い，それを組織する個々を考えるときは複数扱いとなる.

紹介【*shōkai*】indtroduction　例　紹介状を渡します. We furnish you with [give] a letter of *introduction*. / あまり有名な人だから改めて紹介の必要はない. He is such a famous man that no formal *introduction* is needed. ‖ —する introduce　例　田中氏を紹介します. We have pleasure in *introducing* [This will *introduce*] to you Mr. Tanaka. / 君に信頼できる会社を紹介してあげよう. We *introduce* to you some reliable firms. / この商品に関心をもつ貴地の信頼できる輸入商を紹介して頂けるなら有り難く存じます. We shall be obliged if you will *introduce* to us some reliable importers of your city who are interested in this line. / 4月3日付お手紙の御返事として，当社は喜んで東京貿易株式会社を御紹介します. In reply to your letter of April 3, we are glad to *introduce* The Tokyo Trading Co., Ltd. to you. / ロンドン商業会議所から貴社がわが国との貿易に関心を持たれていると紹介されました. Your firm has been *recommended* to us by the London Chamber of Commerce as being interested in trade with Japan.

償還【*shōkan*】refundment; repayment　例　商品は破損したので償還金が支払われた. A *refundment* of money was paid because the goods were damaged. / ローンの返済金は月々4万円. The monthly *repayment* on the loan is ¥40,000. ‖ —手形 reimbursement draft

上記【*jōki*】: —の above-mentioned; stated above; mentioned

above; the said 例 会議の詳細は上記文書に記載. The details of the meeting are given in *the above-mentioned* letter. / 上記の方が会議の主催者です. The person's name *stated above* will be the organizer of the meeting. ‖ —の品 the goods mentioned above 例 上記商品6月6日朝到着します. *The goods mentioned above* will arrive on Monday morning, the 6th of June.

償却【*shōkyaku*】refundment; redemption ‖ 減価— depreciation 例 新鋭設備は償却を急ぐ必要がある. *Redemption* of new facilities needs to be expedited.

商業【*shōgyō*】: —会議所 the Chamber of Commerce (and Industry 商工会議所) 例 当社は東京商工会議所から貴社を紹介されました. Your house has been recommended to us by the Tokyo *Chamber of Commerce and Industry.* / 商店商社の住所は商工会議所で分かる. The address of all business houses can be found at the *Chamber of Commerce & Industry.* ‖ —興信所 credit bureau; mercantile credit agencies 例 銀行は興信所を通じて個人の信用度を知る. A bank can find out an individual's credit rating by getting in touch with the *credit bureau.* ‖ —道徳 commercial laws; principles in business ‖ —送り状 commercial invoice ‖ —信用状 commercial letter of credit; L/C

状況【*jōkyō*】circumstances; situation; background; condition 例 貨物の積み荷状況は申し分ありません. The goods were shipped in a sound *condition.* ‖ —に適した suitable to the occasion; applicable to the circumstances

証券【*shōken*】securities; certificates; document; bond; policy 例 保険証券を送ってください. Please send us your *insurance policy.* / 保険証券は米ドル建てで作成されること. The *insurance policy* is to be made out in U.S. dollars. ‖ 海上保険— marine insurance policy ‖ 船荷— bill of lading ‖ —会社 securities firm [dealer]

条件【*jōken*】condition; term; terms and conditions 例 支払条件御通知ください. Kindly state your *terms* of payment. /

その他の条件は前回と同じ. Other *conditions* are the same as the last. / 同社が当社の条件に同意するか否かは疑問である. It is questionable whether the firm will agree to our *terms*. / 絶好条件で御商談に応じることができます. We are placed in a position to do business upon the best possible *terms*. ‖ ―付きで subject to 囲 貴社承認を条件として品物を売った. We have sold our goods *subject to* your approval. / 即答を条件として売申込をします. We offer firm *subject to* your immediate reply. / 下記商品に対し, 4 日以内に返答することを条件として確定申込をします. We offer you firm the following goods *for* [*subject to*] your reply reaching in [being received within] 4 days. / 貴電受け取り次第売り切れないことを条件としてこれら商品の確定申込をします. We offer you firm these goods *subject to* their being unsold on receipt of your reply by cable. / 売申込は一切先売御免条件です. All offers are *subject to* prior sale. / 取り引きは現金支払が条件. Our business is *subject to* the payment in cash. / 前金払いが条件. We generally do our business *subject to* cash in advance.

証拠 【*shōko*】 evidence; proof 囲 船荷証券の日付けを船積みの日の証拠とみなす. The date of bills of lading shall be taken as *proof* of the date of shipment. ‖ ―金 warrant money; margin ‖ ―を提出する produce evidence

商号 【*shōgō*】 the firm name; the title 囲 商号を石丸商会としました. We have established the trading firm under the *title* of Ishimaru & Co.

詳細 【*shōsai*】 details; particulars 囲 商品の詳細をお知らせください. Please inform us of the *details* of this line. / 値段などについて詳細は同封の市況報告を参照乞う. We refer you to the enclosed market report for *full particulars* as to prices, etc. / 貴製品の全詳細をお知らせください. Please let us have *full details* of your products. ‖ ―な detailed 囲 もっと詳細な情報を追ってする. More *detailed* information will be followed. / 下記会社につき, できる限り詳細な情報を願う. Please give us as *detailed* information as you can of the following firm. ‖

—に in detail 例 詳細は追って手紙でお知らせする. We will write to you *in detail.*

小冊子【*shōsasshi*】(small) booklet; pamphlet 例 小冊子を同封します. We enclose herewith a *small booklet.* Enclosed please find a *small booklet.*

商社【*shōsha*】firm; concern; trading house; trader 例 同商社の信用についてお知らせくださった件は内密にします. Any particulars as to the standing of the *firm* with which you may favor us would be treated in absolute confidence. ‖ 有力— a reliable firm 例 日本製商品の輸入に関心をお持ちの有力商社を御紹介いただければ, 有り難く存じます. We should be very much obliged if you would introduce to us some *reliable firms,* who are interested in the import of Japanese goods. ‖ 一流— a leading firm ‖ 総合— all-round trading firm; general trading company

上昇する【*jōshō suru*】go up; advance; make an advance 例 値段は3月以降漸次上昇しています. Prices have *gone up* steadily since March. / すぐにも市価は上昇する様子なので, 至急このオファーを受諾するようお勧めいたします. As the market is likely to *advance* very soon, we advise you to accept this offer without delay. / 本品の価格は急上昇しました. Prices of these goods have *made a* sudden *advance.*

乗船する【*jōsen suru*】go on board a ship; take a boat 例 彼は箱根丸に乗船して世界一周した. He made a round-world trip *aboard* [*on board*] the Hakone Maru. / 彼は英国船に乗船してアメリカからヨーロッパへ行った. He *took his passage* from America to Europe *by* [*on*] a British *boat.*

状態【*jōtai*】state; condition 例 貴地市場の状態を通知乞う. Please inform us of your market *condition.* / 遺憾ながら御送付の品は不満足な状態にあります. We regret to inform you that the goods forwarded to us are in an unsatisfactory *state.* / 貴積み荷を破損状態で受け取った. We have received your shipments in a damaged *condition.* ‖ 財政— financial standing

承諾【*shōdaku*】consent; agreement ‖ —する be agreeable to;

accept; agree 《to》 **例** 御提案を承諾します. We *are agreeable to* your suggestion. We have *accepted* your proposal. We *accept* your offer. Our company *accepts* the offer from your company. / 3分引き承諾します. We *agree* to allow you a discount of 3%. / 貴社の信用状態が満足いくものであると分かれば, 貴社の申し出を承諾いたします. If your credit standing turns out to be satisfactory, we shall be glad to *accept* your proposal.

商談【*shōdan*】 negotiation; transactions; business talk; sales talk **例** Aとの商談中止しなさい. Break off *negotiations* with A. ‖ ―する talk business with ‖ ―を始める enter into negotiations ‖ ―を進める proceed with business talk

承知する【*shōchi suru*】 agree [consent] 《to》; permit; know **例** 承知する限りでは同店は堅実です. As far as we *know*, they are sound enough. / 彼はそれをすることを承知した. He *agreed* to do it. / 彼はどうしても申し出を承知してくれない. He will never *consent* to our proposal.

譲渡【*jōto*】 transfer; delivery; conveyance; negotiation (手形の) ‖ ―する transfer; assign; negotiate **例** 特許権者は特許を売却により譲渡できる. The patentee may *assign* the patent through sale. / 手形を譲渡できるか知らせてください. Please inform us whether you can *negotiate* our draft. / 御要求により譲渡禁止の B/L を2通同封しました. As requested, two copies of the *non-negotiable* B/L are enclosed. ‖ ―指図書 letter of assignment; tranfer order

商売【*shōbai*】 business; trade; commerce; transaction; commercial activity; dealings **例** 商売はどうですか. How is your *business*? / この商売はもうからない. This *business* does not pay. / 彼の仕事は船長です. He is a captain by *trade*. ‖ ―を営む carry on business in ~; open business; deal in **例** 彼はパリで商売をやっている. He *carries on business in* Paris. / 彼の商売は何ですか. What does he *deal in*? ‖ ―を広げる expand [broaden; develop; increase] the scope of business activities; extend one's business ‖ ―を縮少する reduce one's business

消費【_shōhi_】 consumption　**例** 1人1日の消費高はどれぐらいか.
What is the amount of daily _consumption_ per head?‖ —者
価格 consumer's price

商標【_shōhyō_】 a trade-mark; brand　**例** 当社の商標侵害の報告
あり. It has been reported that our _trade-mark_ has been
infringed. / 月印の自転車. The "Moon" _Brand_ Bicycle. / 商標
を新しく変えました. We have altered the _brand_ to a new
one.

商品【_shōhin_】 goods; commodity; merchandise; wares; article; line　**例** 商品を輸出して50年以上になる. For more than
50 years we have been engaging in exporting _goods_. / 過去
10年世界に当社商品を船積みしてきました. For the last 10
years we have been shipping our _goods_ to all over the
world. / 主な商品は魚網です. Our main _line_ is Fishing Nets./
本商品に関心がありましたら指値を願う. If you are inter-
ested in this _line_, please give us your limit price. / 弊店取引
に不適当な商品です. They are not the suitable _merchandise_
for our trade. / 砂糖は今や世界的商品である. Sugar is now a
world _commodity_. / 売れ行きのよい最新の商品の中から特に精選
したものを送ります. We are pleased to send you a full
selection of our latest best selling _goods_.‖ 缶詰品 canned
goods‖ 流行品 fancy goods‖ 完成品 finished goods‖ 絹製品
silk goods‖ 編み物 knitted goods‖ 反物 piece goods

譲歩【_jōho_】 concession; conciliation　**例** これは最大限の譲歩.
This is the maximum _concession_ we can make.

情報【_jōhō_】 information; report; advice; news　**例** この情報
は正しいと信じて提供しますが, 責任を持つことはできません.
While we furnish you with this _information_ in good faith,
we cannot hold ourselves responsible for it. / いかなる情報
も極秘に扱います. Any _information_ we will treat in strict
confidence. / 完全な情報を送って頂き有り難い. We are very
glad of your sending us the complete _information_. / もちろ
ん貴情報は厳秘にします. Of course your _information_ will be

kept strictly confidential. / 貴信用照会先から受け取った貴社に関する情報は全く貴社に有利なものでした. The *information* concerning you we received from your reference was completely favorable to you.

正味 【*shōmi*】 net　例　支払条件は送り状総額の正味金額. The terms of payment would be *net* on total invoice amount. / 支払条件は3カ月払いは送り状総額の正味金額，もしくは現金払いならば，その1割5分引き. The terms of payment would be three months *net* or 15% discount for cash on the total invoice amount. / 当社正味資産は100万円をこえた. Our *net* worth [assets] exceeded ￥ 1,000,000. ‖ ―値段 net price

証明 【*shōmei*】: ―する certify; prove; confirm; testify ‖ ―書 certificate　例　原産地証明書が入用です. *Certificate* of origin is required. ‖ 領事― consular certificate

商用 【*shōyō*】 (の) business; commercial ‖ ―で on business　例　佐藤氏は商用で貴地に行ってます. Mr. Sato is going to your city *on business*. ‖ ―旅行 business trip; business inspection tour

乗用車 【*jōyōsha*】 (passenger) car　例　たくさんの乗用車メーカーがある. In our country there are many manufacturers of *passenger cars*.

招来する 【*shōrai suru*】 bring about; result in; give rise to; invite; cause　例　本通信が貴我双方の利益を招来するものと信じます. We trust this writing will *result in* a large business to our mutual benefit.

奨励 【*shōrei*】 encouragement; promotion; impetus　例　それは輸出の奨励になるだろう. It will be an *impetus* to exporting goods. / 新協定は両社の貿易奨励につながった. The new treaty has given an *impetus* to the trade between the two companies. ‖ ―する encourage; promote; stimulate　例　政府は輸出入貿易を奨励する政策を取るだろう. The Government will adopt a policy to *encourage* export and import trade. ‖ ―金 bounty; subsidy　例　政府は増産に対して奨励金を出した. The Government granted a *bounty* for increased production.

諸掛かり【*shogakari*】charges; expenses 例 諸掛かりを減らす必要あり．We need to minimize the *charges*. ‖ —向払い charges forward ‖ —着払い charges to collect ‖ —前払い charges prepaid ‖ 船積み— shipping charges ‖ 陸揚げ— landing charges

食料【*shokuryō*】provisions; food; foodstuff ‖ 缶詰食品 canned provisions ‖ —品店 a food store; grocery 例 小売食料品店を開く．We will open a retail *grocery* store. ‖ —品商 a dealer in provisions

職権【*shokken*】authority ‖ —を行う exercise one's authority 例 弊社あて一覧払い手形振出の職権を与える．We *authorize* you to draw upon us at sight.

所得【*shotoku*】income; earnings 例 彼の所得は 2 倍になった．His *income* has been double what it was. / 所得が少ない（多い）．He has a small (large) *income*. ‖ —税 income tax 例 政府は社会事業の支払補助に所得税を徴収する．The Government collects *income taxes* to help pay for community projects. ‖ 未払—税 income taxes payable

処分【*shobun*】disposal; dealing; disposition 例 品物を処分したら残額送金します．We shall remit you the balance for the *disposal* of the goods. ‖ —する dispose of; deal with

署名【*shomei*】signature 例 署名のうえ一通返送ください．Please return one copy with your *signature*. / 岡野氏の署名鑑は下記のとおり．A specimen of Mr. Okano's *signature* is shown below. ‖ —する sign 例 小切手に名前を署名する *sign* one's name to check / 契約書に署名してください．Please *sign* our contract form.

書面【*shomen*】letter; writing; document ‖ —する communicate 例 取引銀行から情報入手次第改めて書面します．We will have the pleasure of *communicating* with you further as soon as we hear from the bankers.

所有【*shoyū*】possession 例 その会社はスミス氏の所有です．The company is in Mr. Smith's *possession* [is *owned by* Mr. Smith]. ‖ —する own; have; hold; be in possesion of 例 彼は大財産を所有している．He *has* a great fortune. / 彼は大きな

カメラ店を所有している. He *owns* a large camera shop. ‖ ―
品 belongings; one's personal property ‖ 株式―権 ownership
of shares ‖ ―地 land; estate

処理【*shori*】management; dealing; disposal; treatment ‖ ―す
る deal with; dispose of; conduct ((business)) 囫 重要物件を
処理した. We *dealt with* the important matter.

書類【*shorui*】documents 囫 船積書類はお送りします. The
shipping *documents* will be forwarded to you. / この書類に買
い手あて積出通知状を同封する. These *documents* are enclosed
with a letter to the buyer advising shipment.

知らせる【*shiraseru*】inform one of; advise one of; notify one
of; acquaint one with; report one a fact; let one know;
write to one; intimate 囫 先方は貴社代理店となりたいと知
らせてきた. They *intimated* to us their wish to obtain the
agency of your company. / 貴注文品を本日船積みしたことを知
らせます. We *inform* you that we have shipped your order
today. / 本日品物は「大洋丸」で発送したことを知らせます. We
inform you that we have despatched the goods today by
M.S. "Taiyo Maru". / 貴地A商会の信用状態を秘密にお知らせ
ください. Please *inform* us secretly of the credit standing
of A & Co. of your city. / この商品がまた入用になるときは電
報で知らせます. We will *let* you *know* by wire when we
are again in want of such goods.

調べる【*shiraberu*】investigate; examine; inquire [look] into;
check up; test; research; make inquiry 囫 貴社にお調べの
ほど願います. We should like you to *examine*. / 政府は航空機
事故の原因を調査の予定. The government is going to *investigate* the cause of the plane accident. / お尋ねの商社に関し
当社は調べました. We have *made inquiries* respecting the
firm referred to [you inquired about].

資料【*shiryō*】material; data 囫 それに関する資料は不十分.
We have insufficient *data* concerning it. / 当社製品に関する必
要全資料を差し上げます. We are glad to give you all the
necessary *data* in regard to our products.

新規【*shinki*】：—申込 fresh offer ‖ —まき直し a new start **例** 機械の故障により新規まき直しをする必要があった. Due to the failure of the machine it was necessary to make *a new start*.

人絹【*jinken*】rayon; artificial silk **例** 人絹物の相場は心持ち弱い. *Rayon* goods are shade weaker. / 人絹20箱送ります. We are shipping 20 cases Rayon.

進行【*shinkō*】：—中 in progress; under way; making progress **例** 工場はまだ建設中でした. The plant was still *in process* of construction.

申告【*shinkoku*】declaration; report ‖ —書 declaration; report; notification; statement **例** 申告書は貴代理店に提出させますか. Shall *declaration* be produced by your agent? ‖ —する report; declare **例** 船荷証券に商品として申告されたい. *Declare* in B/L as merchandise.

紳士【*shinshi*】gentleman; man **例** 紳士用頭文字入りハンカチの見本を送り乞う. Would you please send us samples of *Men's* Initial Handkerchiefs? ‖ —服 a men's suit ‖ —録 a who's who

親切【*shinsetsu*】kindness; goodness; courtesy **例** この件お知らせくださった御親切に感謝します. We highly appreciate [We thank you for] your *courtesy* in bringing this matter to our attention.

迅速【*jinsoku*】rapidity; promptitude **例** 御出荷は最も迅速に願いたい. We must really insist upon greater *promptitude* in regard to deliveries. ‖ —な(に)ready; prompt(ly) **例** 迅速な御配慮を期待します. Your *prompt* attention will be much appreciated. / この商品は売れ行きが早い. These goods command a *ready* sale. These goods sell *quite well* here. / この問題を迅速に解決乞う. You will attend to this matter *promptly*.

慎重【*shinchō*】：—な cautious; careful **例** 慎重な調査が必要. It requires a most *careful* investigation. ‖ —に with consideration [attention; interest] **例** 慎重に調べた. We have examined it *with interest*.

親展【*shinten*】private [confidential]; personal letter [telegram] （書）**例** これは社長あて親展の手紙. This is a *personal letter* to the president.

信任【*shin-nin*】confidence **例** 当社を信任いただき有り難い. We appreciate the *confidence* you show in us. / 御信任を裏切ることはしません. We shall not betray your *confidence*.

信用【*shinyō*】credit (状); confidence; trust **例** この取り引きが成立すれば，電信で信用状を開きます. On concluding the business, we will open a *credit* by cable. / 当社の信用について客観的な情報を求められる場合は東京銀行へお問い合わせください. If you need any objective information concerning our *credit*, please make inquires to The Tokyo Bank Ltd. / 同店と信用取引を結ぶのは好ましくない. It would appear inadvisable to enter into any *credit* transaction with them./その金額に対し信用供与を請け合います. We assure to extend *credit* for the amount. ‖ —状 (letter of) credit (L/C) **例** 信用状は〜日まで有効. *Credit* is available [valid; remains in force] until a certain date. / 信用状は取り消し可能. *Credit* is revocable. / 信用状は〜日に満期となる. *Credit* expires on a certain date. / 信用状条件で取り引きする trade on *Letter of Credit* / 信用状条件で取り引きします. We do our business on a *Letter of Credit* basis. / 至急信用状を開設せよ. Please open your *L/C* immediately. / 信用状を開設願う. We ask you to open the *letter of credit*. / 貴社に信用状を開設. We have opened an *L/C* in your favor. / 貴社への注文にはすべて貴社を受益者として信用状を開設します. For any order we may place with you, we will open *a letter of credit* in your favor. ‖ —状態 credit standing [status]; reference **例** 貴地A商会の信用状態を秘密にお知らせください. Please inform us secretly of [in confidence of your opinion regarding] the *credit standing* of A & Co. in your city. / 当社の信用状態についてはA銀行にお問い合わせください. We will give you the name of A Bank as a *reference*. You may inquire at A Bank about our *credit standing*. We refer you to A Bank as to our *credit standing*. / 同社の信用状態に関して、貴社に問い合わせます. We shall be very glad if you will favour us with your opinion regarding the *credit status* of the firm. / お申し出の会社の信用状態に関し十分な情報を差し上げられません. We are sorry that we can't give you sufficient information regarding the *credit standing* of the firm referred to. / 同社の信用程度をお知らせ乞う. We shall be obliged if you will kindly favor us with *credit standing* and responsibility of the firm. ‖ —照会先 (credit) reference 囫 A商会は信用照会先として貴社名を申し出ています. A Company gave us your name as a *reference*. / これが最初の取り引きですから信用照会をしました. Since this is the first transaction between us, we have made the usual *credit inquiries*. / 貴社信用照会先が有利な報告をくれました. Your *reference* gave us such a favorable report on you [good reports]./ ウィルソン商会は当社と取引の開始を熱望しており、信用照会先として貴社名を申し出ております. Messrs. Wilson & Co. are anxious to open an account with us, and give us your name as a *reference*. ‖ 銀行—照会先 bank reference ‖ 同業者—照会先 trade reference ‖ 無担保—状 clean L/C ‖ 銀行—状 banker's L/C ‖ (無)確認—状 (un-)confirmed L/C ‖ 譲渡可能—状 assignable L/C; transferable L/C ‖ 荷為替—状 documentary credit ‖ 取消可能(不能)—状 (ir)-revocable L/C 囫 取消不能信用状に基づき取り引きします. We do business on an *irrevocable letter of credit* basis. / 東京銀行に貴社を受益者として10,000ドルの取消不能信用状を発行するよう指図しました. We have instructed The Bank of Tokyo here to issue [open] *Irrevocable L/C* in your favor for (the amount of) $ 10,000. / 支払いは通常取消不能信用状に基づく一覧払いの為替手形でしています. Payment is usually made by a draft at sight on an *irrevocable L/C*. ‖ 銀行確認取消不能—状 banker's confirmed irrevocable L/C ‖ —状番号 L/C number ‖ —状発行依頼書 application for L/C ‖ —調査 credit inquiry ‖ 寄託— escrow [impound] L/C

信頼【*shinrai*】 reliance; dependence; trust; confidence ‖ —で
きる reliable; trustworthy 囲 信頼できる筋によれば accord-
ing to a certain *reliable* source / 信頼できる会社名をお知らせ
乞う. Please inform us of the name of a *reliable* firm./信頼
できる会社物色中. We are looking for a *trustworthy* firm./ そ
の会社は信頼できそう. The company appears very *reliable*./
貴地A商会は貴店が最も信頼できる商社の一つだと当社に申し出
ております. Messrs. A & Co. of your city have given us
the name of your firm as one of the most *reliable* concerns.
‖ —する place [put; have; show] confidence in; give one's
confidence to; put trust in one; rely on; depend on; believe 囲 当社を御信頼いただけるものと思います. We believe
that you can *rely on* us quite satisfactorily. ‖ —を裏切る betray one's confidence in

尽力する【*jinryoku suru*】 do one's utmost [best]; make (every)
effort; exert oneself (to the utmost) for (further improvement); spare no efforts 囲 事態改善に尽力ください. *Do your
utmost* to improve the situation.

心労【*shinrō*】 anxiety; cares; worries ‖ —を察する realize one's
anxiety; offer one's sympathy for deep concern 囲 心労お
察しします. You must be very *anxious*.

【す】

遂行【*suikō*】 performance; execution; fulfilment ‖ —する carry
out; give effect to; execute; fulfil; effect; perform; discharge
囲 計画は予定どおり遂行された. The program was *carried
out* [*performed*; *fulfiled*] as planned. / 職務を忠実に遂行した.
He *discharged* his duties faithfully.

推薦【*suisen*】: —する recommend; commend 囲 議長に彼を推
薦する. We recommend him as chairman. / 商工会議所が貴
社を弊社に推薦した. Tokyo Chamber of Commerce and Industry *recommended* you to us. / 本書持参人を推薦します. We
recommend to you the bearer of this letter. / 貴社は岡田氏か

ら業界で最も優良な会社の1つとして当社に推薦されています.
Your firm has been *recommended* to us by Mr. Okada, as one of the best houses in the trade. ‖ —状 a letter of recommendation 例 推薦状を差し上げます. We give you *a letter of recommendation*.

出納【*suitō*】 revenue and expenditure; accounts 例 彼はあの会社の出納をつかさどっている. He is in charge of *accounts* [*revenue and expenditure*] in that company. ‖ —係 cashier 例 東京銀行で出納係をしていた. I have been in the services of The Bank of Tokyo as a *cashier*.

図入り【*zuiri*】: —説明書 illustrated literature [catalog] 例 図入りカタログ同封. Enclosed please find an *illustrated* catalog./新しいコンピュータの使用法に関する図入り説明書がファイルしてある. The *illustrated literature* on the operations of the new computer is in the file.

数字【*sūji*】 figure; numeral 例 3けたの数字 three figures/見積った数字は非常に高い. The *figure* quoted is very high. ‖ —で in figures 例 支払額を数字で書いて頂けますか. Could you write down the amount you paid *in figures*?

数量【*sūryō*】 quantity; volume 例 着々数量を増している輸出 export in steadily increasing *volume*/貴価格が安ければ相当数量の申し込みをします. We shall order in a considerable *quantity*, if your prices are reasonable. / 正確な船積数量を電信ください. Cable the exact *quantity* shipped. / 4月中に全数量を船積みできない. We can't ship all the *quantity* in April. / 輸出品も輸入品も引き続き, その数量を増している. The imports and exports continue to grow in *volume*. / 添付の値段表は各種数量の注文に対し, 数量割引を示しています. Attached is a price sheet which will give you *volume* discounts for orders in various *quantities*. ‖生産高 the volume of manufacturing ‖—過不足容認条件 more or less terms

据え置き【*sueoki*】: —の unaltered; unchanged; standing 例 製品の値段は昨年始めより据え置きになっている. The price of the product has been *unaltered* since the beginning of last year. ‖ —払い deferred payment **例** これら購入品に関しては延べ払いを望みますか。 Do you wish to make a *deferred payment* on these goods purchased?

図解 【*zukai*】 illustration; diagram ‖ —する explain by a diagram; illustrate; figure **例** お問い合わせの設備は小冊子に図解してあります。 The equipment about which you inquire is *illustrated* in the booklet.

図柄 【*zugara*】 pattern; design **例** 当社の図柄は純日本式. Our *patterns* are 100 per cent Japanese.

すぐ 【*sugu*】 at once; immediately; without delay [loss of time] **例** すぐに当社の申し込みを引き受けくださるよう望む. We wish you will accept our offer *without delay*. / すぐオファーを受諾ください. We advise you to accept this offer *without loss of time*.

図示する 【*zushi suru*】 illustrate **例** 製品を図示した折り込みを同封. We are enclosing a folder *illustrating* our goods.

勧める 【*susumeru*】 recommend; advise; urge **例** お買い上げのほどお勧めします. We *urge* you to buy it at once. / 早い御注文を勧めます. We would *recommend* you to place an order as soon as possible. / 貴社の利益のため このオファーを引き受けることを勧めます. We *recommend* you to accept this offer to improve [for] your profits. / 至急お買い上げを勧めます. We *advise* you to purchase the goods immediately. / 契約を結ぶよう勧めます. We *recommend* you to enter into the contract.

捨て売り 【*suteuri*】 bargain sale; sacrifice sale ‖ —する sell at a sacrifice (price) **例** その品物を捨て売りした. We have *sold* out the goods *at a sacrifice*.

ストライキ 【*sutoraiki*】 strike; labour conflict; walkout **例** メーカーの工場にストライキがありました. There have been *labour conflicts* at the plants of our manufacturers. / ストは中止された. The *strike* has been called off. ‖ —する go on (a) strike; walk out (米) **例** ストを決行した They *went on a strike*. ‖ —中 be on (a) strike ‖ ゼネスト a general strike ‖ ス

ト指令 a strike order ‖ 同情スト a sympathetic strike ‖ ―約款
strike clause ‖ スト権を行使する exercise one's right to strike

すなわち【*sunawachi*】viz; namely; that is (to say); i.e. **例**
減価率すなわち，市場価値の下落が増大している． The rate of
depreciation *i.e.* fall in market value has been increasing.

図表【*zuhyō*】chart; graph; diagram

図面【*zumen*】a drawing; a plan; a sketch

【せ】

せい【*sei*】：―である be due [owing] to; be caused by; be
attributed to **例** それはあなたの不注意のせいだ． That *is due
to* carelessness on your part. / いろいろな事情のせいだ． It *is
owing to* various circumstances. / 失敗は全く不注意のせいだ．
Your failure *is* entirely *due to* want of caution.

税【*zei*】tax; taxation（課税）**例** 財産に税をかけた． We charged
a *tax* on an estate. ‖ 無― tax free; free of duty **例** 無税の
品物 an article *free of duties* / 免税品を売る店がいくつかある．
Some shops sell *tax free* goods. / シンガポールは免税自由港．
Singapore is a *tax free* port.

正確【*seikaku*】accuracy; correctness **例** 中味の計量法の正確さ
に関しては自信があります． We are quite confident of the
accuracy with which we weigh the contents. ‖ ―な（に）cor-
rect(ly); accurate(ly); punctual(ly) **例** 7月30日まで品物
が入用ですから正確な積み出しが肝心です． *Punctual* shipment
is essential because we need the goods by the 30th July at
the latest.

税関【*zeikan*】a custom house; the customs **例** 税関を欺くと
厳罰を受ける． The penalties for cheating *the customs* are
very severe. ‖ ―手続 customs formalities ‖ ―手数料 customs
fee ‖ ―送り状 customs invoice ‖ ―代理人 custom broker

請求（する）【*seikyū*】request; demand; claim;（ask for；
charge）**例** 2月2日付手紙で御請求のとおり当社新カタログ1
部お送りします． As *requested* in your letter of February 2,

we are sending you a copy of our new catalog. / 御請求に
従い新定価表を同封します. In accordance with [According
to] your *request*, we enclose a new price list. / 当社最近のカ
タログ御請求の 6 月 1 日付お手紙拝受. We thank you very
much for your letter of June 1, *asking for* [*requesting*] our
latest catalogue. / 当社は喜んで10% の 値引き御請求に応じま
す. We are willing to meet your request for an allowance
of 10%. / 御請求に応じ 本日見本便にて種々の見本を送付しまし
た. As *requested*, we have sent you today by sample post
our samples of various kinds. / これはこの信用状に対して請求
される. This will be *charged* against this credit. / この葉巻は
私の勘定に付けておいてください. *Charge* these cigars to my
account.

制限【*seigen*】 restriction；limitation；limit **例** 現行の制限はさら
に緩和されるでしょう. It is expected that the present *restrictions* will be further relaxed before long. / 織物の輸出その他
の制限が撤廃された. Export and other *restrictions* on Textiles
have been lifted in your country. / 会員となるのに年齢の制限
はない. There is no age *limit* for the membership. ‖ —する
restrict；limit **例** 数(時間)に制限がある be limited [restricted]
in number(time)

成功【*seikō*】 success **例** これが成功すれば貴社からさらに注文を
いただけることになるでしょう. Its *success* will induce you
to send us your further orders. ‖ —する succeed in **例** 特許
を得るのに成功した. We have *succeeded in* obtaining a patent. / 入社試験に成功した. He *succeeded in* the entrance examination of the company.

政策【*seisaku*】 policy **例** 先任者の政策の大綱を踏襲する. I shall
follow the general line of *policy* developed by my predeces-
sor. ‖ 物価— price policies ‖ 継続— a running policy ‖ 営業—
business policy

清算【*seisan*】 liquidation **例** 破産したため会社の資産は清算され
た. The company's assets went into *liquidation* because it
went bankrupt. ‖ —勘定 open account **例** この資材は清算勘

定で当方に付けてください. Please bill the material to us on *open account.*

精算【*seisan*】accurate account; adjustment [settlement] of accounts ‖ —する adjust; settle ((accounts)) 例 海損を精算する *adjust* an average / 海上保険業者は主要港に精算代理人（店）を置いている. Most underwriters maintain *settling* agents at the various principal ports. / 先月1日付貴送り状, 精算のため為替手形を同封する. To *settle* your invoice of the 1st of last month, we enclose draft. / すぐにも精算ください. We hope you will *settle* soon. / 残金を精算ください. Please *settle* the balance to us.

生産【*seisan*】production; manufacture 例 これはクリスマスシーズンの貴社生産計画にうまく入ると思う. We believe it will fit into your *production schedule* for the coming Christmas season. ‖ —地 producing center ‖ —高 output; turnout ‖ —目標 goal of production ‖ —物 products ‖ —者（天然物）a producer;（加工物）a manufacturer ‖ —する produce; manufacture 例 オーストラリアでは大量の羊毛が生産される. A great deal of wool is *produced* in Australia. / 貴市場向けに新しい異なった型の車を生産しています. We are going to *manufacture* different types of vehicles for your market.

製造【*seizō*】manufacture; production 例 お問い合わせの品物第4号は目下製造しておりませんが, 同じような品物第5号なら供給することができます. The model No. 4 you asked for is out of *manufacture*, but we can supply the similar article No. 5. ‖ —する manufacture; produce 例 この工場では車を製造している. They are *manufacturing* automobiles in this factory. / 当社は多年漁網の製造に従事. For many years we have been engaged in *manufacturing* Fishing Nets. / 製造経費として当社が受けている利益は常に低価格という形で貴社に還元しています. Any advantage we receive in the way of *manufacturing* costs is passed on to you as lower prices. / 次の品物を製造している工場の住所を教えてください. Kindly tell us the address of factories which *produce* the following

goods. ‖ —業者 manufacturer 例 多数の製造業者と連絡があ
る. We are in connection with many *manufacturers*. ‖ —能
力 manufacturing capacity

ぜいたく 【*zeitaku*】 luxury 例 彼はぜいたくに暮している. He
is living in *luxury*. ‖ —な luxurious 例 私達はぜいたく品を
好む. We like *luxurious* goods very much.

精通する 【*seitsū suru*】 be well [thoroughly] acquainted [con-
versant] with; be well versed [posted] in; possess a good
knowledge [command] of; be at home in; familiarize oneself with 例 私は外国貿易実務に精通しています. I *am well
acquainted with* foreign trade practice. I *am thoroughly con-
versant with* the routine of foreign trade business. / 当社は
当地の事情に精通しています. We are *well acquainted with*
the conditions in this district.

製品 【*seihin*】 manufacture; product; manufactured goods 例
当社製品に興味を持っていただいて有り難うございます. We
thank you very much for your interest in our *products*. / 貴
社製品の最新カタログと値段表をお送り乞う. Please send us
the latest catalog and price list of your *manufactures*. / それ
らが当社製品です. They are the *manufactures* of our company. / これは自国(外国)の製品である. This is of home (foreign) *manufactures*. / この時計は日本の製品である. This watch
is *of* Japanese *make*. This watch is *made* in Japan. ‖ 皮—
leather goods

税率 【*zeiritsu*】 tax rates; tariff 例 ちかぢか税率の変更がある
と思われる. Alteration of *tariff* is expected in the near
future.

精力 【*seiryoku*】 energy ‖ —的な energetic 例 精力的な業者
energetic businessmen / 本社は非常に精力的な経験ある販売力
を持っています. We have a most *energetic* and experienced
sales force at our headquarters.

世界 【*sekai*】 world; universe ‖ —的 international; world-wide;
universal; global ‖ —銀行 the World Bank (国際開発銀行 the
International Bank for Reconstruction and Development の

通称)

積送【sekisō】 shipment; consignment (委託品)　例 航空機 (汽車，トラック，船舶) による積送 *shipment* by air (rail; truck; ship) / 本品は箱根丸で積送手配中です. The goods are preparing for their *shipment* per M.S. Hakone Maru. / 積送品をそのまま引き取ることにしました. We have decided to accept delivery of the *consignment* as it is. ‖ ―する ship　例 委託販売として下記商品を積送しました. We have *shipped* to you the following goods on *consignment*. / 御注文品は本日神戸丸で積送いたしましたことを御通知申し上げます. We inform you that we have *shipped* today your order by "Kobe Maru".

責任【sekinin】 responsibility; liability (支払いの)　例 それに責任はない. We have no *responsibility* for that. / 彼は責任感が強い. He has a strong sense of *responsibility*. / 責任を負わない. We accept no *responsibility*. / 貴社の責任においてなすべきである. You must act on your own *responsibility*. / これは個人的意見にすぎません. それに対しては当社はなんらの責任も取りません. This is no more than a personal opinion, for which we take no *responsibility*. ‖ ―がある be responsible; liable　例 取引能力や信用状態について何ら責任ある意見を言うことはできません. We can not supply any *responsible* opinion on the business capability and credit standing. / 責任を取って頂きます. We shall hold you *responsible* for any loss. / 財産が付保されている額を超えた損失分について会社は責任を負わない. The company is not *liable* [*responsible*] for the part of the loss in excess of the amount for which property is insured. ‖ ―者識別記号 identification marks

積極【sekkyoku】: ―的 positive; active ‖ ―的に actively; with [in] a positive attitude　例 積極的に取り引きを進めたい意向を持つ. We have an intention of cultivating business *with a positive attitude*.

絶対【zettai】: ―の (に) absolute(ly); positive(ly); definite(ly); complete(ly); by all means　例 元金は絶対安全です. Your capital [principal] is *completely* safe.

設置【*setchi***】** establishment ‖ ─する establish; set up; organize; found; form **例** 日本貿易 K.K. の名称のもとに会社を設置しました. We have *formed* a company under the name of Nippon Trading Co., Ltd. / 空調装置を設置することが必要です. It is necessary to *install* [*set up*] a complete air-conditioning system.

設備【*setsubi***】** equipment; installation; facilities; accomodation; arrangements **例** 当社は近く設備を一新して新しい建物に営業所を移す予定です. Our firm expects shortly to move its business offices into the new building that has entirely new *equipment*. / このホテルは2千人を収容する設備がある. This hotel has *accomodations* for 2,000 guests. ‖ ─の良い well-equipped **例** このホテルは設備がよい. This hotel is *well-equipped*. ‖ ─投資 equipment investment ‖ ─資金 equipment fund

切望【*setsubō***】:** ─する desire [hope] earnestly; be really anxious for **例** 面倒をかけないよう切望します. We *earnestly hope* that you will not give us trouble. / 平和的解決を切望する. We *are really anxious for* a peaceful solution. ‖ ─して with a keen desire to; with one's wishes to

説明【*setsumei***】** description; explanation **例** 一層詳細な説明を要する. A more detailed *description* is required. / 将来の製品に関し簡単な説明をしておきました. We made a brief *explanation* about our future products. ‖ ─する explain; account; clarify **例** 最近の値下がりはそのような理由では説明できない. The recent price decline cannot be *accounted* for by such reason. ‖ ─を要しない self-explanatory

設立【*setsuritsu***】** establishment; foundation ‖ ─する establish; found **例** 横浜貿易会社は輸出商として設立されました. The Yokohama Trading Co., Ltd. was *established* as Exporters. / 密接な取引関係を設立したい. We wish to *establish* a close connection with you. ‖ ─登記 registration of incorporation

世評【*sehyō***】** public opinion; popularity; reputation **例** その会社の世評について御意見を賜われば幸甚. We shall be obliged

if you will kindly let us have your frank opinion on their
reputation.

是非とも【*zehitomo*】without fail; at any cost; at all costs; in
any event; by all means　例 是非とも御注文のほどをお願い
します．We ask that you will place orders with us *without
fail.*

世話 【*sewa*】kindness; assistance; care　例 お世話になりまし
た．Thank you for your *kindness.* / 彼には大変世話になった．
He did a great *deal* for us. / 余計なお世話だ．That's none
of your business. / 航空機内には旅客サービス係がいてお世話を
します．Aboard our plane you also get *assistance* from the
officer of passenger service．We are glad to take *care* of you.

全額【*zengaku*】total amount; sum total　例 購入商品の総額は
10万円に達した．The *sum total* of all goods purchased came
to ￥ 100,000. ‖ ―決算 settlement in full　例 未払手形に対し
全額決算がなされた．*Settlement in full* has been made for
the outstanding bill. ‖ ―払い込み済み fully paid

全危険担保【*zenkiken tanpo*】Against All Risks; A.A.R.　例 信
用状は「全危険担保の保険」としてある．The credit stipulates
"Insurance *against all risks*".

前記【*zenki*】: ―の foregoing; above-mentioned; the said; previously stated　例 前記の会社がそのビルに必要な電気製品を供
給するだろう．The *above-mentioned* company will supply the
electrical goods needed for the building.

占拠【*senkyo*】occupation ‖ ―する occupy; grab　例 その製品は
市場の10％を占拠している．The products have *grabbed* 10%
of this market.

専業【*sengyō*】speciality ‖ ―とする specialize in　例 弊社は中東
及び極東貿易を専業としています．We *specialize in* Middle and
Far Eastern trade.

船艙【*sensō*】a hatch; a hold　例 米は船艙に積み込まれた．
The rice was loaded into the *hold* of the ship. ‖ ―貨物 hatch
cargo ‖ ―口 a hatch

戦争【*sensō*】: ―危険 war risks　例 工場位置を設定する場合戦

争危険を考える必要がある. *War risks* need to be considered when planning the location of factories. ‖ —約款 War Clauses ‖ —保険 war risk insurance

船側【*sensoku*】: —渡し Free Alongside Ship; F.A.S.; ex-ship

全損【*zenson*】total loss 例 火災のため全在庫が全損となった. Due to the fire there was a *total loss* of all stock. ‖ —担保 Total Loss Only; T.L.O.

船体【*sentai*】hull 例 今後12ヶ月間同船体に対する保険を更新願います. We wish you to renew the insurance on the *hull* for 12 months hence.

選択【*sentaku*】selection; option; choice 例 選択できるように3種の見本を送ります. We are sending you 3 different samples so that you may make a *selection.* / 選択を誤った. You made a bad [wrong] *choice.* / 特に協定のない限り船積港は売り手選択のこと. Unless expressly agreed upon, the port of shipment shall be at the seller's *option.* ‖ —できる alternative 例 選択できる航路について意向をお聞かせください. Please give us an idea of possible *alternative* routes.

宣伝【*senden*】advertisement; propaganda 例 宣伝は製品の売上高に大きく影響する. The *advertisement* has serious influence on the proceeds of products.

船舶【*senpaku*】vessel; ship ‖ —賃貸料 charterage 例 船舶の賃貸料は1日10万円. The *charterage* fees for the *vessel* are ¥100,000 per day.

船腹【*senpuku*】ship [freight; cargo] space; tonnage; bottom ‖ —を予約する secure [reserve] space 例 貴社注文に対する船腹を獲得するよう最善の努力を払う. We will do our best to *secure* space for your order. ‖ —不足 scarcity of space ‖ 可能 — available space

専務取締役【*senmu torishimariyaku*】managing director 例 専務取締役は副支配人の決定に対し拒否権を持つ. The *managing director* usually has the power to veto decisions made by his sub-managers.

専門【*senmon*】speciality; line; major 例 当方はその製造が専

門です. We *make a speciality* of [are *specialized in*] the manufacturing. / 御専門は何ですか. What is your *line* [*speciality*;
major]? ‖ ―の special; specialized 圀 専門の電信係 *specialized* cable clerk ‖ ―家 specialist 圀 せっけん化粧用具専門 soap
and toilet *specialists* / 綿製品の専門店です. We are *specialists*
in Cotton Goods. / 真珠の輸出専門店です. We are *specialists*
in the export of pearls. ‖ ―とする specialize in 圀 合成樹脂
が専門. We *specialize in* plastics.

【そ】

総 【*sō*】:―重量 gross weight [gr. wt.] (net weight 正味純量) ‖
―売上高 turnover 圀 月の総売上高は250,000円に達した.
The monthly *turnover* amounted to ¥250,000. ‖ ―経費 over-
head expenses ‖ ―額 the aggregate amount

増加 【*zōka*】 increase; addition ‖ ―する increase 圀 月給を
10,000ドルに増やす *increase* one's salary to $ 10,000 / 商
売は漸次増加(減少)している. Trade is gradually *increasing*
(decreasing). / 同社は資本金を1万ポンドから2万ポンドに増加
した. The company has *increased* the capital stock from
£10,000 to £ 20,000. / 値段が2割上がった. It has *increased*
20 per cent in price.

総会 【*sōkai*】 a general meeting [assembly] ‖ 株主― general
meeting of stockholders

送金 【*sōkin*】 remittance [remit.; remt.; rem.] 圀 都合つき次第
早く送金ください. We shall be glad to have your *remittance*
at your earliest convenience. Please send us your *remittance*
as early as possible. We hope you will favor us with your
remittance as soon as possible. / 折り返し送金ください. Please
let us have your *cheque* per return. / 貴送金は未着です. Your
remittance has not been received yet. / 電信送金で願います.
We request you to remit by T.T. (telegraphic transfer)
remittance. / 貴電拝見，御希望どおり送金しました. Have received your cable. Made *remittance* as requested. ‖ ―手形

remittance bill‖—する remit 例 何日にいくら送金できます
か. How soon can you *remit* and how much？/ 差し上げた商
品に対し御送金ください. We shall be greatly obliged if you
will *remit* us a cheque for the goods supplied to you.

総計【*sōkei*】total; sum total 例 小麦の取り引きは総計わずか
50 俵でした. The *total amount* of wheat sold amounted to
only 50 bales. / 損害は総計 10 万円になる. The *total* loss
amounts to ￥100,000.‖—で in all 例 当社は事務員が総計
で 40 人いる. There are forty clerks *in all* in this office.

倉庫【*sōko*】a storehouse; a warehouse; a godown 例 貴倉庫に
保管願っている漁網 10 俵A商会あて積送ください. Please ship
10 bales of our Cotton Fishing Nets in your *warehouse* to
A Co.‖—に入れる store; warehouse 例 先方の指図に接する
まで当分貨物を倉庫に保管していただきたい. Please *store* the
goods and hold them at our disposal pending instructions
from our clients. / 貨物を倉庫に保管していただきたい，回送に
関しては後日お知らせします. You may *warehouse* the goods
for the present, and we shall instruct you later as to the
forwarding. / 大洋丸積み貨物は当地に陸揚げの上倉庫に収めま
した. The cargo of the "Taiyo Maru" has been landed and
warehoused here./ しばらくこの品物を倉庫に預けてください.
Please *warehouse* these goods for a while.‖—料 storage
例 倉庫料は保管しない時の料金を含む. The *storage* includes a
storing and unstoring charge.‖—渡し ex warehouse 例 引
き渡しは 5 月，当地倉庫渡し. Delivery in May, *ex warehouse*
here.‖ 保税— bonded warehouse‖—証券 warehouse warrant

相互【*sōgo*】：—の(に) mutual(ly) 例 相互利益のために取り引
きをしたい. We want to open an account with you for our
mutual interests. / 相互に助け合わねばならぬ. We must help
mutually [*each other*]. / 各国家は相互の安全と利益を尊重せね
ばならない. Nations must respect their *mutual* safety and
interests. / 御返事を是非いただきたく取り引きが成立してその
結果相互の利益になるように切望します. We shall be glad to
hear from you and trust that business may result to our

mutual benefit.

総合【*sōgō*】general; comprehensive 例 総合計画 *comprehensive* program / 弊社は総合輸出商社です．We are *general* exporters and importers.

増進【*zōshin*】increase; promotion ‖ ―する increase; develop; promote; further 例 A氏は企業の利益増進のため全才能を振るうでしょう．Mr. A will exert all his abilities to *further* the interest of the firm. / 十分な休養が能率を増進する．Sufficient rest will *develop* [*increase*] efficiency.

総代理店【*sōdairiten*】sole [exclusive; general] agent 例 わが国の本品総代理店はロンドンのノードン商会です．The *general agents* for this article in this country are Messrs. Noden of London.

相当【*sōtō*】: ―な substantial; considerable; reasonable; sufficient 例 年に相当量の取り引きをして，貴社に仕えることができました．We could do a *substantial* turnover for you annually. / 彼は相当の金を使った．He spent a *considerable* sum of money. / それ相当の値で売れた．The article was sold at a *reasonable* price. / 相当の理由がなければ会社を休んではならない．You must not stay away from the office without a *sufficient* reason. / 紛争が生じた場合は相当額の値引きを認めて解決せよ．In case of dispute, you (should) settle it with a *reasonable* allowance. / 仕事に相当する金額であれば給料はいくらでも結構です．I should be willing to start at whatever figure is [seems] right *for* the job. ‖ ―する be equal to 例 1ドルは230円に相当する．One dollar *is equal to* 230 yen.

総トン数【*sōtonsū*】gross tonnage 例 その橋の制限総トン数は1,000 kg. The *gross tonnage* restriction on that bridge is 1,000 kg. ‖ 総トン当たり per gross ton [p.g.t.] 例 ニンジンの総トン当たり値段は6％下落した．The price *per gross ton* of carrots has fallen by 6%.

相場【*sōba*】quotation; market [current] price; rate 例 時価1ドル230円の相場 the *quotations* at 230 yen per dollar / 下記商品に対し最低値段（相場）お知らせください．Kindly let us

have your lowest *quotation* for the following goods. / 相場騰貴
の原因は大手筋の買い入れによるものでした. The real reason
for the improvement in *prices* was the heavy buying by
leading speculators. / 相場表を持参します. We will call upon
you with *price* current. / お申し越しあれば見本と相場表（値段
表）を喜んで差し上げます. We shall be pleased to forward
samples and *quotation* if you will command us. ‖ 公定— public
quotation ‖ 現物— spot quotation ‖ 先物— forward quotation
‖ 買い—buying rate ‖ 売り— selling rate ‖ 上げ— rising rate
‖ 下げ—falling rate

双方【*sōhō*】: —の mutual; both 例 この契約は双方合意の上成立
した. This contract was closed by *mutual* agreement. / 双方の
利益のため大量の受注を希望します. We hope you will obtain
large orders to our *mutual* benefit. / 双方の利益のため貴社と
仕事をしている. We are working with you to our *mutual*
advantage.

創立【*sōritsu*】establishment; foundation 例 本日は当社創立
50年祭です. This is the 50th anniversary of the *foundation*
of our company. ‖ —する establish; found 例 わが社は明治
40年に創立された. Our company was *established* [*founded*]
in the 40th year of Meiji. ‖ —者 a founder ‖ —費 organization
costs ‖ —趣意書 a prospectus

総量【*sōryō*】gross weight 例 コンテナーの総量には中に入っ
ている在庫品も含まれた. The *gross weight* of the container
included the stock contained inside. ‖ —条件 gross weight
terms ‖ 船積—条件 gross shipped weight terms ‖ 陸揚—条件
gross landed weight terms

促進【*sokushin*】promotion; acceleration; stimulation ‖ —する
promote; stimulate; hasten; expedite 例 その計画の実現を
促進するため部長が渡米した. The manager went to America
to *hasten* the realization of the program [plan]. / 科学は文明
の進歩を促進する. Science *expedites* the progress of civiliza-
tion. / 会議は世界平和を促進するため開かれた. The conference
was held to *promote* world peace. / 電子計算器の発達は数学の

問題を解く際にスピードを上げる必要によって促進された. The development of electronic computers was *stimulated* by the need to increase speed in solving mathematical problems.

速達【*sokutatsu*】express [quick] delivery; dispatch 例 速達で手紙を送ると少し余計にかかる. To have a letter send by *express* usually costs a little more. / 為替は速達で送られた. The money order was sent by *quick delivery*. ‖ ―で送る send a letter by express

続騰【*zokutō*】: ―する advance; (じり高) rise slowly [rather high] 例 値段は続騰中. The prices are *advancing*.

底値【*sokone*】bottom [lowest] price 例 底値をつく. The *prices* touch *the lowest* point. (反 reach the top) / 財布の底をはたいた. I have emptied my purse to *the last penny*. / テレビの底値（最低値段）は 2 万円. The *bottom* [*lowest*] *price* for the television set is ￥20,000.

組織【*soshiki*】: ―する organize; form; compose 例 A氏と組合を組織した. We *formed* a partnership with Mr. A. / 彼は調査団を組織した. He *organized* an investigation team. ‖ ―的 systematic 例 組織的な方法 *systematic* method ‖ 社会の― a social organization ‖ 会の―を改める change the constitution of a society; reorganize a society

即金【*sokkin*】immediate payment; cash (down); spot cash [payment] 例 彼は何でも即金で買う. He buys anything for *cash*. / 即金なら 1 割引きにする. We shall take off 10% for *cash*. / 条件は即金払いです. Our terms are *spot cash*. ‖ ―で払う pay in cash

措置【*sochi*】treatment; attention; arrangement; measure; step 例 本件至急御措置願います. Please give this matter your prompt *attention*. / 適当の措置を取られたい. Let proper *measures* be taken. ‖ ―を誤る take wrong measures [steps]

続行する【*zokkō suru*】proceed; continue; go on; pursue 例 皆は討議を続行した. They *proceeded* with discussions. / 彼は研究を続行した. He *pursued* his studies. / 今月末まで注文の製造を続行するな. Do not *proceed* with manufacturing our order until the end of this month.

率直【*sotchoku*】: —な frank; candid **例** この問題に関し，率直な御意見をお聞かせくだされればまことに有り難く存じます． We shall be most grateful if you will give us your *frank* opinion on this matter. / 貴社の率直な意見をお聞かせください． Please oblige us with your *candid* [*frank*] opinion.

その結果【*sono kekka*】 as a result **例** 結果として需要が増えた． *As a result* the demands increased.

損益【*son-eki*】 profit and loss **例** 損益相償う． The *profits* cover the *losses*. ‖ —計算書 profit and loss statement ‖ —を勘定する balance *profit and loss*

損害【*songai*】 damage; injury; harm; loss **例** 10万円の損害 ￥100,000 worth of *damage* / 当方の不完全な包装によって起こった損害に対し深く遺憾の意を表します． We express our regret for the *damage* caused by our imperfect packing. / 事故は彼らの事務所に大した損害を与えなかった． The accident didn't do much *damage* to their office. / 火災で当社は大損害を蒙った． We suffered a serious *loss* in the fire. / ただちに決定しないなら大きな損害を受けよう． If you do not decide at once, you will suffer a great *loss*. / 損害賠償の支払いを命ぜられることがある． You may be compelled to pay *damages*. ‖ —を受ける damage **例** 貨物の一部が潮ぬれの損害を受けた． Goods were partially *damaged* by sea water.

損失【*sonshitsu*】 loss **例** 船積みによる当社の損失はどれくらいになる見込みですか． What do you estimate our *loss* will be by last shipment? / 損失を埋め合わせるために5,000円の小切手を送ります． We are sending you our check for ￥5,000 to cover the *loss*. / 当方で損失価額を決定します． We shall decide upon the amount of the *loss*. ‖ ～を与える inflict a loss

損傷【*sonshō*】 damage; injury **例** 弊店の品物は事故で損傷を受けた． Our goods received *damage* in the accident. ‖ —を受ける damage; injury **例** 損傷貨物に対する弊店賠償要求を支持してくれますか． Will you support our claim for the *damaged* goods against the insurace company?

損する【*sonsuru*】lose　例　その投資はもうからないまでも損には
　ならないつもりです．We shall *lose* nothing if not gain on the
　investment.

損料【*sonryō*】hire; charge; rent

【た】

～台 【*dai*】 level; mark　囫　株の値段は3,000円台に達した．The price of the shares has reached a *level* of 3,000 yen. / 船の積み荷は500トン台に達した．The ship's load has reached the 500 ton *level*.

代案 【*daian*】 alternative plan; alternative　囫　他に代案はない．There is no other *alternative plan*.

第1位 【*dai-ichii*】 top; the first; first ranking　囫　三菱は日本のトップ会社の1つ．Mitsubishi is one of the *top* companies in Japan. ‖ ―を占める be ranked first; be at the top　囫　その会社は製品売り上げ第1位を占めた．The company was *ranked first* in products sold.

第1便 【*dai-ichibin*】 the first opportunity available　囫　その商品を第1便に船積みくださるようお願いします．We ask you to ship the goods by *the first opportunity available*.

第1船 【*dai-issen*】 the first available ship　囫　第1船に船積みする手配をした．We made arrangements to shipment by *the first available ship*.

滞貨 【*taika*】 congested cargo; stockpiles; accumulated stocks　囫　滞貨一掃 clearance of the *stocks* / 需要低下により在庫が増えだした．Due to the fall in demand the *stocks* began to *accumulate*. / 一層の値上がりにそなえて油が備蓄されている．Oil is being *stockpiled* for fear of further price rises.

代価 【*daika*】 money; price; cost ‖ ―を払う pay the price for ~　囫　当社は新しい設備の代価を払います．Our company will *pay the price for* the new equipment. ‖ ―と引き換えに in exchange for the money ‖ ―前払い payment in advance　囫　値上げを食い止めるため代価を前払いした．*Payment* was made *in advance* to beat the price rise. ‖ ―後払い payment on credit

対外 【*taigai*】 international; foreign; （市場）foreign market　囫　日本には広範の対外市場がある．Japan has an extensive *internatioal trade network*.

大海損 【*daikaison*】 heavy average 　例 多くの保険会社は南シナ海の大海損をおそれています. Many of the insurance companies are dreading the *heavy average* to which they are exposed on the South China Sea.

耐久力 【*taikyūryoku*】 lasting quality; durability ‖ —のある durable 　例 高額品には耐久性と持続性がある. Expensive goods are usually *durable* and *of lasting quality*.

代金送付 【*daikin sōfu*】 remittance 　例 何とぞ～の代金を御送金ください. Please favour us with [send us] your *remittance* for ～.

代金引き換え払い 【*daikin hikikae barai*】 cash on delivery; C.O.D. 　例 同社の注文はすべて代金引き換え払いでした. All their orders were paid for *cash on delivery* of goods.

代行 【*daikō*】 vicarious execution ‖ —業務 agency business ‖ —者 agent; proxy ‖ —する act for a person; execute as proxy 　例 代行者による契約では, だれかが欠席者の代行をする. In an agreement by *proxy*, someone is *substituted for* an absent *proxy* member.

対抗する 【*taikō suru*】 be sufficiently competitive with ～; compete (sufficiently with ～); face; stand against 　例 その会社は他社と対抗するためコンピュータ技術を導入する必要があった. The company needed to introduce computer technology to *be sufficiently competitive with* other companies. / その会社は変容する市場に対抗できず崩壊した. The company collapsed because it failed to *compete with* the changing market variations.

第3次産業 【*daisanji sangyō*】 tertiary industry 　例 第3次産業は, 1次, 2次産業より多くの人を雇用している. *Tertiary industry* employs more people than primary and secondary industry.

第三者 【*daisansha*】 a third (party); outside 　例 第三者の保険はすべての自動車に必要だ. *Third party* insurance is necessary for all motor vehicles.

大使 【*taishi*】 ambassador 　例 駐米大使は本日退任を発表した.

The *ambassador* for the United States announced his retirement today. ‖ —館 embassy

大事 【*daiji*】 serious matter; important affair ‖ —を取る act with caution [be cautious] 例 株を購入する場合は特に大事を取らなければならない. It is necessary to *act with caution* when buying shares. ‖ —ではない insignificant [of no consequence] 例 新しい競争も, その会社のナンバーワンの地位にとってはたいしたことではなかった. The introduction of new competition *was no consequence* to the company's No. 1 standing.

大至急 【*daishikyū*】 emergency 例 品物は大至急積送ください. Please ship the goods *with all speed*.

貸借 【*taishaku*】 loan; debit and credit ‖ —対照表 balance sheet [B/S] 例 会計係は貸借対照表のバランスをとり, 財務諸表を作るよう訓練される. Accountants are trained to balance *debits and credits* in a *balance sheet* and produce financial statements. ‖ —関係 loan accounts

大衆 【*taishū*】 public ‖ —化 popularization ‖ —に受ける be popular among the public 例 新しい冬用衣料は大衆に受けることがわかった. The new range of winter clothes has proved to *be popular among* the public. ‖ —向きの popular [appealing to the public mind]

大小取り混ぜ 【*daishō torimaze*】 in large and small sizes mixed 例 大小取り混ぜて40個ください. I want forty pieces, *large and small all mixed together*.

退職する 【*taishoku suru*】 retire 例 同氏は退職しました. He has *retired* from our firm.

対処する 【*taisho suru*】 cope with; meet with; tide over; bridge over 例 需要の変化に対処するのは時に難しい. It is sometimes difficult to *cope with* changes in demand.

滞船料 【*taisenryō*】 demurrage 例 10日間以内に荷物の積み下ろしをしない場合は, 時間当たり1割の割で滞船料がつく. If cargo is not discharged within 10 days, *demurrage* shall accrue at the rate of 10 per cent per hour.

滞納 【*tainō*】 nonpayment; failure to pay; arrears (金)　例 滞納処分 disposition for *failure to pay* / 納付金の滞納で会社は罰金を課せられた. The company was fined because of the *nonpayment* of the fees. / ローン返済は滞納となっている. Repayments on the loan are in *arrears*.

大半 【*taihan*】 the greater [most] part (of it); a large proportion; mostly; great majority　例 大半は売れ残った. *The greater part* of the goods remained unsold. / 新しいビルの大半は完成している. The construction of a new building is *nearly* completed.

代表 【*daihyō*】 representative　例 いつでも当方の代表者を差し向けます. We shall be pleased to send you our *representative* at any time. ‖ —する be represented by　例 弊社は御地では山田氏が代表しています. We are *represented* in your district *by* Mr. Yamada. / わが社は東京は，スミス社によって代表されています. We are *represented by* the firm of Smith, Tokyo.

代品 【*daihin*】 replacement　例 当方の負担で至急代品を空輸します. We send immediately the *replacement* to you by airplane for our account.

怠慢 【*taiman*】 negligence ‖ —により through neglect of duty　例 貴店の怠慢により，注文を失っているしだいです. We are losing orders *through* your *negligence*.

代理 【*dairi*】 agency; representation　例 弊社にわが国の一手代理権をお与えください. Please give us your exclusive *representation* of our country. / 当地で，当社に代理業務をさせていただきたい. We have pleasure in recommending our *agency* business here.

代理者 【*dairisha*】 representative; legal representative (法定)　例 当社は東京に有能な代理者をもっています. We now have an able *representative* in Tokyo.

代理店 【*dairiten*】 agent　例 弊社は大丸株式会社の輸出代理店である. We are export *agents* of Daimaru Co., Ltd. / 弊社は，貴国に一手販売代理店を持っていることを，お知らせしなければなりません. We have to inform you that we have a firm who work for us as our sole selling *agent* in your country. / 当社はアメリカにたくさんの代理店があります. We have many *agencies* in America. / この代理店契約は 6 カ月間有効です. This *agency* agreement shall remain in force and effect for a period of six months. / 東京でこれまで取り引きがありましたが, まだ適当な代理店をもっておりません. Although we have already done some business in Tokyo, we have no proper *representative* there.

代理人【*dairinin***】**agent　**囫**　代理人は, 販売促進に必要な時間と努力を払うことに同意する. *Agent* agrees to devote such time and effort as may be necessary for sales promotion.

大量【*tairyō***】**large quantity; mass; bulk; volume　**囫**　弊社は, 貴社に大量の注文を出せます. We shall be able to give you *large orders*. / 本品の大量のストックが, 昨年度から持ち越されています. A *heavy stock* of these goods have been carried over from last year.

代用品【*daiyōhin***】**substitute　**囫**　当社は, 代用品を送るよう命じました. We ordered a *substitute* to be sent.

高い【*takai***】**dear; expensive; high in price; high-priced　**囫**　値が高い. The price is *high*. / 品物が高い. The article is *dear* [high in price; costly; expensive]. / 生活費が高い. The cost of living is *high*. Living is *dear*.

互いに【*tagaini***】**mutually　**囫**　貴社の積極的な協力は互いに取引関係を順調に進めるでしょう. Your active cooperation will lead *mutually* to a prosperous business relationship.

高値【*takane***】**high price　**囫**　高値気配. *Prices are in upward* tendency. / 市場は高値が続く. The market remains of a *high level*. / 市場は高値を唱えている. The market rules *high*. / この品は高値を唱えている. These goods are quoted *high*. / 当市場では現在のところたいへん高値に持ち合っています. *Prices* are ruling *high* just now in this market.

高見込み【*takamikomi***】**upward trend　**囫**　市況は, 底固くなお高見込みです. The market is steady with *an upward trend*. / 値段が上がり気味. Prices *tend upward(s)*.

託する【takusuru】entrust a person with a thing; charge a person to do something; place a thing in one's hands; charge a person with a duty 例 貴市の当社代理店を，貴店に託することにしました．We have decided to *entrust* to you our agency for your city.

託送【takusō】consigning ‖ ―品 consignment ‖ ―する consign goods to; send ～ under the care of; send ～ by favor of 例 支払いは売却待ちという了解でその会社に託送した．The goods were *consigned* to the company with the understanding that they will not be paid for until sold.

妥結【daketsu】agreement ‖ ―する reach an agreement; come to a settlement 例 この月曜までに新しいマネジャーを雇用することに関し妥結することが必要．It is necessary to *reach an agreement* on the employment of a new manager by next Monday.

出し抜く【dashinuku】get [have] the start of; forestall; circumvent; outwit 例 新しい競争相手を出し抜くことが必要だった．It was necessary to *circumvent* the new competitor. / 長官は警察に準備させて暴動を出し抜いた．The magistrate *forestalled* a riot by having the police ready.

多少【tashō】more or less 例 貨物をいちいち検査したところ，各個とも多少漏出していました．We have examined them one by one and found each of them leaks *more or less* [*somewhat*; *rather*]. ‖ ある程度 to some extent; in a degree

但し書き【tadashigaki】((with)) proviso ((that)); ((on)) condition ((that)) 例 入社試験に合格するという但し書きつきでマネジャーは雇われた．The manager was employed with the *proviso* that he pass the entrance test. / 医療給付金が含まれるというのが契約の但し書きだった．The inclusion of health benefits was a *condition* in the contract.

ただちに【tadachini】at once; immediately; straight; right away 例 ただちに電信をください．Please cable us *immediately*.

立場【tachiba】situation; position; standpoint; footing ‖ ―から from a viewpoint 例 商業上の立場からみれば，ことは重要で

ある．The matter is important *from* a commercial *standpoint* [*point of view*].

立ち寄る【*tachiyoru*】drop in　例 お立ち寄りくださいますれば，喜ばしく存じます．We shall be most pleased if you *drop in* at our store.

脱税【*datsuzei*】tax evasion; a tax dodge　例 A社は脱税で取り調べを受けた．The A company was examined about *tax evasion*. ‖ —する evade [avoid; dodge] a tax ‖ —品 smuggled goods

建て値【*tatene*】quotation　例 当方の建て値は，値引きの余地がありません．There is no room for a reduction in our *quotation*.

打電【*daden*】telegraphing; sending telegram　例 確定売申込は，打電時から 48 時間有効とする．Firm offers are to remain effective for forty-eight hours after the time of *dispatch*. ‖ —する telegraph; send a telegram; cable; wire

棚卸し【*tanaoroshi*】inventory; stock taking; clearance ‖ —品 stock in the inventory ‖ —する clear; inventory; take stock; make an inventory of articles　例 月々 1 回棚卸しする店もある．Some shops *inventory* their stock once a month. ‖ —表 inventory ‖ —商品 (merchandise) inventory　例 店主は棚卸し品を減らすため売り出しを行った．The shop keeper had a sale to reduce his *inventory*.

他人資本【*taninshihon*】borrowed capital　例 他人資本は年末までに返金される．The *borrowed capital* will be paid back by the end of the year.

楽しみ【*tanoshimi*】pleasure; delight; interest　例 お返事を楽しみにお待ちしています．We *look forward to* hearing from you *with much interest*.

旅【*tabi*】travel; journey; trip; tour　例 山田氏は，関西地方に商用で行かれます．Mr. Yamada is making a business *tour* in the Kansai districts.

多忙【*tabō*】rush of business　例 弊社は，商売に多忙をきわめています．We have a great *rush* [*press*; *pressure*] *of business*. /

事務多忙. We are *pressed with business* [We are *in a whirl of business.*] / 店は多忙です. We are doing *brisk business.*

試し 【*tameshi*】 trial; test; (に) on trial; by way of experiment 例 今回は試し注文ですから, 十分注意して御調達ください. We wish to recommend to you careful execution because this is a *trial* order. / 見本や値段受け取り次第試し注文をします. On receipt of your samples and prices, we shall place with you an order *as a trial.* / 当社製品の品質は優良なので, 貴社が試し注文をくださるようになることを信じています. We trust that the high quality of our products will induce you to place a *trial* order.

ために 【*tameni*】 (目的) in order to; for the purpose of; with a view to; with the object of 例 契約を履行するために生産を上げる必要がある. *In order to* fulfill the contract it will be necessary to increase production. / 会社は能率アップのためワードプロセッサーを入れた. The business purchased a word processer *for the purpose of* increasing efficiency.

(利益) for (the benefit of); for the sake of; in the interest of; in the service of; in behalf of; in favor of; in honor of 例 田中君のために送別会を開きます. We give a farewell party *in honor of* Mr. Tanaka. / 将来のために全力を尽くしましょう. We will do our best *for the sake of* future business.
(理由, 原因, 結果) for; from; of; through; by; because of; on account of; on the ground of; in consequence of; owing to; thanks to; due to 例 職務怠慢のために 叱られた. He was blamed *for* neglect of duty. / 戦争のために物価が上がった. The prices rose *owing to* ⌊*in consequence of*⌋ the war.

たやすく 【*tayasuku*】 readily; easily; without difficulty 例 日本製万年筆は, 20 ドルでたやすく売れます. Japanese fountain pens sell *readily* at 20 dollars per piece.

単価 【*tanka*】 unit price 例 日本製ミシンの単価は 50 ドルです. The *unit price* of Japanese sewing machine is 50 dollars.

短期 【*tanki*】 short term; short time 例 その企業は利益を短期金融市場に投資した. The business invested its profits in the *short-term* money market. / 彼はほんの短期間エンジニアとして雇われた. He was employed only for a *short time* as an engineer. ‖ ―貸付 short-term loan 例 短期貸付のため利率は高かった. The interest rate was very high because it was a *short term loan*. ‖ ―取引| short transaction ‖ ―資金 short-term fund ‖ ―融資 call loan ‖ ―手形 short bill [draft; exchange]

断言【*dangen*】 positive statement; assertion; affirmation ‖ ―する assert; affirm; be positive about; we assure you 例 若干の商売上の投機で彼らが重大な損失を被っていることは, 断言できる. It is now *positively stated* that they have suffered severe losses in several mercantile speculations.

担当【*tantō*】 charge ‖ ―する take [be in] charge of 例 取締役は企業経営を担当する. Directors have *charge* of business management. / 山田氏はＰＲ担当だ. Mr. Yamada *is in charge of* public relations.

単独海損【*tandoku kaison*】 particular average [P.A.] ‖ ―担保 with particular average [W.P.A.] ‖ ―不担保 free from particular average [F.P.A] 例 「箱根丸」の積み荷に対し金額3万ドル単独海損担保の保険お引き受けください. Please insure us for $30,000 W.A. on the shipment per M.V. "Hakone Maru".

単独手形【*tandoku tegata*】 solo bill 例 出合売買のため単独手形が買い手に送られた. Due to the singular sale a *solo bill* was sent to the buyer.

担保【*tanpo*】 security; mortgage; hypothec 例 御来示の担保では, 融通できぬ. Cannot make a loan on the *security* offered. / 為替手形の担保に何を差し入れてよいか. What *security* do you require for the bill? ‖ ―条件(海上保険) marine insurance terms [conditions] ‖ ―物件 a mortgage; a security; a collateral ‖ ―に入っている lie [be] in pledge ‖ ―付き secured by [with securities] ‖ ―付き社債 secured debenture ‖ ―貸し loan on security ‖ ―付き約手 a collateral [secured] note

段ボール【*danbōru*】 corrugated (card)board 例 商品は, 各50反入り段ボールで包装してあります. The goods are packed in *corrugated board* case each containing 50 pieces.

単名手形【*tanmei tegata*】single name bill　**例** 総代理店は単名
手形を受け取った．The sole trader received a *single name bill.*

反物【*tanmono*】piece-goods　**例** 毛製反物のスリランカ向け輸出
に関心を持っています．We are interested in exporting *piece-
goods* to Sri Lanka.

単利【*tanri*】simple interest　**例** 貸し付けの単利率は 7 ％だった．
The *simple interest* rate on the loan was 7 ％.

【ち】

地位【*chii*】position; status; situation; standing　**例** 今朝の新聞
に御広告の会計係の地位に申し込みます．I wish to apply for the
position of accountant advertised by you in this morning's
paper. / 本田氏は顧問の地位に従って，相当多額 の取り引きを貴
店といたしました．Mr. Honda did a considerable business with
you acting in the *capacity* of an adviser. / 彼は職務怠慢のた
め地位を失った．He lost his *place* through neglect of duty.
‖ ─の高い人 a man of (good social) standing

地域【*chiiki*】area; region; zone‖ ─別 regional; by area　**例** こ
れらの品物の価値は地域によって違っています．The value of
these goods makes a difference *in some areas.*

遅延【*chien*】delay; retardation　**例** これ以上の遅延は待てませ
ん．We can not wait for the *delay* any longer. / この遅延に
より貴社に御不便をかけて申し訳けありません．We are afraid
we have much inconvenienced you by this *delay.*

力【*chikara*】power; ability; authority‖ ─の及ばぬ out of [be-
yond] our power [control]　**例** 政府決定を変えるのは力の及
ばないことだった．It was *out of our power* to change the
Government's decision.

蓄積【*chikuseki*】accumulation;（する）store　**例** 過剰在庫は次
のシーズンまで蓄積しておく必要があった．It was necessary
to *store* the excess stock till next season.‖ ─円 deposited
[accumulated] yen

遅滞【chitai】 delay; arrearage; balance due 例 船積みの遅滞に対し貴社にまったく責任を感じます. We hold you entirely responsible for *the delay* in shipment. ‖ ―なく without delay; losing no time; with dispatch; immediately; directly; promptly 例 貴社がこの提案を考慮くださるつもりなら，遅滞なくその旨電報してください. If you are inclined to consider this proposal, cable us to that effect *without delay*. / 値段は特に魅力的であるから遅滞なくこの申し込みを引き受けることをお勧めします. The prices being specially attractive, we advise you to accept this offer *without delay*.

着船【chakusen】 arrival of a vessel ‖ ―渡し ex-ship ‖ ―通知書 arrival notice 例 着船通知書は支配人のオフィスにある. The *arrival notice* of the vessel is in the manager's office.

着地沖渡値段【chakuchi okiwatashi nedan】 [運賃保険料込値段] C.I.F. [Cost, Insurance and Freight] price

着荷【chakka；chakuni】 goods arrived; arrivals ‖ 新規― new arrivals 例 新規着荷はまず倉庫に入れられる. The *new arrivals* of stock are first stored in the warehouse. ‖ ―渡し delivery on arrival ‖ ―払い payment on arrival; Cash on Delivery

注意【chūi】 attention; note; caution; advice ‖ ―を促す draw [call] one's attention; bring to one's notice ‖ ―する pay attention; give heed to; take care [notice] of; be careful of 例 貴社御注文は，念入りに注意をいたします. Your order will receive our best *attention*. / 7月3日付貴信の本件に関する御注意感謝します. We thank you for *calling our attention* in your letter of July 3. / 貴社がこの取り引きに最善特別の注意をお払いくださるようお願いします. We hope that this business will receive your best and prompt *attention*. / 当社は上等品を望みますから，この点に特に注意ください. As we require the goods of superior quality, we ask you to *give* [*pay*] *your best attention to* this matter. / 品物の品質は貴見本のそれと同等であることに注意してください. Please *see to it* that the quality is equal to that of your sample.

仲介【chūkai】 intermediation ‖ ―者の手を経て through agent ‖

—貿易 intermediary trade **例** 仲介貿易契約は荷渡しと品物が使えるようになる間に 3 週間の猶予を求めている．The *intermediary trade* agreement requires a lapse of 3 weeks between delivery and use of the products.

中級品【*chūkyūhin*】 fair average quality **例** 中級品を基礎としてお取り引きしたいと思います．We shall be glad to work with you on the basis of *fair average qualities* [*F.A.Q.*].

仲継【*chūkei*】 transmission; relay **例** 新設備の情報はいまメーカーから小売店へ仲継されている．The information on the new equipment is now on *relay* from the manufacturer to the retailer. ‖ —する relay; transmit; convey ‖ —港 transit [intermediate] port **例** マニラはロンドンから東京へコンテナを送るときの仲継港とされていた．Manila was used as a *transit port* in the delivery of containers from London to Tokyo. ‖ —貿易 entrepot trade

忠告【*chūkoku*】 advice; warning; caution ‖ —に従って on a person's advice ‖ —に従う follow a person's advice **例** 不慣れな地域では他人の忠告に従うことも時に必要である．It is sometimes necessary to *follow a person's advice* in unfamiliar areas. ‖ —をきかない disregard a person's advice

仲裁【*chūsai*】 (裁判) arbitration **例** 労働者の賃金のクレームは労使間の仲裁で解決した．The workers' pay claim was settled through *arbitration* between the union and the management. ‖ —裁判所 arbitration tribunal [court] ‖ —裁判に持ち込む bring into arbitration

中止【*chūshi*】 discontinuance **例** 同店事業中止のため目下辞任を考えています．I am now leaving their employment on account of their *discontinuance* [*discontinuation*; *suspension*] of business.

ちゅうちょ【*chūcho*】 hesitation ‖ —せずに without loss of time; without the least delay; without hesitation ‖ —する hesitate **例** それゆえ，お申し越しの金額に対して信用を与えることをちゅうちょします．We *hesitate* therefore to extend credit for the amount mentioned.

注目【*chūmoku*】attention; notice ‖ —に値する worthy of note; notable 　例 注目すべきものが輸入されることもある. Some of the most *attractive* things are imported.

注文【*chūmon*】order; indent; ordered goods (品)　例 電報にてこの注文確認書をお送りください. Kindly let us have the confirmation of this *order* by telegraph. / 3月1日付注文書を受け取りました. We have received your *order* of the 1st March. / 注文品は注文殺到のため売り切れました. The recent rush of *orders* has exhausted our stock of the article you *ordered*. / 現在当社の電気製品には注文が殺到しています. At present the electric appliances of our company are being *rushed with orders*. / 注文書を受け取った. We have received the *Order Sheet*. / 報告書に記載の事項は完全に満足ですので, ただちに御注文に応じさせていただきます. We are pleased to *fill your order* at once, since the information in the statement is entirely satisfactory. / 6月22日付御注文第520号, 入帳いたしました. We have the pleasure of *entering your order* No. 520 of the 22nd June. / 注文と同時に半額現金をいただき, 残額は現品引き換え払いといたします. Must have half *cash with the order*, and balance on delivery. / 貴社に注文品を送りました. We sent you the *ordered goods*. ‖ 追加— a further [additional] order ‖ —と同時に現金払い C.W.O. (Cash With Orders) ‖ 再— repeat order ‖ —を受ける accept [book] order 　例 双方の利益のために大量受注するよう希望する. We hope you will *book* large *orders* for our mutual benefit. / 相当多額の御注文をいただきたいと存じます. We hope that you will be able to *book substantial orders*. / このような安値では御注文を引き受けることはできない. We regret that we are unable to *accept* your *order* at such a low price. ‖ —を果す execute order; fulfill contract ‖ —する place an order with one for a thing 　例 下記商品に対し注文いたします. We *place an order with* you *for* the following. We pass you an *order* for ~. We *order* the following goods from you. / 下記商品を試験的に注文します. We are glad to *place* a trial *order with* you *for* the following goods. / 下記の通り貴社に注文をいたします. We have much pleasure in *placing an order with* you as following. / 親切にも大量注文をくださり喜びにたえ ない. It was a pleasure to receive the sizeable (large) *order* which you were kind enough to *place with* us. ‖ —を断わる decline order 囲 an order は注文, 注文品, 注文書

超過 【*chōka*】 excess; (額) surplus 例 超過価格は 6 割 4 割で貴社と配分します. We'll split with you the *overprice* 60/40. ‖ —する exceed 例 輸出超過 600 万ドルに及ぶ. Export *exceeds* import by six million dollars.

長期 【*chōki*】 long term; long period of time 例 長期的には利益の増進が望まれる. In the *long term* it is hoped that profits will improve. ‖ —取引 long-term transaction ‖ —信用 long-term credit ‖ —計画 long-range plan ‖ —契約 long-term contract 例 政府と三菱との間で三菱が電気設備を供給する長期契約ができていた. There has been a *long term contract* between the government and Mitsubishi that Mitsubishi should supply electrical equipment.

兆候 【*chōkō*】 indication; inclination; sign 例 輸出取引が活発になる兆候がある. There are *signs* that our export business is about to rally.

調査 【*chōsa*】 survey; investigation; analysis; research 例 当社は今月末をもって, オーストラリアの市場調査を打ち切ることにする. We decided to discontinue the *market research* of Australia at the end of this month. ‖ —する investigate; inquire; make inquiries 例 貴社の価格を慎重に調査しました. We have *investigated* with interest your quotations. / お尋ねのその商社に関し直ちに調査しました. We have *made inquiries* respecting the firm referred to [you inquired about].

調製 【*chōsei*】 manufacture; preparation ‖ 注文の— execution of order

調整 【*chōsei*】 adjustment; arrangement; coordination ‖ —する adjust 例 この件, 御満足のゆくよう調整したいと思います. We wish to *adjust* the matter to your satisfaction.

調達【*chōtatsu*】 procurement; accomodation; execution 例 貴社御注文品の調達につきましては，必要な手続きを踏みました．
Regarding our *execution* of your order, we have taken the necessary procedures. ‖ —する procure; execute 例 御満足のいただけるように，その品物を調達いたします．We shall spare no trouble to *execute* the order to your satisfaction.

調停【*chōtei*】 mediation; arbitration; intervention 例 生産ストップを解決するには経営者と工場労働者間の調停が必要だった．
Mediation between the manager and the factory worker was necessary to solve the breakdown of production. / 航空管制官のストライキを政府は調停した．There was government *intervention* in the air traffic controllers' strike. ‖ —する arbitrate in a matter; mediate a quarrel ‖ —員 claim adjuster ‖ —書 adjustment letter

調度品【*chōdohin*】 fixtures 例 調度品はすべて漏れなく当店に取りそろえてございます．All *fixtures* are completely assembled in our shop.

帳簿【*chōbo*】 book ‖ —をつける keep accounts; book 例 新しい仕入品は店主の日誌に記帳された．The new supplies were *booked* into the storeman's log. ‖ —を締め切る close the book 例 政府は事業利息に関し帳簿を締め切る必要があった．It was necessary for the government to *close the book* on its business interests. ‖ —を検査する check records; look over the book 例 会計係が帳簿を検査すると赤字が増えたことがわかった．When the accountant *looked over the book*, he found that the deficit had increased.

直接【*chokusetsu*】: —課税 direct taxation 例 直接税はすべての勤労者が支払う．*Direct taxation* is paid by all workers. ‖ —貿易 direct trade 例 現在日豪間で直接貿易が行われている．There is now a pattern of *direct trade* between Australia and Japan. ‖ —交渉 direct negotiations ‖ —費 direct cost

直航船【*chokkōsen*】 direct steamer [vessel; boat] 例 貴社にその荷物を直航船で送ります．We will send you the goods by *direct steamer*.

直輸出【*choku yushutsu*】direct export 囫 新しい機械は工場か ら直接海外に送られたので，直輸出であった．The new machinery was a *direct export* because it was sent overseas straight from the factory.

直輸入【*choku yunyū*】direct import 囫 車の新しい受け渡しには 関税の支払いがなかったので，直輸入だった．The new delivery of cars was a *direct import* because there was no duty to be paid.

貯蔵【*chozō*】storage; storing 囫 かさ高の品物の貯蔵費は高く つく．The *storage* cost of bulky articles is often high.‖ ─す る store; have things in store; have a store of goods 囫 古い在庫は倉庫に入れてある．The old stock is being *stored* in the warehouse. / 市況が変わる場合は品物を貯蔵する必要が あ る．It is necessary to *have things in store* in case of a change in market trends.

賃借【*chinshaku*】hire 囫 会社は車を 5 台賃借している．The company has the use of five *hire* cars. / その会社は賃借料支払 いのため 10 万円借り入れた．The business borrowed ￥100,000 to pay for the *lease*.‖ ─する hire; lease land; rent a house ‖ ─条件で on rental basis

沈滞【*chintai*】stagnation; dullness; depression ‖ ─している dull; depressed; inactive 囫 目下市況は沈滞気味である．The market situation is *dull*.

沈没【*chinbotsu*】sinking; submersion; foundering ‖ ─船 sunken vessel ‖ ─する sink; founder 囫 難波船が沈没している．The damaged ship is *foundering*.

陳列場【*chinretsujō*】a show room 囫 新型車が陳列場に並んで いる．The new model cars are on display in *the show room*.

【つ】

追加【*tsuika*】addition; appendix; supplement ‖ ─予算 supplementary budget ‖ ─する add 囫 貴社の製品を 30 ダース追 加します．We *add* thirty dozen of your goods to our order.

追伸【*tsuishin*】postscript [P.S.] 例 手紙の終りに追伸が書かれていた. A *postscript* was added to the end of the letter.

通運【*tsūun*】transportation; forwarding; express 例 商品の通運はどの事業にも必要だ. The *transportation* of goods is necessary in every business. / 悪天気のため備品の通運は遅延した. The *forwarding* of the equipment was delayed by bad weather. ‖ ―機関 transportation facilities

通貨【*tsūka*】currency 例 ニュージーランドは, 通貨の呼称を「ドル・セント制」に切り替えるはず. The New Zealanders are scheduled to switch the denomination of their *currency* to the new dollar and cent.

通関【*tsūkan*】entry; (custom) clearance 例 貨物の通関および受け渡しの御用をいたします. We offer you our services for the *clearance* of cargoes through the customs and delivery. ‖ ―業者 customs broker ‖ ―手続き customs procedures ‖ ―用送り状 customs invoice ‖ ―する pass the customs house ‖ ―手続きをする clear the goods through customs

通産省【*tsūsanshō*】Ministry of International Trade and Industry [MITI]

通商【*tsūshō*】commerce; trade 例 通商協定は, まもなく締結される. The *trade* agreement will be signed before long.

通信【*tsūshin*】correspondence (文); communication 例 通信の記録をすべて取っておかなければならない. You ought to keep records of all *correspondence*. ‖ ―費勘定 communication's account ‖ ―機関 means of communication ‖ ―網 network of communication

通知【*tsūchi*】notice; information; advice ‖ ―払 advise and pay ‖ ―あり次第 on receipt of one's notice ‖ ―する give a person notice; inform a person; notify 例 至急関係者一同に御通知していただきたい. Please *notify* immediately all parties concerned. ‖ 追って―あるまで until further notice

通訳【*tsūyaku*】interpretation; interpreter 例 日米両社の契約をまとめるには, 通訳を必要とした. It was necessary to use an *interpreter* to finalize the contract between the Japanese and American companies.

通用【*tsūyō*】common use ‖ —期間 stipulated period **例** この機械の使用は通用期間のみだった. The use of the machinery was for a *stipulated period.* ‖ —する be available; be good for

尽きる【*tsukiru*】become exhausted; be consumed **例** 最初の在庫品は尽きました. The original stock is *exhausted.*

着く【*tsuku*】reach; arrive at; get to **例** その船は多分, 月曜日にサンフランシスコに着くでしょう. The ship will probably *reach* San Francisco on Monday.

尽くす【*tsukusu*】render; serve; exert oneself; do 《a service》 **例** 彼はあなたに尽くすだろう. He will *do you a service.*

償う【*tsugunau*】compensate (one for damage); make amends for; make up for; make reparation for **例** 今期の利潤は, 営業費用も償っていません. The profits realized at this season do not *cover* the working expenses.

付け値【*tsukene*】bid; quotation **例** 貴社問い合わせの当社ビールの付け値は, 1 ダース9 ドルです. Our *quotation* of beer which you inquired is nine dollars per dozen.

付ける【*tsukeru*】bear; attach; stick **例** すべての木箱は, 荷印を付けなくてはならない. All wooden cases have to *bear* shipping marks.

都合【*tsugō*】: —により for certain reasons; owing to circumstances ‖ —のよい時に at one's earliest convenience **例** 送り状金額を都合つき次第早く送金してください. For the invoice amount, we shall be glad to have your remittance *at your earliest convenience.* / 都合のよい折に面会くださいますようおねがいします. I would welcome a personal interview *at your convenience.* ‖ —する arrange; accommodate a person with **例** 御注文量は, 多分御都合できます. Probably it is possible for us to *accommodate you with* the quantity required.

積み送り【*tsumiokuri*】consignment (品) **例** この商品は積送品である. The goods are on *consignment.* ‖ —人 consignor **例** Y氏はこの商品の運送に責任のある積送人です. Mr. Yamoto is the *consignor* responsible for the transport of the goods. ‖ —

宛名 consignee ‖ —する consign **例** 山田氏にこの商品を急便で積み送りする. We will *consign* the goods to Mr. Yamada by express.

積み替え 【tsumikae**】** transhipment **例** 貨物の積み替えはその港で行われました. The *transhipment* of the cargo has taken place at the port. ‖ —る tranship **例** その品物は，香港で積み替えられるはずだ. The goods are to *be transhipped* at Hongkong.

積み込み 【tsumikomi**】** shipping; loading; shipment **例** 積み込み港は横浜です. The port of *loading* is Yokohama. / 貴社の貨物は積み込みを拒絶されました. Your goods are *shut out*. / 残念ながら「カナダ」丸に積み込みかねます. We regret that we can not *catch* the "Canada Maru". ‖ —する ship **例** 均等に3カ月分割で積み込みする ship goods in equal three monthly instalments

積みすぎ 【tsumisugi**】** overloading **例** トラック会社は積みすぎのため罰金を科せられた. The trucking company was fined for *overloading*.

積み高 【tsumidaka**】** loading quantity; shipping weight **例** この船への積み高は200キロである. The *loading quantity* for the ship is 200 kg. / 小荷物の積み高は20キロから15キロに下げられた. The *shipping weight* of the parcel was reduced from 20 kg to 15 kg.

積み出し 【tsumidashi**】** shipment **例** 積み出しはなるべく取り急ぎいたします. *Shipment* of the goods will be made as soon as possible. / 当社は遅くとも7月31日までに品物が入用ですから正確な積み出しが肝心です. Punctual *shipment* is essential because we need the goods by the 31st July at the latest. ‖ —係 shipping clerk ‖ —品質条件 shipment quality terms ‖ —人 shipper ‖ —費 shipping charges ‖ —案内 shipment advice ‖ —港 port of shipping ‖ —をする ship; forward; [effect] shipment **例** 注文品は本日浅間丸で積み出しました. 右御通知します. We wish to advise that we have *shipped* today your order per M.V. "Asama Maru." We are glad to advise having *shipped* today by M.S. "A" the goods you ordered.

積み立て【*tsumitate*】 reserving; accumulation 例 新事業を開始するため資金を積み立てている. There is an *accumulation* of funds to initiate a new venture. ‖ ―金 reserve ‖ ―金繰り入れ additions to reserves ‖ ―る save money; deposit; reserve 例 企業は不況にそなえて利益を積み立てている. The company is *reserving* its profits for stagnation.

積み付け【*tsumitsuke*】 stowage 例 小麦の積み付けに3時間かかった. The *stowage* of the wheat took three hours. ‖ ―明細 stowage plan ‖ ―人 hatch [hold] man

積み荷【*tsumini*】 cargo; freight; load; goods ‖ ―目録 manifest ‖ ―案内状 shipment advice; advice of shipment ‖ ―港 port of shipment; shipping [loading] port ‖ ―料 stowage ‖ ―書類 shipping documents ‖ ―を陸揚げする discharge 《cargo》‖ ―を下ろす unload a ship 例 当社の積み荷は, 来週横浜で陸揚げします. Our *cargo* will be *unloaded* [*discharged*] at Yokohama port next week.

積み残し【*tsuminokoshi*】 short shipment; shutout 例 積み残し品は, 倉庫に送られました. The *shutouts* were sent to the warehouse. ‖ ―になる be short-shipped; be shut out of the vessel 例 10個積み残す short-shipped by 10 pieces / 当社の貨物は積み残されました. Our goods were *shut out*.

積み戻し【*tsumimodoshi*】 reshipment; re-exportation ‖ ―品 reshipments ‖ ―する reship; re-export; ship back 例 関税未納なら, 貨物積み戻しねがいます. *Reship* the goods unless duty has been paid. / 貨物がなお保税倉庫にあるなら積み戻してよろしいか. Shall we *reship* the goods, if they are still left in bond?

積む【*tsumu*】 ship; load ‖ 船に― ship goods by a vessel; load a ship with cargo; load goods in a ship; freight a ship 例 横浜で荷物を積みました. We *loaded* the goods at Yokohama. / 綿花の船荷を積んだ. The ship *took on a cargo* of cotton.

つもり【*tsumori*】 intention; plan; design 例 この国のどこにも代理店を置く考えはありません. We have no *mind* [*intention*]

to open [establish] agents in any part of this country. ‖ 意図
する contemplate　例 当社は, 製品を空輸するつもりはありませ
ん. We do not *contemplate* sending the goods by air transportation.

強気【*tsuyoki*】bull; bullish tone　例 市況は強気である. The
market has a *bullish feeling* [is *strong*].

強含み【*tsuyofukumi*】firm; steady　例 市況はたいへん強含みで
す. The market is very *firm* [*steady*].

つり合う【*tsuriau*】balance; be proportionate to　例 会計係は勘
定の借方貸方のバランスをとる必要があった. It was necessary
for the accountant to *balance* the debit and credit sides of
the account. ‖ つりあった balanced; well-matched; well-
balanced ‖ つりあってない ill-balanced; ill-assorted

【て】

提案【*teian*】suggestion; proposal; proposition　例 御提案を受
諾できる. We are agreeable to your *suggestion*. / 貴社がこ
の提案を考慮してくださるつもりなら遅滞なくその旨電報くださ
い. If you are inclined [feel disposed] to consider this
proposal, cable us to that effect without delay. / 当社は貴社の
御提案に同意することに決めました. We have decided to agree
to your *suggestion*. ‖ ーする suggest [propose] (that)　例 B
の代わりにAを取り上げてはいかがですか. We should like to
suggest that you take up A instead of B. / 彼らは船積みする
ように提案した. They *proposed that* the shipment should be
effected. / この申し出をお受けになってはいかが. May we *suggest that* you avail yourself of this offer?

定価【*teika*】fixed [list] price　例 定価から6％の割引をする
make a six per cent discount off our *list price* ‖ ーで売る
sell at a fixed price　例 定価の2割引で売る sell the goods at
20 per cent off the fixed price ‖ ー表 price-list　例 現在の定
価表を送付乞う. Will you send us your present *price-list* for
the goods? / 当社商品の定価表を同封します. We enclose a

price-list of our goods. / 定価表記載の値段は，予告あるまで有効ですから御承知おきください．Please note that the *prices* given in the *list* are good till further notice.

低開発国【*teikaihatsu koku*】underdeveloped countries　囫 アフリカには低開発国が多い．There are many *underdeveloped countries* in Africa.　囲 開発途上国 developing country ‖ 中進国(新興工業国) newly industrializing country　囫 ブラジルは新しい産業発展の中心だから，新興工業国のお手本である．Brazil is an example of *a newly industrializing nation* because it is now the center of new industrial expansion.

定期【*teiki*】regular [fixed] period [time; term] ‖ ―預金 fixed deposit　囫 定期預金の利息は高い．*Fixed deposits* earn higher interest. ‖ ―船 liner ‖ ―相場 time bargain ‖ ―便 regular service ‖ ―便 (航空機) an air liner　囫 船は定期に出発している．The ship starts *at regular intervals*.

提供【*teikyō*】offer; provision　囫 彼から千円の提供を受けた．We received *an offer* of 1,000 yen from him. ‖ ―する offer　囫 この品を 1,000 円で提供する．We *offer* you this article for 1,000 yen. / 品物を 20%引きで提供する．We *offer* the article at 20% reduction.

提携【*teikei*】cooperation ‖ ―する work together; co-operate with; be affiliated with ‖ ―して in operation with; in alliance with　囫 当社はA社と提携して薬品を発売した．We have put the drug on sale *in* cooperation [*in conjunction*] *with* A company.

停止【*teishi*】suspension; stop; stoppage　囫 商売は停止状態だ．Business is at a *standstill*. ‖ ―する suspend; stop　囫 ～まで業務一切を停止します．All business will be *suspended* until ～. / 支払いを停止した．They *suspended* payment. / やむなく注文停止する．We have to *suspend* the order. ‖ 営業― the suspension of business

定時【*teiji*】scheduled [regular; fixed] time　囫 航空機は定時に到着した．The airplane arrived *on schedule* [*on time*]. / 列車は定時に発車します．The train leaves *at the scheduled*

time. 囲 定時外労働 overtime work

呈示【*teiji*】 presentation 例 呈示あり次第受け取ってください.
Please accept on *presentation.* / 呈示された際は貴社手形を引き
受けます. On *presentation* of security we shall duly protect
your draft. / 当社は貴社あて一覧後 30 日払い 10,000 ドルの為替
手形を振り出しました. 呈示のさいはどうぞお引き受けください.
We have drawn on you a draft at 30 d/s for \$ 10,000, which
please accept on *presentation.* ‖ —する present; show; exhibit;
introduce 例 貴手形銀行より呈示がありました. Your draft
was presented by the bank.

提出【*teishutsu*】 submission; introduction; presentation ‖ —する
present; submit 例 商品は提出の見本通りではございません.
The goods are not in accordance with the sample *submitted.* /
必要書類は 5 日までに提出のこと. You are requested to *submit*
the necessary forms not later than the 5th.

訂正【*teisei*】 amendment; correction 例 送金が別の条件で行わ
れる時は訂正のため返還します. Remittance sent on any other
basis will be returned for *correction.* ‖ —する correct; revise;
amend 例 信用状の文字を訂正してください. Please *amend*
the words in the letter of credit. / 付せんの箇所を訂正するこ
と. The parts labelled are to be *corrected.* / 下記文句を訂正く
ださい. Please *amend* the following clause.

抵当【*teitō*】 mortgage; security; a collateral; a guarantee 例
会社は国債を担保として提供した. Government bonds were
offered as *collateral* by the firm. ‖ —をとって金を貸す lend
money on security ‖ —権設定 settlement of mortgage ‖ —に
入れる mortgage; give a thing as security 例 独力の商人に
とって資本を増やすには家屋を抵当にする必要があった. It was
necessary for the sole trader to *mortgage* his house in order
to raise more capital.

低落【*teiraku*】 decline; depreciation; fall 例 目下早期低落の兆
しない模様. No indication of an early *decline* at present.

手薄【*teusu*】 scanty; scarce; slender 例 在庫品は手薄である.
The stock is *small* [*scarce*].

手かぎ無用【*tekagi muyō*】Do not use a dog hook. Use no [No] hooks.

手形【*tegata*】bill; draft; note 例 手形は6月10日に満期になります。The *bill* falls [becomes] due on the 10th June. / その手形の期限は経過している。The *draft* is overdue. / 手形を支払う。We must *meet* your *draft*. / 手形は東京銀行で支払います。The *bill* will be domiciled at The Bank of Tokyo. / 手形の延期について取引銀行と打ち合わせた。We have arranged with our banks to extend the *draft*. / 一覧後30日で手形を振り出す。We draw a *draft* at 30 d/s. / 当方振り出し手形は大阪銀行を通じ買いとられた。Our *draft* was negotiated through The Osaka Bank, Ltd. ‖ 約束— a promissory note ‖ 為替— a bill of exchange ‖ 銀行— bank draft ‖ 無為替— clean bill ‖ 商業— commercial draft ‖ 融通— accomodation draft ‖ 一覧払い— sight draft ‖ 一覧後60日払い— 60 days' draft [draft at 60 days after sight] ‖ 荷為替— documentary draft ‖ 不渡り— dishonored draft ‖ —を振り出す draw (a draft for the amount on a person) 例 ～銀行をとおして手形を振り出した。We have *drawn* upon you through ～ Bank. / 当社は送り状金額に対し一覧後60日払いの為替手形を貴社あてに振り出します。呈示あり次第手形の引き受け支払いをしてくださることを信じます。We *draw a draft* upon you for the amount of the invoice at 60 d/s and trust you will meet the *bill* on presentation. / 貴社あて貴地A商会受け取り，金額1万ドルの為替手形を振り出した。We have *drawn* on you a *draft* for $10,000 in favor of Messrs. A & Co. of your city. ‖ 貨物を引き当てに—を振り出す draw a draft against goods ‖ 一覧払いで—を振り出す draw a draft at sight ‖ ～あての—を振り出す draw a draft in favor of～ ‖ 信用状に基づいて—を振り出す draw a draft under an L/C ‖ —借り入れをする get a loan on a draft ‖ —呈示時に支払う honor [protect] a draft on presentation ‖ —を取り組む negotiate a draft ‖ ～に—を引き受け（支払い）のため呈示する present a draft to ～ for acceptance (payment) ‖ —を取り戻す recall a draft ‖ 支払いを拒絶して—を差し戻す return a draft

unpaid ‖ —を撤回する withdraw a draft ‖ 為替—を不渡りにす
る dishonor a bill ‖ —引き受け船積書類渡し documents against
acceptance [D/A] ‖ —支払い船積書類渡し documents against
payment [D/P] **例** 弊社は手形支払い船積書類渡しの条件で取
り引きを許されている. We are permitted to do business on
a *D/P basis*. ‖ —買い取り指図書 letter of instruction ‖ —買い
取り支払い授権書 authority to purchase [pay]

出方【*dekata*】 one's behavior; one's attitude; a move **例** 先方
の出方を見よう. Let's wait and see what *move* they will
make. / 先方の出方で対応を考えよう. We will deal with them
according to their *attitude*.

手紙【*tegami*】 letter; mail; message; correspondence ‖ —で by
mail; via airmail ‖ —で知らせる inform ~ of something by
letter ‖ —による注文 order by mail; mail order **例** カタロ
グにある商品を手紙で注文した. The goods in the catalogue
were *ordered by mail*.

適する【*tekisuru*】 (be) fit; suit; be suitable; be adapted; be
qualified; be good **例** この商品は貴地に適しています. These
goods would *be suitable* for your country. / この水は飲用に適
する. This water *is good* [*fit*] to drink. / 寒い気候はリンゴに
適する. A cold climate *suits* the growing of apples. / 船は使
用に適す（任務にたえる）. The ship *is fit* for use (service)./
彼は最もその任に適している. He is *the very* man for the post.
/ 貴社の価格が割安で製品が当社の営業に適するならば，大量に
注文します. If your prices are reasonable and your goods
suit our trade, we shall order large quantity.

適正【*tekisei*】 propriety; pertinence; reasonability ‖ —な proper;
right; reasonable 《price》 **例** 貴社の考え方は適正でない. Your
way of thinking is not *reasonable*. / 適正な判断を下すことは
容易でない. It is not easy to form [pass] a *just and proper*
judgement on anything.

摘要【*tekiyō*】 remarks **例** 摘要欄 the remarks column / 右の欄外
に摘要が記載してある. *Remarks* are given in the right margin.

適用【*tekiyō*】 application **例** この規則は適用範囲が広い. This

rule has an extensive range of *application.* ‖ —する apply 例
この規則は貴社には適用されない. This rule does not *apply* to
your company. / 規則の適用を誤った. They *misapplied* the
rule. / 本覚書は貴我間の全取り引きに適用されるべきものです.
This memorandum is to *be applied* to all transactions between us.

できる【*dekiru*】can do; be realized; (商売が) do a business
例 品質がよければよい商売ができると思います. If your quality
is good, we *can* promise you good results. / 値段が安ければ
商売が大いにできると思う. If your price is reasonable, considerable business will *result* [*be realized*]. / 貴社と相当取り引
きができることを期待しています. We expect to *be able to do
a good business* with you. / 残念ながら御依頼に応ずることはで
きません. We regret to say that we are not in a position to
comply with your request.

できる限り【*dekiru kagiri*】as ～ as possible 例 できる限り貴社
の御要求にそうよう努力します. We will try to meet your requirements *as far as possible.* / かなり大量の注文をするつもり
ですから，できる限り安い値段を申し出るよう願います. As we
intend to place a fairly large order with you, we ask you to
give [quote] us your *lowest prices possible.* / 市場価格がまもな
く上がりそうですから，できる限り早く注文くださるようお勧め
します. As the market prices are likely to rise very soon,
we can advise you to place your order *as early as possible.*

手数料【*tesūryō*】commission; fee; charge; handling fee 例 手
数料は5ドル. The *fee* is five dollars. / 当分の手数料は3分に
させていただきます. Our *commission* would be 3%. / 関税
額，手数料などはこの金額から差し引きで取り立てること. The
amount of duty, *commissions*, etc. to be charged against this
sum. / CIF に当方の手数料6%込みの最低値段を出してくださ
い. Will you quote the best possible prices CIF including
our *commission* of 6 per cent. / 手数料を払ってもらいたいと主
張した. We insisted on having our *fee* paid. / 売上高に5分，
代金支払い保証に2分，銀行手数料に1分の手数料を 要求しま

す. The *commission* we require would be 5% on the amount realized, *del credere* 2% extra, bank *commission* 1%. ‖ 販売― selling commission ‖ 買付― buying commission

撤回する【*tekkai suru*】withdraw; retract; take back; recede from 例 要求を撤回した. They *withdrew* their claims. / 約束を撤回した. We *retracted* our promise. / 提案を撤回した. They got the proposal *abandoned*.

手続き【*tetsuzuki*】procedure; arrangements; formalities; proceedings 例 法律上の手続き legal formalities / 輸入割当を入手するため複雑な手続きが必要. You must take the complicated *procedures* to obtain import quotas. / 同意あり次第金額を調整する手続きをとります. Upon receipt of your consent, we will *take* the necessary *procedure* to adjust the amount. / 渡米手続きはどうしたらよいか. What *procedure* is necessary for going to America? / 入社手続きを済ませたか. Did you go through the entrance *procedure* at the office?

鉄道【*tetsudō*】railway; railroad; rail 例 鉄道便により至急お送り乞う. Please forward at once *per rail*. / 鉄道便で送りました. We have dispatched the goods by *rail* to your address. ‖ (米)―運賃(客) railway charge [fare] ‖ ―運賃(貨物) a railway freight rate ‖ ―貨物受託書 railway consignment note

手取り【*tedori*】net profit; net income; net proceeds 例 手取り5万円で売る sell at 50,000 yen *net* / 手取り500円 500 yen *in hand* / 貴殿受け取りの正味手取金はお指図あるまで保管します. The *net proceeds* due to you we hold at your disposal.

手に入(れ)る【*te ni hairu*】obtain; secure 例 早速注文下されば多量入手できる見込み. More can be *obtained* if ordered promptly. / 前回同様の値段と条件で多少とも手に入るか. Can you *secure* more at the same price and terms as last?

手荷物【*tenimotsu*】(米) baggage; (英) luggage 例 駅に手荷物を預けてある. I have my *baggage* checked in at the station. ‖ ―を預ける check one's baggage ‖ ―一時預かり所 (米) checkroom; (英) cloakroom ‖ ―受取所 baggage counter

手ぬかり【*tenukari*】omission; a slip; mistake; oversight; fault

囫 当方の手ぬかりにより貴社に迷惑をかけました. We sincerely regret that we have much troubled and inconvenienced you through our *oversight*. ‖ —なく with care [caution]

手配【tehai】 arrangement; attention **囫** 本件に対する手配感謝します. We thank you for your *attention* to this matter. / 貴社商品を手配しました. We have made *arrangements* for your goods. / 貴社御注文の手配については当社は必要な手続きをとりました. Regarding our *execution* of your order we have taken the necessary procedures. / 信用状の有効期限は6月30日ですから, 7月15日まで延長するよう貴取引銀行に手配願います. The expiration date of the credit being June 30, we would like to request that you make an *arrangement* with your banker to extend it until July 15. ‖ —する fix; arrange (for); prepare; cover / すぐ貴社注文の調達を手配させます. We shall *proceed* at once with the *execution* of your order. / 輸出業者はその積み荷の船腹予約を受け付ける手配をする. The exporter *prepares* to book ocean freight space for his cargo.

手はず【tehazu】 preparation; arrangement ‖ —を決める make arrangements beforehand; arrange; prepare (for) **囫** 御注文品はちかちか発送の手はずがすべて整っていますから御安心ください. Rest your mind, as everything *is prepared for* shortly dispatching the goods ordered. / 会議の手はずが整った. Everything *was arranged for* the conference. / 計画は手はずが狂ってしまった. The plan *went wrong*.

手間【tema】 labor; trouble; time ‖ —取る delay; take time; tardy **囫** 貴社の信用状を送るとき手間取らないよう注意ください. Please take care not to *delay* in sending your credits. / 事務所を探すのに手間取った. It *took* a lot of *time* to find out your office. ‖ —が省ける save trouble **囫** こうすれば大分手間が省ける. It will *save* a lot of *time and labor*.

手持ち【temochi】 stocks; stock on hand **囫** 当社は品物を手持ちしておりますから受注次第発送できます. As we *have* the goods *in stock*, we can dispatch them at once on receipt of your orders. / 手持品の中から提供できます. We can furnish them from the *goods on hand*. / 手持品はほとんど尽きた. The *stock on hand* is almost exhausted. / 7月2日付お手紙に関連して, 当社はお問い合わせの商品を手持ちしていることを申し上げます. Referring to your letter of July 2, we are glad to say we *have in stock* the goods asked for.

手元【*temoto*】 in one's hands **例** お手元の報告書を見ていただけばわかります. If you look at the report *in your hands*, you will understand.

テレタイプ【*teretaipu*】 teletype; teleprinter **例** テレタイプは1つの会社から他の会社へ情報を伝送する. A *teleprinter* relays information from one business to another.

テレックス【*terekkusu*】 telex (国際加入電信) **例** テレックスは会社から海外の会社へメッセージを送ることができる. A *telex* machine can send messagges overseas from one company to another.

テレビ【*terebi*】 television; (英) telly ‖ ―番組 TV program ‖ ―放送する telecast; televise **例** 新しいオフィスのオープンはテレビ放送される. The opening of the new office will be *telecast*.

展開【*tenkai*】 development; progress **例** 局面の展開を待っている. We are awaiting *developments* of the situation. ‖ ―する develop; extend; turn **例** この計画は有利に展開しよう. This plan will *turn* to advantage.

電気器具【*denki kigu*】 electric appliances **例** 弊社の電気器具に対する引き合いに対し感謝します. We thank you very much for your inquiry of our *electric appliances*. / 過去20年高級電気器具を扱ってきました. We have been a dealer of high-class *electric appliances* for the past 20 years.

点検【*tenken*】 inspection; examination **例** 点検用として見本3組同封します. We are enclosing three sets of samples for your *inspection*. ‖ ―売買 sale on approval ‖ ―する examine; inspect **例** 発行銀行は書類点検のために相当の時間が与えられる. The issuing bank shall have a reasonable time to *examine* the documents.

電子【*denshi*】 electron **例** 原子はすべて電子と陽子で構成されて

いる. All atoms are composed of *electrons* and protons. ‖ —工
業 electronic industry 例 ソニーは電子工業界の有力メーカー
である. Sony is a leading producer in the *electronic industry.*
‖ —顕微鏡 an electron microscope

電子計算機【*denshi keisanki*】 electronic computer 例 在庫の明
細を電子計算機を使って作成した. A detailed inventory was
made with the use of an *electronic computer.*

電信【*denshin*】 telegram 例 暴風雨で電信が不通になった. The
telegraphic communication has been interrupted [cut off] by
the storm. / 本社へ～と電信した. We sent a *telegram* to the
head office to the effect that ～. ‖ —にて by cable [telegram] ‖
—略号 cable [telegraphic] address ‖ —回線 telegraphic circuit
‖ —料 telegram [cable] charges ‖ —為替 T.T. telegraphic
transfer ‖ —する cable; telegraph 例 そのことについて至急
電信ください. Please *cable* us immediately about that. / 至
急電信で確定売申込をされたい. Please *cable* your firm offer
immediately. / 正確な船積数量を電信せよ. *Telegraph* exact
quantity shipped.

転送【*tensō*】 transmission ‖ —する transmit; convey; forward
例 その貨物を転送してください. Please *transmit* the goods. /
貴社の伝言を東京へ電信にて転送した. We have duly *transmit-
ted* [*conveyed*] your message to Tokyo by telegram.

天地無用【*tenchi muyō*】 this end up; this side up; do not turn
over 例 ガラス器具の積み荷には天地無用と書いてあった. The
cargo of glasses was labeled "*This Side Up*".

転任【*ten-nin*】 transference; change of post ‖ —する be transferred 例 東京本店より名古屋支店へ転任となりました. I was
transferred from Tokyo main office to Nagoya branch office.

転売【*tenbai*】 resale ‖ —する resell 例 損傷した商品は転売せね
ばならない. It was necessary to *resell* the damaged goods.

伝票【*denpyō*】 a slip; a memo 例 株式仲買人は発行株券の伝票
を作った. The stock broker made a *memo* of the shares
issued. ‖ 支払— a paying memo ‖ 入金— a receiving memo ‖
振替— a transfer memo

添付する【*tenpu suru*】attach　例　この書状に小切手を添付くださ
れば最も簡単な支払方法です．If you *attach* your cheque to
this letter, it will be the simplest way of payment. / 添付の
ごとく申込書のコピーを参照ください．Please refer to applica-
tion copy as *attached*. ‖ — して herewith attached [hereto]

電報【*denpō*】telegram; wire; telegraphic message　例　10 時に
電報を打った．We sent [dispatched] a *telegram* at ten. / 向う
に着いたら電報で知らせてください．Please let us know by
wire [*cable*; *telegram*] when you get over there. / 11 月 5
日付弊電に対する御返事を待っています．We are waiting for
your reply to our *telegram* of November 5. / 昨日付電報受け
取りました．We received your *cable* of yesterday. / 下記の
とおり電報を打ちましたことを確認申し上げます．We wish to
confirm having *cabled* you as follows. ‖ — 確認 confirmation
of telegram ‖ 至急 — urgent telegram ‖ 暗号 — code telegram
‖ — 料 telegram charge ‖ — の本文 text ‖ — の前段 preamble
‖ — 不着 miscarry; non-delivery ‖ — 誤配 wrong delivery ‖ 写
真 — photo telegram ‖ — 為替 telegraphic transfer (T.T.) ‖ —
で送金する remit by telegraphic transfer ‖ 普通語 — plain language telegram

転落【*tenraku*】fall; collapse; bankruptcy ‖ — する fall　例　市
価は転落（暴落）．The market *falls sharply*.

電話【*denwa*】telephone ‖ — を引く install a telephone ‖ — で呼
ぶ call on the phone　例　払い戻しの責任者を電話に呼んだ．I
called the man responsible for refundment *on the phone*. ‖
話し中 the line is busy ‖ — 不通 line is interrupted ‖ — 帳
telephone directory ‖ 代表 — 番号 key number ‖ — 交換手 telephone operator

【と】

問い合わせる【*toiawaseru*】apply to; refer to; (make an) inquiry of [about; after; for]　例　詳細は事務所にお問い合わせ
ください．For particulars *apply to* the office. / 弊社はそのこ

とについて問い合わせをしました. We have *made an inquiry* about that. / わが社の財務状態に関しての情報は銀行にお問い合わせください. We *refer* you to the bank for information as to our financial standing. / 御希望の品物につきましては御遠慮なくお問い合わせください. You are at liberty to *make inquiries* about the goods in which you are interested. / 貴質問を当社ロンドン支店に問い合わせ御返事します. We will *refer* your question to our London Office for reply.

同意する【*dōi suru*】 agree to (物); agree with (人); accept; approve 例 当社は6月1日付の電報の貴社の価格に同意します. We *agree to* your prices cabled June 1. / 契約を変更することに同意した. We have *agreed with* them in amending the contract.

騰貴【*tōki*】 rise; advance; price-hike ‖ ―する rise; advance 例 価格は騰貴する見込み. Prices are expected to *advance*. / これらの品の値段は近日中にきっと騰貴します. The price of these goods is sure to *rise* before long. / 当社市場は活発で, 値段はいっせいに騰貴した. Our market is very active and prices have *risen* all round.

投機する【*tōki suru*】 speculate 例 過度に投機をやっている噂です. It is reported that the firm has *speculated* excessively.

等級【*tōkyū*】 grade; class; rating 例 これらの商品は御要求の等級のものです. These goods are of the required *grade*.

同業者【*dōgyōsha*】 competitor; fellow trader 例 貴社がもっと低い価格を示さなければ弊社は他の同業者と取り引きするかもしれません. We may do business with other *competitors* if you do not lower your prices. / 貴社の同業者における評判は非常によろしい. You have a fine reputation in the *community*. / この品を割引なしの52ドイツマルクという値段で同業者にオファーできます. We are able to offer the goods to *the trade* at a price of DM 52 net. / 正味価格500ポンド以上の注文にはすべて4分の特別同業者割引をすることにしています. We are prepared to offer *a special trade discount* of 4% on all orders over £ 500 net.

当局【*tōkyoku*】 authorities; authorities concerned 例 関係当局

から輸出免状を得るため必要な手続きを取りました．We have taken the necessary procedures to get the export permission from *the authorities concerned*.

当座 【*tōza*】 the present; the time being; current ‖ —預金 current deposit ‖ —貸越 overdrawn account; overdraft ‖ —借越 overdrawing account ‖ —勘定 current account　例 販売は当座勘定で行われる．Sales are made on *open account*.

投資【*tōshi*】investment　例 その事業には多大の投資がなされている．The industry has large *investments of capital*. / 確かな古物を買うのは利回りのいい投資になる．A good antique is a good *investment*. ‖ —する invest [put out] money in ～ ‖ 対外— overseas investment ‖ 公共— public investment ‖ 設備— equipment investment ‖ —信託 investment trust

同時 【*dōji*】 same time; synchronism　例 同時に2つのことはできない．You can not do two things *at a time*.

当事者【*tōjisha*】 party; party concerned; man in charge　例 この規定はすべての関係当事者を拘束する．This provision is binding upon all *the parties concerned* [*the persons in charge*].

当社 【*tōsha*】 our company　例 当社は1950年に一般輸出入業として創立しました．*We* were established in 1950 as general importers and exporters. / 同封の当社あて切手添付の封筒により御返事ください．We hope to receive your reply using the enclosed *self-addressed* and stamped envelope.

当初 【*tōsho*】 at the beginning [commencement; outset] ‖ —の計画 the first [initial] schedule; the plans at the outset　例 よそでも当初は同額の給料をお願いしたく存じます．I should ask for the same salary to *commence* with elsewhere.

統制 【*tōsei*】 (する) control　例 政府は米価を統制した．The government *has controlled* the price of rice. ‖ —価格 controlled prices ‖ —の枠 limitation [restriction] of control ‖ —解除 decontrol ‖ —を強化する tighten the control ‖ —を撤廃する remove control on ～

到着する 【*tōchaku suru*】 arrive at [in; on]; reach; get to　例 貴社の船積品はひどい破損状態で到着しました．Your shipments

have *arrived* in a badly damaged condition. / 貴社の信用状
は船積みに十分間に合って到着しました. Your credits *arrived*
here fully in time for the shipment. / 品物が故障なく到着する
だろうと信じます. We trust the goods will *reach* you in good
order and condition.

同封する 【*dōfū suru*】 enclose 例 この商品のカタログを同封し
ます. We are *enclosing* a catalog of these goods. / 貴社の御
希望の新型カメラのパンフレットを同封しました. We *enclosed*
the pamphlet of the new type camera that your company
requested. / 同封のカタログを他社の方に見せてくださってもよ
い旨の了解を得ています. We are permitted to let you show
the *enclosed* catalog to other firms. / 定価表同封の 6 月20日付
お手紙受け取りました. We have received your letter of the
20th June, *enclosing* a price list. / 同封の注文書に記入しすぐ
送り返してください. We suggest you complete the *enclosed*
order form and return it to us immediately.

同文電報 【*dōbun denpō*】 multiple telegram 例 同文電報が関心
ある会社すべてに送られた. A *multiple telegram* was sent to
all the companies interested.

同様 【*dōyō*】 same; identical; similar 例 これは新品同様だ.
This is *as good as* new.

通り相場 【*tōri sōba*】 ruling price 例 通り相場は一個あたり30ド
ルです. *The ruling price* is $ 30 per piece.

登録 【*tōroku*】 registration; registry ‖ ―商標 a registered trade-
mark ‖ 船籍― registration of nationality ‖ ―する register 例
弊社の電信あて名は中央郵便局に登録されている. Our cable
address is *registered* at Central Post Office.

得意先 【*tokuisaki*】 customer; client; connection 例 貴市場に
はたくさんの得意先をもっています. We have many *connections* [*customers*] in your market. / 弊社はお得意様からの御用
命をただちに調達します. We are in a position to fill all the
requirements of our *customers* at once. / 商売を得れば得るほ
ど得意先も増える. The more business standing we gain, the
more *customers* we can have. / お得意様はその商品を急いでい

るようです．The *customers* seem to be in a hurry for the goods. / お得意先は当方商品に少なからず満足のようすを示しています．*Customers* seem to be very much satisfied with our goods. / お尋ねのその会社は長年当社のお得意先です．The firm you inquired about has been a *regular customer* for many years.

特色 【*tokushoku*】 feature; characteristic 囫 軽いのがその車の特色です．Lightness is *characteristic* of the car. / その博覧会は幾多の興味ある特色をもっています．The exhibition has many *features* of interest. ‖ —がある be featured by; make a distinctive feature of; the (principal) features are that; have a speciality of; be characteristic of ‖ —とする be specialized [specialize] in

特製品 【*tokuseihin*】 speciality 囫 過去4半世紀にわたって特製品の製造を行っています．They have been manufacturing this *speciality* for the last quarter of a century.

独占 【*dokusen*】 monopoly; (事業 a monopoly; monopolistic enterprise) 囫 同会社がその商売を独占している．The company has a *monopoly* of that trade. / 当社は缶詰商品を専売する．We make a *monopoly* of canned goods.

特徴 【*tokuchō*】 characteristic; feature 囫 この金属の最も重要な特徴は，その強さである．The most important *characteristic* of this metal is its strength. / 優秀なシステムの独特の特徴は，同封資料に詳細に説明してある．The unique *features* of this excellent system are shown in the enclosed literature.

特定品 【*tokuteihin*】 specific goods 囫 特定品は直接仕向港に船積みせよ．Ship our *specific goods* direct to port of destination.

特に 【*tokuni*】 specially; particularly 囫 特にこれという仕事もありません．We have nothing *particular* to do.

特約店 【*tokuyakuten*】 agent 囫 AはBをシンガポール地域における漁網の特約店に委嘱する．A hereby appoints B as its *agent* of fishing nets for the territory of Singapore.

独立 【*dokuritsu*】 independence; self-supporting ‖ —採算制 self-supporting [independent] accounting 囫 弊社は独立で営業し

ています. We are carrying on business *on our own account*.

土地改革法【*tochi kaikakuhō*】 land reform law 囲 新しい土地
改革法は土地のない農民が所有者になるような機会をふやした.
A new *land reform law* increased opportunities for landless
peasants to become land owners.

途中【*tochū*】 on the way [road]; en route; halfway; in transit;
in mid course 囲 その商品は輸送の途中で損害を受けた. The
goods got damaged *on the way* to transport.

特価【*tokka*】 special price; bargain price ‖ —品 bargain-priced
articles 囲 その商品を特価で買いました. We bought the
goods *at a special price*.

特許【*tokkyo*】 patent 囲 特許取得に成功した. We succeeded in
obtaining a *patent*. / 政府は特許を与える権限をもっています.
The government is authorized to grant *patents*. / 特許権者は
もし望むならその特許を売ることができる. The *patentee* may,
if he desires, sell the *patent*. ‖ —出願中 patent has been applied
for ～ ‖ —権 patent right ‖ —権使用料 royalty ‖ —権の侵害
infringement of patent right

特権【*tokken*】 privilege; special right; concession 囲 大きな特
権を得て好調な売れ行きをあげられるものと確信します. With
this large *concession* we trust you will enjoy a good sale.
‖ —を与える grant person a privilege; privilege 囲 弊社はそ
の商品を売る特権がある. We *are privileged* to sell the goods.
‖ —階級 privileged classes

滞りなく【*todokōri naku*】 duly; without hitch; smoothly 囲
同品は滞りなく貴社に到着すると思います. We trust the goods
will reach you *in due course*. / 貴注文58号の貨物は今朝滞り
なく船積みしました. We have *duly* shipped your order No.
58 this morning.

唱え値【*tonaene*】 quotation; price quoted 囲 弊社は貴社の唱え
値を検討した. We have examined your *quotations*.

とにかく【*tonikaku*】 anyway; anyhow; at all events 囲 とに
かく御期待にそいたい. *At any rate*, we want to meet your
expectations.

ドラムカン 【*doramukan*】 drum 例 油はドラムカンに入れた．
The oil was stored in a *drum*.

トランジスタラジオ 【*toranjista rajio*】 a transistor radio

取扱品 【*toriatsukaihin*】 handling commodities [articles]; hand-
led items; specialties 例 弊社の取扱品の主なものは西ドイツ
製のフォルクスワーゲンです． Our *handling items* are mainly
West Germany's Volkswagen. / わが社の取扱品はカタログに出
ています． Our *specialties* are pictured in our catalogue.

取り扱う 【*toriatsukau*】 treat; handle; deal 例 取扱注意．
Handle with [With] care. / そのニュースは極秘に取り扱います．
The news *will be treated* in strict confidence. / 弊社は各種
日本商品を取り扱います． We *deal in* all kinds of Japanese
goods. / 当社はこの見本がどんな手荒な取り扱いにも耐えること
を確信しています． We are confident that they will stand up
to the roughest *handling*.

取り替える 【*torikaeru*】 replace; renew; exchange 例 まち
がった商品は正しい商品と取り替えます． We will *replace* the
incorrect goods with correct ones.

取り決め 【*torikime*】 arrangement; settlement; agreement ‖ ―る
(契約を) conclude (a contract)　(売り(買い)を) register a
sale (purchase)　(商売を) combine (a business)　(値段・運
賃を) establish; fix　(条件を) decide; fix; establish　(準
備・相談事を) arrange　(代理店を) appoint 例 取り決めの通
り船積みをするつもりです． We will effect the shipment *as
arranged*.

取り消す 【*torikesu*】 cancel; call off; withdraw; take back 例
その品物の注文を取り消した． We *cancelled* their order for
the goods. / 弊社はこれによって貴社あてに取消不能信用状を開
設します． We hereby open an *irrevocable* letter of credit in
your favor. / 注文を取り消してもらいたい． We wish to have
the order *cancelled*. ‖ 取り消し cancellation 例 船積みが半年
遅れますから，注文の取り消しに応じる． We have to comply
with your *cancellation* of order since there is a 6 months'
delay in our shipment to you.

取り立て【*toritate*】 collection (of money) ‖ —手形 collection bill ‖ —る collect 例 借金を取り立てた. They *collected* debts.

取引【*torihiki*】 business; trading; dealings; transaction 例 弊社は通常信用状条件で取引しています. We usually do our *business* on a letter of credit basis. / 取引はすべて富士銀行を通じて行う. All *transactions* are done through the Fuji Bank. / 貴社とは初取引ですから, 信用照会先銀行名をお知らせ乞う. As this is our *first transaction* with you, please tell us the name of the bank to whom reference can be made. / 取引上の失敗にもかかわらず, お互いの友好関係が続くことを信じます. We trust that our cordial relations will continue in spite of this *loss of business*. ‖ —がある keep an account with; doing business with; have dealings with ‖ —する have dealings with; deal with; carry on transactions 例 過去5年間この商社と取引している. We have *dealt with* the firm for the last five years. ‖ —を始める open an account with; enter into business; do business with 例 突然ながら貴社と取引したく御連絡申し上げます. We take the liberty of approaching you with a proposal to *open an account with* you. / 実際の取引をする前に同社の誠意を判断しなければならない. We have to judge their sincerity before *doing* actual *business*. / 価格と条件が適切なら取引します. We are prepared to *do business* with you if your prices and terms are good. / 貴地の信頼できる商社と取引したい. We desire to *enter into business* with some leading firms in your district. ‖ 現物— spot transactions ‖ 先物— forward transactions; dealings in future ‖ 現金— cash transactions; business for cash 例 当社の製品はすべて現金取引で行っています. All our goods are performed by *business for cash*. ‖ 信用— dealings on credit ‖ —高 volume of business; a turnover; transactions ‖ —銀行 one's bankers; a bank reference 例 当社取引銀行に照会願います. We refer you to *our bankers*. ‖ —先 a customer; a client

取引関係【*torihiki kankei*】 business relation; business connection 例 弊社は貴社と取引関係を締結したい. We hope to enter into *business connections* with you. / 同社と特別の取引関係に入る可能性について目下検討中です. We are now discussing the possibility of coming to special *business relation* with them./ この取引が気持のよい取引関係の初めになることを望んでいます. We sincerely hope that this is the beginning of pleasant *business relationship.* / 取引関係の成功を期待しています. We look forward to our successful *business relations.* / 当社は日本の主要なメーカーときわめて良好な取引関係にあります. We have very good *connections* with the leading manufacturers in Japan.

取引条件 【*torihiki jōken*】 terms and conditions of business 例 取引条件については, なにとぞ取引条件協定書を御参照ください. As regards *the terms and conditions of business*, please refer to Agreement on Terms and Conditions. / 価格表と取引条件をお知らせください. We would like to have your price lists and *terms and conditions of business.* / 当社と取引の御意向があれば取引条件をお知らせください. If you are interested in doing business with us, please inform us of your *terms and conditions of business.*

度量衡 【*doryōkō*】 weights and measures 例 正確を期して度量衡はチェックしなければならない. The *weights and measures* must be checked for accuracy.

取り寄せる 【*toriyoseru*】 obtain; procure 例 見本は取り寄せた. We have samples *forwarded.*

ドル手形 【*doru tegata*】 dollar draft [bill] 例 ドル手形はロバート氏によって振り出された. The *dollar bill* was drawn by Mr. Robert.

トン 【*ton*】 (英) long ton ‖ (米) short ton ‖ キロ— metric ton ‖ 重量— weight ton ‖ 容積— measurement ton

問屋 【*tonya*】 commission house; agent; wholesaler 例 問屋の手数料は1割だった. The commission of the *wholesaler* was 10%.

【な】

内外【*naigai*】home and foreign ((affairs)); at home and abroad
圀 内外の識者の意見を聞くことにする. We are to consult the
best *Japanese and foreign* opinions. / その商品の名は国の内外
に知られている. The name of the goods is known both *at
home and abroad*

内国【*naikoku*】inland; home ‖ ―水路貨物受託書 inland waterway consignment note ‖ ―水路船荷証券 inland waterway bill
of lading

内定する【*naitei suru*】decide unofficially; come to informal
[unofficial] decision

ない場合【*nai baai*】(なければ) without (ないので) in the
absence of; for want of 圀 信頼できる代理店がないので, 当
社は自ら販売を続けます. *In the absence of* a reliable agent,
we will continue to do our own marketing. / 運転資金がな
ければ何もできない. *Without* working funds, we could do
nothing.

内密【*naimitsu*】confidence ‖ ―に in confidence 圀 御報告は
ごく内密にします. Your information will be treated *in absolute confidence.* / 貴社の情報はいつものごとく慎重, 内密に取
り扱います. Your information will be held, as usual, *in strict
confidence.* / 同社が信頼できるかどうか内密にお知らせ乞う.
Please let us know *in confidence* whether the firm is reliable
in their dealings. ‖ ―の confidential 圀 A氏の信用能力および
一般の評判に関し, 内密の御意見は貴行に問い合わせるよう申し
出がありました. We have been referred to your Bank for a
confidential opinion of the trustworthiness, ability and general
reputation of Mr. A.

仲買【*nakagai*】broker; intermediary ‖ ―口銭 brokerage; commission 圀 仲買手数料はちょうど1割. The brokerage rate
is a flat 10%.

仲間割引【*nakama waribiki*】trade discount 圀 当社の定価は5%

の仲間割引をします. Our price is subject to 5% *trade discount.*

中味【*nakami*】 contents　囫 荷造不良, これより生ずる中味不足および事故は無関係. Insufficient packing. N/R for consequential loss or shortage and condition of *contents.*　囶 N/R Non Responsible

投げ売り【*nageuri*】 dumping; selling at a loss [sacrifice]; bargain sale‖ーする sacrifice; dump　囫 不景気のため織元は品物を投げ売りしている. Owing to depression, the weavers are *sacrificing* their goods. / 商人は本国の相場を保つため品物を外国市場へ投げ売りすることがある. Merchants sometimes *dump* their goods at a foreign market to avoid lowering home price.

投げ出し無用【*nagedashi muyō*】 Not to be thrown down.

納得【*nattoku*】 consent‖ーさせる convince one of ～; make one consent [agree; accede]; persuade one to consent‖ーする consent to; assent to; comply with; think reasonable　囫 代理店を拡張するのが得策であることを納得いただけるでしょう. We shall *convince* you of the advisability of extending the agency. / 見本を御検討いただければ, 当社の値段が他社のとうてい及ばないことを納得していただけると思います. We invite your comparision of our samples with those of other firms, and *are convinced* that our prices will be found most advantageous. / すでに納品してから3カ月も経た品物に対する支払いをさらに2カ月も待たされることは納得できません. We *think it unreasonable* to have to wait two more months for payment for the goods supplied three months ago.

何【*nani*】: ーするにしても whatever you may do‖ー気なく casually‖ーとなく somehow‖ーとかかんとか somehow; in some way or other‖ーも手に入らぬので none being available‖ーやかやと one way or another‖ーやかやと多忙で due to pressure of work

なにとぞ【*nanitozo*】 kindly; please; be good enough to　囫 最低値段をなにとぞお知らせください. Would you *kindly* quote us your lowest prices. / なにとぞ御許可願います。 You *will be pleased to* grant us permission.

何分にも【*nanibun nimo*】 anyway; anyhow; at any rate; as you are aware 例 何分にも，こんな少量では売っても利益がでない。 *As you are aware*, we cannot sell such small amounts profitably.

何分よろしく【*nanibun yoroshiku*】 例 We leave it entirely to your discretion [kind consideration]. I hope we shall get on well together. I'm glad to have made your acquaintance.

並の【*namino*】 (に) common(ly); ordinary(-rily) 例 高い関税を欧米並に課そうとしている。 They have a plan to levy a duty *as* heavily *as* in Europe and America.

悩む【*nayamu*】 suffer from; be troubled; be worried about 例 食糧不足に悩む国々が多い。 Many countries *suffer from* food shortage. / インフレに悩む国はイタリアである。 One of the countries *troubled by* inflation is Italy.

成り立つ【*naritatsu*】 consist of; realize; be concluded; hold good 例 契約が成り立つまで2カ月かかった。 Two months had passed before the contract *was concluded* [*signed*]. / 貴説はこの場合成り立たない。 Your theory does not *hold good* in this case.

なるべく早く【*narubeku hayaku*】 as soon as possible; at the earliest possible date; at one's earliest convenience 例 御注文品をなるべく早く船積みすべく全力を尽くしています。 As to your orders, we are now doing our best to ship them *at the earliest possible date*. / なるべく早く返事をください。 Please reply *at your earliest convenience*. / なるべく早く御注文なさるようお勧めします。 We would recommend you to place an order *as soon as possible*. / このオファーをなるべく早く受諾されるようお勧めします。 We advise you to accept this offer *without loss of time*.

難関【*nankan*】 difficulty; hardships; crisis 例 難関が前途に横たわっている。 *Difficulty* is foreseen.

難局【*nankyoku*】 difficult situation; difficulties 例 この難局を

何としても切り抜けねばなら ない. We must tide over this *difficulty* by any means. / 会社はいまや難局に立っている. We are now in a *difficult situation*. / 全力を傾けてこの難局に当たるべきだ. We must cope with this *crisis* with might and main.

難色を示す 【*nanshoku o shimesu*】 raise [make] difficulties; defy; disapprove; oppose; object 例 産業界は新しい増税案に難色を示すだろう. The industry will *raise* some *difficulties* in the bill for increased taxation.

軟調 【*nanchō*】 sluggish; dull; idle 例 現在需要は軟調. Demand is *sluggish* at present.

何とかして 【*nantokashite*】 by any means; at all costs 例 今年は何とかして成功させねばならぬ. The company must succeed this year *at all costs*.

何とかする 【*nantoka suru*】 manage to; see one's way to (do) 例 わが社の新製品で何とかして貴市場に進出していただきたい. Please *see your way to* making inroads into your market with these novelties of ours.

【に】

荷 【*ni*】 a load (重荷) a burden (船荷) a cargo (手荷物) baggage (米); luggage (英) (貨物) goods ‖ ―を積む (下ろす) (un)load; get a cargo 例 車に荷を積んでくれ. *Load* the cart. / 船は横浜で荷を積んだ. The ship *got a cargo* at Yokohama. / 車から荷を降ろした. We *unloaded* the car.

荷揚げ 【*niage*】 discharge; landing ‖ ―賃 landing charge ‖ ―港 port of discharge ‖ ―する unload a vessel; discharge cargo from a vessel 例 あの大きさの船は荷をおろすのに4時間かかる. It takes 4 hours to *unload a vessel* of that size.

荷扱い注意書 【*niatsukai chūisho*】 Side [Care] Marks

荷受け 【*niuke*】 receiving; receipt of goods ‖ ―する take delivery ‖ ―を受諾する accept delivery ‖ ―を断る reject to take delivery of ～ ‖ ―人 consignee 例 荷物4個は不引き渡しの旨の通知が荷受人からきたところです. Information has just been received from our *consignees* that four parcels have not been delivered.

荷おろし 【*nioroshi*】 discharge; unloading ‖ —する discharge; unload; discharge into lighters **囫** コンテナ化がすすんでいるので荷おろし時間は半減した. Since the advent of containerization, *unloading* time has been halved.

荷為替手形 【*nigawase tegata*】 documentary bill [draft] **囫** 荷為替手形不備につき，新規作成御送付願います. Since *Documentary Bills of Exchange* are not in order, please produce and send new ones. ‖ 〜あてに—を組む draw a documentary bill on a person ‖ 荷為替信用状 Documentary L/C ‖ 引受渡— documents against acceptance; D/A ‖ 支払渡— documents against payment; D/P ‖ —副書 general letter of hypothecation

荷印 【*nijirushi*】 mark; shipping mark **囫** 買い手から直接に荷印の指図があるはずです. Buyer will send you instructions about *marking* directly. / すべての木箱には荷印をつけなくてはならない. All wooden cases should have *shipping marks*. / 輸出荷物には外側に荷印をつけなければならない. All packages for export must be provided on the outside with *shipping marks*.

日限 【*nichigen*】 fixed date; time limited; deadline **囫** 日限までにこの書類を提出してください. Please submit these papers by the *fixed date*. / 日限を1週間延ばしてください. Please extend the (*fixed*) *date* for a week.

2通 【*nitsū*】 (に) (in) duplicate (3通 triplicate; 4通 quadruplicate; 5通 quintuplicate) **囫** 貴社の価格表を2通送ってください. We hope you will send us your price list *in duplicate*.

荷造り 【*nizukuri*】 packing; 小型たる詰め in kegs; たる詰め in barrels; 袋入り in bags; 俵入 in bales (B/S); ドラム缶入 in drums; 箱詰め in cases (C/S) **囫** 荷造り指図は追って航空便にて通知する. *Packing* instructions will follow by airmail. / 荷造り不良これより生ずる中味不足および事故無関係. *Insufficient packing*. N/R for consequential loss or shortage and condition of contents. / 荷造り不良のため，大安売りしなければならなかった. Owing to the defective *packing*, we are compelled to dispose of the goods at much reduced prices. / この損害は不完全な荷造りに基因するものと思います. The damage appears to have been caused by the faulty *packing* of the goods. ‖ —する pack 例 入念に荷造りされるよう御留意のほど希望します. You will take care that the goods are carefully *packed*. / 荷造りはいつものように願います. Kindly have them *packed* as usual. / この商品はパッキングしやすい. This article *packs* well. / 商品は海洋輸送の危険にたえられるよう荷造りすること. Goods should be *packed* to withstand the hazards of ocean transportation. ‖ 荷解きする unpack ‖ —リスト packing list ‖ —費 packing charge ‖ —不良 insufficient packing ‖ 紙箱 paper packing case ‖ 輸出向— packed for export ‖ 箱詰めにする pack in case ‖ 包装費別勘定 packing extra ‖ 包装費無料 packing free ‖ 包装費込み packing included ‖ —の手違い a mistake made in packing the goods

日産【*nissan*】daily output 例 弊社は日産5万トンを誇っています. Our company boast a *daily output* of 50,000 tons.

日本製【*nihon sei*】Japanese made 例 日本製生糸の輸出商として開店した. We have just established ourselves as exporters of *Japanese made* silk.

荷役日【*niyakubi*】working day 注 working day of 24 consecutive hours: 荷役港において日曜, 祭日等の休日を除いた平常荷役の行われる日, 継続24時間をもって1作業日とする.

入庫【*nyūko*】warehousing ‖ —する warehouse 例 商品は十月末日までには入庫の予定である. The goods will *be warehoused* by the end of October.

入港【*nyūkō*】entry into port; arrival in port; docking ‖ —する enter a port; sail in; arrive in; dock at a port 例 フーバー号は今夕横浜に入港する. The Hoover will *arrive in* Yokohama this evening. ‖ —予定日 expected time of arrival [ETA]

入札【*nyūsatsu*】tender; bid 例 入札には激烈な競争が予想される. Keen competition is anticipated in *the tender*. / 工作機械の入札があるそうすで. We hear *a bid* is invited for machine tools. / 入札を受理します. We are prepared to entertain *bids.* / その事業はまもなく入札になるでしょう. The project will be presently up for *bid.* ‖ —する make a bid for; submit [offer] a tender; tender for 囲 入札希望者は1週間以内に申し出ること. Any person who desires to *bid* for the above shall apply within a week. ‖ 一般— open [public] tender [bid] ‖ 指名— private tender ‖ —価格 bidding price; price tendered

入手【*nyūshu*】procurement; availability; receipt ‖ —する get; obtain; receive; procure; be available 囲 その品物は市場に近いところで入手できる. The goods *are available* close to the market. / これらの商品はわが社で単価720円で入手できます. These goods *are available* at our office for only ¥720 each. / 貴社のカタログを入手いたしました. We are *in receipt of* your catalog.

入用【*nyūyō*】need; want; necessity ‖ —である (be in) want; be needed; require 囲 貴社商品至急入用ですから引き渡しのできる最も早い日時を教えてください. Please state the earliest date you can deliver, as they *are* urgently *needed.* / この商品がまた入用になるときは電報でお知らせいたします. We will let you know by wire when we *are* again *in want of* such goods. / 貴社が当社商品を入用とされているかどうかぜひ承りたいと存じます. We are anxious to know if you now *require* our goods. / 今朝の新聞で会計助手入用との広告を見つけました. I happened to see your advertisement *for a* young assistant in this morning's paper.

入用品【*nyūyōhin*】requirement; necessity 囲 先方の入用品は月々総計1,000ポンドまででしょう. Their *requirements* may be to the amount of £1,000 monthly.

荷渡し【*niwatashi*】(する) (make) delivery 囲 早速荷渡しのお約束ができればインド綿花ベンガル百俵御注文します. If you can promise early *delivery*, we shall be pleased to pass you an order for 100 bales Indian Cotton Bengal. ‖ —指図書 delivery order [D/O]

認可【*ninka*】authorization; permission; approval ‖ —する au-

thorize; approve 【例】貴社の取引先が同封カタログを見ること
を認可します. We are permitted to *authorize* you to let your
business friends see the catalogs enclosed.

人気【*ninki*】popularity; boom 【例】市場の人気をあおる stir up
the bullish (buying) *sentiment* of the market / 市場の人気
はどうか. How is the *tone* of the market? / この事業の人気は
どうか. How is the *popular feeling* towards this enterprise? /
一般の人気はよい(悪い). The *general sentiment* is in its favor
(against it).‖ーがある be popular; be booming; be popularized; be received with favor 【例】市場の人気がよい(悪い).
The market is *brisk* (*dull*). / ビデオレコーダは西独で人気があ
ります. Video tape recorders *are popularized in* W. Germany.

認識不足【*ninshiki fusoku*】lack of knowledge [understanding];
ignorance 【例】市場について詳しい認識が不足していたので, 会
社は倒産した. The *lack of* detailed *knowledge* of the market
led to the company's failure. / 現状について認識不足だ. They
have little *understanding* of the present situation.

認証【*ninshō*】approval; certification‖輸出(入)ーexport (import) validation‖銀行ー certificate 【例】到着と同時にこの銀行
認証を税関に提出してください. Please present this *certificate*
to the customs officials on arrival.‖ー輸出額 validated export
amount

任命【*ninmei*】appointment; commission‖ーする appoint 【例】
彼は社長に任命された. He has been *appointed* president. /
当社はシカゴのバナデューム・スチール社の総代理店に任命され
た. We have been *appointed* the sole agent for the Vanadium
Steel Co., Chicago.

【ぬ】

抜かす【*nukasu*】omit 【例】うっかり名簿にこの名まえを抜かした.
I carelessly *omitted* this name in the list.

抜き荷【*nukini*】pilferred goods; pilferage 【例】抜き荷の率は前
年比 7 %増えた. The rate of *pilferage* has increased by 7%

over last year.

濡れ損 【nureson】 water damage 　例 密封コンテナの利用で濡れ損の危険性は減った。The risk of *water damage* has been reduced through the use of sealed containers.

濡れ荷 【nureni】 wet goods; sea-damaged goods 　例 濡れ荷は4割引きで売ります。Our *sea-damaged goods* are sold at a 40% discount.

【ね】

値上がり 【neagari】 rise in price; increase in value; advance in price 　例 本品は値上がりの見込みです。The price of these goods are expected to *advance*. / 最近の値上がりは長続きしないだろう。The recent *advance* cannot be maintained. / 値段は上がっている。Prices are on *the advance* [*going up*]. / 市場価格がまもなく上がりそうですから，できるだけ早く御注文くださることをお勧めします。As *the market prices* are likely to rise very soon, we can advise you to place your order as early as possible.

値上げ 【neage】 raise the price; increase in price 　例 1割だけ値上げのやむなきにいたりました。We are now compelled to *raise* our *prices* by 10%. / 若干の値上げを認めていただけない限り品質の優秀さは保持できそうにありません。We shall be unable to maintain our quality without any *increase in price*.

値うちがある 【neuchi ga aru】 be of value 　例 これは御使用くだされば値うちものであることが確信いただけると存じます。If you give it a trial, you will be confident of its *being of value*.

値切る 【negiru】 beat down the price; cheapen 　例 値段を2割値切れるなら，値うちものになるだろう。If we can *beat down the price* by 20%, it will be good value.

値ごろ 【negoro】 reasonable [moderate] 　例 これは値ごろだ。This *price* is *reasonable* for us. / どの値ごろの品をお望みですか。What *price range* are you interested in?

値段 【nedan】 price; value; quotation; figure; cost 　例 当方の

値段は極めて競争的であることを保証します．You are assured that our *quotations* will be most competitive. / 弊社値段が意にかなわない場合は希望値段をお申しこしください．Should you not find our *price* acceptable, please tell us your *price* ceiling. / 弊社は値段を切り下げる予定である．We intend to cut down *prices*. / 興味をもって貴社の値段を調べました．We have studied your *quotations* with interest. / これらの品物の値段を出してください．Will you please *quote* for these items. / この商品の時価は一そろい 5,000 円．The current *price* for this line of goods is ￥5,000 per set. / 当社の値段は同業者の値段より千円も安いことがわかるでしょう．You will find our *prices* are lower than those of other competitors by ￥1,000. / 現在この値段は騰貴の模様がみえます．At present the *prices* seem to have still an upward tendency. / 一番勉強した値段をください．Please quote [give] us your very best *prices*. / 下記のとおり当社の最低値段を申し上げます．We quote you our lowest *prices* as follows. ‖ 買値 buying price ‖ 売値 selling price ‖ 工場— factory price ‖ 法外— excessive [extravagant; exorbitant] price ‖ 競争— competitive price ‖ 決着— rock-bottom price ‖ 見切り— a cut price ‖ 仲間— trade price ‖ 現場渡し— loco price ‖ 貨車渡し— F.O.R. (free on rail) price; F.O.T. (free on truck) price ‖ 本船渡し— F.O.B. (free on board) price 　囫　これらの値段は日本の港本船渡し値段です．These *prices* are quoted on F.O.B. Japanese port. ‖ 石炭本船渡し— F.O.B. & Trimmed price ‖ 埠頭渡し— Ex Quay price ‖ 船渡し— Ex Ship price ‖ 船側渡し— F.A.S. (free alongside ship) price ‖ 陸揚げ渡し— Landed Terms price ‖ 保税倉庫渡し— In bond (Bond) price ‖ 停車場渡し— At Station price ‖ 運賃保険料為替費用込み— C.I.F. & E. price (cost, insurance, freight and exchange) ‖ 運賃保険料および利子込み— C.I.F. & I. price (cost, insurance, freight and interest) ‖ 運賃保険料および手数料込み— C.I.F. & C. price (cost, insurance, freight and commission) 　囫　値段は運賃，保険料込みニューョーク渡しを基礎としております．The *prices* are based on C.I.F. New

York. ‖ 運賃込み— C. & F. (cost and freight price) ‖ 持ち込み— Franco (Franco Domicile; Free Rendu) price ‖ 諸掛込み— all-round price ‖ 通関済み— Duty Paid price; Ex Customs Compound price ‖ 通関未済— Duty Unpaid price ‖ —をつける(見積もる) quote on [for] the goods ‖ —を申し出る offer a price ‖ 値上(下)げする raise (lower; lessen) a price ‖ —を切り下げる cut down a price ‖ 値引きする reduce a price ‖ —を割引く make a discount off a price ‖ —が上がる rise [advance; go up] in price ‖ —が下がる fall [decline; come down] in price

値段表 【*nedanhyō*】 price list 例 当方の取引条件の詳細 を 添え て, 値段表は手紙と同封します. Our *price list* is enclosed with the letter, together with details of our trade terms. / 貴社の最低値段表を御送付くだされば幸甚です. We shall be happy to receive your lowest *price list.* / メーカーは代理店に対し製品の値段表を提供すること. Manufacturer shall furnish agent with *price lists* for the products. / 値段のお問い合わせの返事として最近の値段表を同封お送りします. In reply to your inquiry for prices, we are pleased to enclose our latest *price list.*

熱気無用 【*nekkimuyō*】 keep away from heat 例 製品は熱に近づけないでください. Please *keep* these products *away from heat.*

値引き 【*nebiki*】 reduction in price; discount; allowance; deduction; concession 例 この値引きはその日以降は適用されません. This *price concession* will not apply after that date. / 弊社は貴社に5分の特別現金割引を与えます. We allow you a special cash *discount* of 5%. / 御要求の値引きはまったく不合理です. The *deduction* required by you is entirely unreasonable. / 値引きで注文をお引受します. We are willing to accept the order for an *allowance.* / 貴社が要求する値引きは弊社としては承諾できません. We cannot accept the *allowance* you demand. / 当社は貴社に特別の値引きをするつもりでいます. We will give you a special *allowance.* / 大量の注文には相当の値引

きをします．A substantial *reduction* is made on large orders. /
貴方の値引き要求が相当と存じ送り状価格の 10 ％値引きします．
Considering your *allowance demands* reasonable, we allow
you 10 percent of total invoice price. / 長い取引関係を考えて
値引きに応ぜざるをえません．In view of long business rela-
tions we are compelled to accept your demand for *discount*. /
これ以上の値引きはできません．We are not in a position to
make any further *discount*. / 買い手は 1 割の値引きを要求して
います．Our buyer is claiming a 10% *allowance* off the price
from us. / 本注文は利益がほとんどないので，特に 8 ％の値引き
を認めていただきたい．The margin on this order being very
small, we wish you to allow us an extra *discount* of 8%. ‖
—する reduce the price; make [offer; grant; allow] a reduction in price 例 トン当たり 350 ドルに見積書を値引きできま
すか．Can you *reduce* your quotation to $ 350 per ton? / 損
傷の賠償として 5 分の値引きをなさい．Allow us a *discount* of
5% for the damage. / 少し値下げくだされば注文できると思い
ます．We may give you an order if you can *reduce the price*
to some extent. 困 わずかの値引き abatement ‖ 劣等品のため
の値引き allowance ‖ 買い手よりの要求に応じ譲歩時に行う減額
concession ‖ 支払い総額からの値引き deduction

年間【*nenkan*】 yearly; annual 例 日本の対米輸出額は年間 1,000
億ドルに達する．The export of Japan to the U.S. amounts
to $ 100 billion a *year*. / 年間利率は 6% です．The *annual* in-
terest rate is 6 percent.

念のため【*nen-notame*】 by way of precaution; to make sure;
for caution's sake （用心のため） 例 念のため同社に注意して
おいた．We warned them *by way of precaution*. / 念のため証
文を書かせた．We made them sign a paper, *to make sure*.

年利【*nenri*】 interest rate per annum [p.a.]; annual interest
例 年利 8 分 the *interest rate* of 8% *p.a.* / 年利 5 分は有利．An
interest rate of 5% *p.a.* is very reasonable these days.

【の】

納期 【nōki】 (appointed date of) delivery **囫** 納期は注文後2週間以内. *Delivery* is made within two weeks after order. / 納期はもっとも早いものです. The *delivery* is the nearest possible. / 納期については詳細に通知する. We will advise you in detail as to *the time of shipment*. / 貴納期と価格が満足できる限り引き続いて注文する用意がある. We are prepared to make repeat order, providing your *delivery* and prices are satisfactory.

能率 【nōritsu】 **囫** efficiency ‖ ―を上げる increase [promote; raise] efficiency ‖ ―を下げる diminish efficiency ‖ ―の低い inefficient **囫** その原因は能率の低い農法と肥料の不足にあります. The trouble can be traced to *inefficient* farming knowledge and shortage of fertilizers. ‖ ―のよい efficient **囫** 能率のよいポケット型電卓デジタルI型を製造できる. We can produce *efficient* pocket-size electronic calculator, Digital I.

能力 【nōryoku】 capacity **囫** 工場は全能力をあげて操業している. The factory is running at full *capacity*.

残り 【nokori】 balance **囫** 残量を次船で船積みしてよろしいでしょうか. May we ship the *balance* by the next steamer?

～の条件で 【no jōken de】 subject to; providing; provided; on condition that **囫** ～の条件付きで確定売申込みをする. We make a firm offer *subject to* ～.

望ましい 【nozomashii】 favorable **囫** A社は貴社に関して望ましい報告をしてくれた. A company gave us such a *favorable* report on you.

望む 【nozomu】 desire; want (熱心に得がたいものを望む); hope (実現できると思われるものを期待して望む); expect; look forward to **囫** 今年は売り上げが相当に伸びることを望む. We *hope* to increase our sales considerably this year.

～のため 【no tame】 on account of; due to; owing to; because of; for **囫** 品質劣等のために *on account of* inferior quality / 船積み遅延のために *on account of* late shipment / 破損状態のために *on account of* damaged condition / 雨天のため船積みが遅延しています. The shipment has been delayed *due to* rainy weather.

～の通り【*no tōri*】 in accordance with; according to; as per　**例** 御指示のとおり, 貨物に付保しました. *In accordance with* your instructions, we have fully insured the cargo.

のばす【*nobasu*】 (伸ばす) extend; lengthen; stretch　(延ばす) defer; postpone　**例** ロンドンとの為替不利の状態にありますので, 数日中は 250 ポンドの手形売方を延ばす考えである. The unfavorable rate of exchange with London induces us to *defer* the sale of the £ 250 draft for a few days.

伸びなやみ【*nobinayami*】 slackened increase [growth]

のびる【*nobiru*】 (伸びる) increase; rise; extend; stretch; lengthen　(延びる) postpone; put off; prolong　**例** 売り上げは昨年の 7 ％増し. Sales registered a *7% increase* over last year. / それはゴムのようによく伸びる. It *stretches* easily like rubber. / 出発が 6 月 1 日に延びた. Our departure has been *postponed* [*put off*] till June 1. / 国会の会期は 1 カ月延びた. The session of the Diet was *prolonged* for a month. / わが国は輸出入ともに伸びている. Our trade, both export and import, is steadily *increasing*. / 日本の貿易はまだ伸びる. Japan's foreign trade is capable of further *growth* [*expansion*]. / その売り上げは年 1,500 万ドルと急速に伸びた. Its sales *shot up* to fifteen million dollars a year.

延べ払い【*nobebarai*】 deferred payment　**例** 延べ払い制度が導入された. A *deferred payment* system has been introduced.

述べる【*noberu*】 state; mention; express　**例** 貴社の手紙の中に述べてある条件について, いくつかの疑問があります. We have some doubts about the terms *expressed* in your letter.

乗り気になる【*noriki ni naru*】 become interested in; take an interest in; show much interest in; be enthusiastic　**例** その計画に乗り気になった. They *took an interest in* the program. / この事業に非常に乗り気になっている. They enter into the enterprise *with enthusiasm* [*much interest*].

乗り出す【*noridasu*】set about; start doing; undertake; embark in; launch out on; go into 《business》; enter 例 彼は若くして事業に乗り出した. He *set about* the enterprise in his youth. / 父の死後，すぐ政界に乗り出した. He *went into* politics soon after his father's death. / 彼は投機に乗り出した. He *ventured* on a speculation.

【は】

場合 【baai】: __に in the event of; in case; in case of; on the occasion of; sometimes **例** 火災が生じた場合直ちに保険会社に通知していただかなければならない. *In the event of* fire damage, the insurance company must be immediately notified. / 貴社の場合はそれを例外としなければ ならない. *In your case* we must make an exception. / 場合によっては1週間ほど米国に滞在するかもしれない. Depending *on the circumstances*, we may stay in America for a week or so. / 万一汽車に乗り遅れた場合はバスに乗りなさい. Take a bus *in case* you miss the train. / いざという場合には手前どもを頼りなさい. Ask us for help *in time of* emergency. / 正直者がバカをみる場合もある. Honesty *sometimes* does not pay.

倍 【bai】 times; fold; (2倍 double; twice; twofold / 3倍 treble; triple; threefold / 4倍 quadruple; fourfold / 5倍 quintuple; fivefold) **例** この橋はあの橋の1倍半の長さだ. This bridge is *one and a half times* as long as that bridge. / わたしの荷物はきみの2倍も重い. My baggage is *twice* as heavy as yours [has *double* the weight of yours]. / 彼は人の倍も働く. He works *twice* as hard as others. / 彼の所得は以前の2倍だ. His income is *double* what it was. / その額は予期していた4倍であった. The amount turned out to be *fourfold* (of) what we expected. / 二重の魅力 *twofold* charm / 三重の喜び *treble* pleasure / この時季の消費者需要は4倍に増えた. There was a *fourfold* increase in consumer demand this season. / 人口は5倍に増えた. The population increased *fivefold*. / 昨年貯金は倍増した. My savings *doubled* last year.

賠償 【baishō】 compensation; reparation **例** バス会社に損害賠償を請求する. We demand the bus company to make *compensation* for the loss. / わが国の戦争賠償は膨大なものだ. Japanese *reparations* for the war come to enormous sums. ‖ 金銭— reparation in cash ‖ 役務— reparations in service ‖

現物— reparations in kind

配船【*haisen*】allocation of vessels 例 東京行の船は5月中配船がない. No *steamer* to Tokyo *is available* during May.

配船表【*haisenhyō*】shipping list 例 5月分の配船表を同封します. We are pleased to enclose our *shipping lists* for you. / この配船予定表は予告してか, または予告なしに変更することがあります. This *shipping schedule* is subject to change with or without notice.

敗訴【*haiso*】: —になる lose a case ‖ —側 losing party 例 敗訴側は, 関係諸費を負担すべきである. The *losing party* shall bear the expenses thereof.

配置する【*haichi suru*】arrange; post; layout; staff 例 カウンターには〜を配置している. The counters *are staffed by* 〜.

配当【*haitō*】dividend 例 貴社が配当を怠ったのは遺憾です. To our regret, you defaulted on *a dividend*. ‖ 株式— stock dividend 例 株式配当は年2回払います. A *stock dividend* is paid biannually.

倍増する【*baizō suru*】double; increase [grow] twofold 例 過去10年間の輸出は, 10億ドルに倍増しました. Exports in the past decade have grown *twofold* to $ 1 billion.

売買【*baibai*】buying and selling; purchase and sale ‖ —確認書 sales confirmation; purchase confirmation ‖ 現金— cash sale 例 現金売買には大幅の割引をします. The company offers a considerable discount for *cash sales*. ‖ 現物— spot sale ‖ 先物— future sale ‖ 委託— consignment sale and purchase ‖ —する deal in 例 彼は油の売買をしている. He *deals in* oil. ‖ —契約書 sales contract 例 別便にて売買契約書を送ります. We are sending you under separate cover a *sales contract*. / 後日売買契約書を送付します. We will send you a *sales contract* at a later date. ‖ —手数料 sale commission ‖ —条件 terms and conditions of transaction 例 売買条件はきわめて有利. *The terms and conditions of the transaction* were very favorable.

廃品【*haihin*】waste materials; disused articles 例 廃品は海洋に投棄される. *Waste materials* are dumped into the ocean.

売品【*baihin*】 goods for sale

売約書【*baiyakusho*】 sales note　**例** 売約書２通同封いたしました. We enclosed *Sales Notes* in duplicate. ／ 本売約書は，下記商品を下記条件にもとづいて貴社あてに売約したことを示す. This *Sales Note* covers our sale to you of the undermentioned goods on the terms and conditions set forth below.

売約品【*baiyakuhin*】 goods sold　**例** 売約品は，各契約で規定された期間内に船積みすべきこと. The *goods sold* shall be shipped within the time stipulated in each contract.

入り込む【*hairikomu*】 get in; step in [into]; enter; come into　**例** 日本の会社にうまく入り込んだ外人がたくさんいる. Many foreigners have *got a good berth in* [have *found their way into*] a Japanese firm.

配慮【*hairyo*】 attention; patronage; consideration　**例** 親切な御配慮をいただけるものと前もって感謝します. Thank you in advance for your kind *consideration*. ／ まずは，大至急御配慮のほどを願い上げます. We trust this will have your prompt *attention*. ／ 品質はどの点からみても合格するように配慮ください. Please *see* that the quality is in every way up to the mark. ／ その点よろしく御配慮ねがいます. We ask for your kind *consideration* about the matter. ／ 貴社の注文品には最善の配慮をしますから，御安心ください. You may rest assured that our best *attention* will be given to your order. ／ この注文に対し，迅速かつ特別の配慮をねがいます. Please give this order your prompt and careful *attention*. ／ 当方の満足のいくよう貴社の最高の御配慮をお願いする. We would like you to give this transaction your best *consideration* to satisfy us.

歯が立たない【*haga tatanai*】 out of one's reach　**例** 貴社の現在の価格は，非常に高いので競争他社の価格に歯が立たない. Your present prices are *out of their reach*, because they are very high compared with those of your competitors.

計り知れない【*hakari shirenai*】 immense　**例** この商品は，計り知れない価値がある. The goods are of *immense* value.

白紙に戻す【*hakushi ni modosu*】 call off　**例** 明日の会合はたぶん

白紙に戻るだろう． They will probably *call off* tomorrow's meeting.

白書【*hakusho*】a white paper; a government report　例 委員会の公害白書は業界に無視された． The committee's *white paper* on pollution was ignored by the industry.

ばくだいな【*bakudaina*】huge　例 弊社はばくだいな研究投資を必要としています． We are in need of *huge* investment in research.

薄利【*hakuri*】narrow margin; small [slight] profit　例 当店は薄利多売主義です． Our principle is to sell much at a *small profit*.

はけ口【*hakeguchi*】outlet; sales output; market　例 弊社は，これらの製品のはけ口を求めています． We are seeking for an *outlet* for these products.

激しい【*hageshii*】keen; hard; severe　例 取引における競争は激しかった． There was *keen* competition in business. / この商品における競争は激しかった． Competition in this line was *keen*.

派遣する【*haken suru*】dispatch; send　例 その会議に多数の代表を派遣した． We *sent* [*dispatched*] many representatives to the conference.

箱【*hako*】case; box; carton; chest　例 200 箱の茶 200 *chests* of tea / お茶は，ブリキ裏付木箱に包装しなければ ならない． Green tea must be packed within a tin-lined wooden *case*.

端境期【*hazakaiki*】off season　例 端境期にはホテル料金は安くなる． Hotel rates are much cheaper in the *off season*.

破産【*hasan*】bankruptcy　例 松本商会は破産以来，非常 な困難のもとに努力しています． Since the *bankruptcy* of Matsumoto & Co., they are laboring under great difficulties. ‖ —する go bankrupt; drive into bankruptcy　例 その会社は破産するだろう． The firm will be *driven into bankruptcy*. / 銀行が破産した． The bank *went bankrupt*.

始まる【*hajimaru*】start; begin; commence; open; initiate　例 取引が始まる． The business *is opened*. / 会期は毎年 5 月 1 日に

始まる. The session is *called on* the lst of May every year. /
弊社は問屋業を始めました. We have *commenced* business as
commission agents.

外れ 【*hazure*】 miss; failure; the end; the outskirts ((of a town))
圏 当たりか外れか. Hit or miss？‖ ― る miss ((one's aim)); fail;
go wrong 圏 今年は当てが外れた. This year we have *missed
our aim.* / 期待(目算)が外れた. Our scheme has *failed* [*gone
wrong*].

破損 【*hason*】 damage; breakdown 圏 貴商品には破損が多い.
There are many *breakdowns* in your goods. ‖ ― する be
damaged; be broken 圏 製品は修繕の見込みがないほど破損
しております. The products have been irreparably *damaged.* /
貴積み荷を破損状態で入手した. We have received your shipment in *damaged* condition.

果たす 【*hatasu*】 accomplish [effect] ((one's purpose)); discharge
((one's duty)); fulfil; perform; achieve; execute; carry out
圏 契約をきちんと果たしてくれることを信じます. We trust
that you will duly *fulfil* the contract. / 同社は必ず約束を果た
す. They always *keep* [*fulfill*] their promise. / 無事使命を果
たした. We have *carried out* our mission successfully. / 義務
を果たさなければならない. We must *perform* [*fulfill*] our
duty. / ついに目的を果たした. We have *accomplished* [*attained*]
our purpose at last.

場違い 【*bachigai*】 out of place; out of one's way 圏 彼のいま
の地位は場違い. He is *out of place* in his present position.

八条国 【*hachijōkoku*】 the (I.M.F.) Article 8 status country 圏
日本は八条国に属してから 15 年になります. It is fifteen years
since Japan joined the *I.M.F. Article 8 status country.*

発案する 【*hatsuan suru*】 suggest; propose; mastermind 圏 彼
から発案があった. The plan was *masterminded* [*suggested*;
proposed] by him.

発揮する 【*hakki suru*】 display; exhibit; demonstrate; give play
((to)) 圏 天分を発揮する make (it) clear what one has / 才
能を発揮できる事業をせよ. Engage in the work which will

give play to your abilities.

はっきり【*hakkiri*】precisely; clearly; apparently; certainly 例 貴社ははっきりと支払い条件を示すべきだ. You should show *clearly* your terms of payment. ‖ ―言う to be frank [candid] with you; to speak definitely; to put it flatly 例 はっきり言えば貴社は信頼できない. *To be frank,* your firm can't be relied upon. / はっきりいえば, 貴社の現在の価格は非常に高い. *To be* more *precise,* your present prices are very high.

パッキング【*pakkingu*】packing; package →荷造り

発行依頼人【*hakkō irainin*】applicant for the credit 例 発行依頼人は松本商会. Matsumoto & Co., Ltd. is the *applicant for the credit.*

発行する【*hakkō suru*】issue; raise; open; publish 例 右保険に対し仮保険証券を発行ください. We ask you to *issue* a covering note for the insurance. / 貨物に百万円の保険証券を発行させること. To *take out* an insurance policy for ¥1,000,000 on the cargo.

抜粋【*bassui*】extract; summary; quotation 例 レポートからの抜粋文について貴社にお知らせします. We inform you of an *extract* from the report.

発する【*hassuru*】place; issue; give out 例 綿花300こりの注文を発した. We have *placed* an order for 300 bales of Cotton.

発送【*hassō*】despatch [dispatch]; forward; send 例 本日品物は「大洋丸」で発送いたしました. We inform you that we have *despatched* the goods today by M/S "Taiyo Maru". / 本日鉄道便で商品を発送しました. We have *forwarded* the goods by rail today. / 何とぞ至急保険証券を御送付ください. Please *put* policies *forward* at once. / 契約品を至急発送してください. Please *forward* our contracts immediately. ‖ ―費 delivery expense 例 発送費は輸出商もち. The *delivery expense* will be borne by the exporter.

ハッチ【*hatchi*】hatch 例 積み荷はハッチでなされる. The ship will be loaded through the *hatch.*

発展させる【*hatten saseru*】develop; expand 例 事業を発展さ

せる *develop* [*expand*] one's business

発動 【*hatsudō*】 motion; operation ‖ ―機 motor ‖ ―機船 motor ship(M/S); motor vessel(M/V) **例** その商品は東京丸で積送された. The goods were shipped by the *M/S* "Tokyo Maru".

発売する 【*hatsubai suru*】 sell; put on sale; put on the market; be on sale (発売中) **例** これらの品は, どこでも発売されています. These things *are on sale* everywhere. / 弊社は昨年新しい機械を発売した. We *put* a new machine *on sale* last year.

波止場 【*hatoba*】 wharf; dock (揚げ場, 岸壁); pier (桟橋) **例** 大洋丸はいま波止場に係留中. The M.V. Taiyo Maru is now moored at the *wharf*. ‖ ―使用料 wharfage

話 【*hanashi*】 talk; story; account; subject **例** 同社と長い話をした. We had a long *talk* with them. / ちょっと～について話があります. We have *something to talk* to you about ～. / K氏と何度か話をしたことがある. We have had several *conversations* [*talks*] with Mr. K. / 話のタネにそれを見ておこう. We will look at it for a topic of *conversation*. / 耳寄りな話がある. We have good *news*. / ここだけの話だが, 当社は商売をやめる積りです. *Between you and us*, we are going to give up our present business. ‖ ―合いの場 common grounds ‖ ―を打ち切る close the discussions; break up the negotiations **例** 弊社はその件については, すでに話を打ち切りました. We had already broken up the *negotiation* about the matter. ‖ ―を進める go into details; push the negotiation ‖ ―をもちかける approach; make proposals to ‖ ―がまとまる come to an agreement ‖ ―にならない out of [beyond] the question

話合い 【*hanashiai*】 consultation; agreement; conference **例** 話合いはシンガポールで行われる予定. The *conference* is to be held in Singapore.

話す 【*hanasu*】 (have a) talk; tell; speak **例** 彼と親しく話した. I *had a talk* with him in person. / その秘密をだれにも話してはいけない. *Keep the secret* to yourself. / お話ししたいことがある. We have something to *tell* you.

早積み 【*hayazumi*】 prompt [immediate] shipment

早出料 【*hayaderyō*】 despatch [dispatch] money 例 早出料がわ
ずかあるだけで, 他に利益はない. We can expect no profit
from this shipment except small income of *despatch money*.

早める 【*hayameru*】 hasten; advance; expedite; accelerate 例
支払い期日を早めてください. Please *advance* the due date. /
船積みを早めてください. Please *accelerate* your shipment.

はやる 【*hayaru*】 be popular; be in vogue [fashion]; be fashion-
able 例 当節スポーツカーがはやっているようです. The sports-
car seems to *be in fashion* [*vogue*].

払い 【*harai*】: ―すぎ overpayment ‖ 現金― cash payment ‖ 一
覧― payment at sight ‖ 持参人― payable to bearer ‖ 指図人―
payable to order ‖ 手形― payable by bill ‖ 内金― payment
on account ‖ 割賦― payment by instalment ‖ 前金― payment
in advance

払い込み済み 【*haraikomi zumi*】 paid-up 例 全額払い込み済み会
員です. He is fully a *paid-up* member of the club.

払う 【*harau*】 pay 例 貴社の提案があれば直ちに十分な注意を払
います. We shall *pay* our immediate and careful attention
to your proposal. / 前金で払うにはおよびません. You need
not *pay* in advance.

ばら 【*bara*】 bulk 例 荷物はばらで積まれた. The goods were
loaded in *bulk*. 囲 ばら荷 a bulk cargo; a cargo in bulk

バラスト 【*barasuto*】 (底荷) ballast 例 弊社は, 横浜から神戸ま
で底荷だけで本船を出さねばならない. We shall have to let
our ship sail from Yokohama to Kobe in *ballast*.

波乱 【*haran*】 trouble; disturbance ‖ ―のある stormy 例 市場
の波乱は免れない. *A stormy* market is inevitable.

版 【*han*】 edition 例 10月4日付新聞地方版 the local *edition* of
October 4 issue

範囲 【*han-i*】 scope; range; extent; limits; sphere 例 (信用照
会) 調査範囲 one's *field* of inquiry / 利益範囲内 within our
sphere of interest / 活動範囲が広い. He has a wide *sphere*
[*field*] of activity. / 交際範囲が広い. They have a large *circle*

of acquaintances. / この行為は，彼の代理範囲を逸脱している.
The act is outside the *scope* of his agency. ‖ がわたる range
例 応募者の年齢は 20 歳から 50 歳の範囲. The age of the applicants should *range* from 20 to 50.

半額【*hangaku*】a half amount 例 弊社の勘定書の半額だけ即刻
御送金ねがいます. Please remit to us *half the amount* of our
statement immediately.

半期【*hanki*】half term; six months' period 例 本年度上半期,
外国を旅行するアメリカ人の数は，着実な増加を続けています.
The number of Americans who travel abroad continued its
steady increase in the first *six months of the year* [*half-year
period*; *six months' period*]. 圏 四半期 a quarter year

番号【*bangō*】number 例 俵番号 B/♯ (Bale *number*)/箱番号 C/♯
(Case *number*) / 注文は，つねに番号にておねがいします. Please
order by *number* always.

万国博覧会【*bankoku hakurankai*】World's Fair 例 当社商品は
万博で販売促進された. Our goods were promoted at the
World's Fair.

反して【*hanshite*】contrary to 例 期待に反して販売は第三四半
期に落ちこんだ *Contrary to* expectation, sales dipped in the
third quarter.

半製品【*hanseihin*】semi-manufactured goods; half-finished
goods 例 半製品は低率の課税対象. *Semi-manufactured goods*
attract a lower rate of quarter duty.

万全【*banzen*】perfection; all precautions; every effort 例 今
後このようなことが再発しないよう万全を尽くすことをお約束し
ます. We assure you that *every effort* will be made in future
to prevent any repetition of such mistakes.

反対【*hantai*】contrast; opposition; reversal ‖ —の counter 例
この取引に反対申し込みをしたい. We wish to make a *counter
offer* to this business. / 貴社の反対申し込みは安価過ぎる. Your
counter offers are always too low. / 6 月23日付貴社からの反
対売り申し込みを有り難く受けます. We thank you for your
counter offer of June 23. ‖ —になる reverse 例 事態は反対に

なった. The situation has been *reversed*.

判断 【handan】 decision; conclusion; judgement ‖ —を下す pass a decision; draw the conclusion 例 市場調査により判断を下されることを望みます. We hope you can *draw* some *conclusion* from the market survey. ‖ —がつきかねている be perplexed; be at a loss

番手 【bante】 S＝count 例 20番手綿糸 20*s* cotton yarn ／ 綿プリント地60番手100反をお送りします. We send you 100 pcs. Cotton Prints, 60*s*. ‖ 細— high count ‖ 太— low count

反応 【han-nō】 reaction; response 例 新しいがん具の着想に対する当方の反応をお尋ねの10月22日付貴状拝受. Thank you for your letter of October 22 asking our *reaction* to your ideas for new toys.

販売 【hanbai】 sale; selling; marketing 例 この商品の販売はセンセーションを起こすでしょう. This *sale* of goods will cause a sensation. ‖ —経費 selling charges ‖ —収益 margin ‖ 見本— sale by sample ‖ 明細書— sale by specification ‖ 標準— sale by standard ‖ 予約— sale by subscription ‖ 大安売 bargain sale ‖ 蔵払い clearance sale ‖ 委託— consignment sale ‖ 掛け売り credit sale ‖ —係 selling clerk; salesman ‖ —店 store; shop; dealer ‖ —課 a sales department ‖ —価格 selling price ‖ —人 a seller; a dealer ‖ —する sell; trade; deal in; market 例 中国人向けのゴム靴多数を販売する好機です. We have an excellent opportunity to *dispose of* Rubber Shoes suitable for Chinese in large numbers. ／ 当店は最近のあらゆる種類の男子一般向き肌着を販売しています. We *carry* a full line of the currently popular types of men's underwear.

販売権 【hanbai ken】 selling right 例 当社は，ヨーロッパに販売権をもっている. We have the *selling rights* in Europe.

販売促進 【hanbai sokushin】 sales promotion; marketing procedures 例 当社の広告代理店は販売促進の最新方法を有効に用いることができます. Our advertising agency makes efficient use of the latest *marketing procedures*.

販売代理店 【hanbai dairiten】 selling agent 例 当社は，貴市場

に多くの販売代理店をもっています．We have many of our *selling agents* in your market.

販売部長【*hanbai buchō*】sales manager　例 その店はオースチン氏を販売部長にしたところです．The firm has just made Mr. Austin *sales manager*.

販売網【*hanbaimō*】sales network; distribution channel　例 当社は，販売網を拡張するためにあらゆる手を打っております．We are taking every opportunity to promote [extend] our *distribution channels*. / 同店は，比較的小地域までも販売網を伸ばしたいと望んでいます．The firm hopes to expand its *sales networks* into smaller areas. / この品目については，当社は強力な販売網をもっています．We have an extensive *sales network* for this line of goods.

販売力【*hanbai ryoku*】sales force　例 メーカーは，御社の販売力に大いに期待しております．The manufacturers are quite willing to rely on your *sales force*.

販路【*hanro*】outlet; market　例 弊社新製品の販路の探求に御尽力ねがいます．Endeavour to find good *outlet* for our new products. ‖ ―開発する cultivate [find; exploit; seek after] a new market ‖ ―拡張する expand business; develop sales　例 貴市場で販路を広めるために価格を切り下げた．We have cut our prices in order to *develop* our *sales* in your market. / さらに販路を拡張するため，貴市場を開拓したいと存じます．In order to *expand business* [*promote the sales*], we are desirous of selling in your market.

【ひ】

ひいき【*hiiki*】favor; support; sponsorship; patronage　例 毎度御ひいきにあずかり，ありがとうございます．It is always a pleasure to have the opportunity of serving our *old customers*. / これを機会として今後ずっと御ひいきにねがいます．We sincerely hope that this is the beginning of a long and pleasant business relationship. / 御ひいきを感謝し，できる限

りサービスをさせていただきます．We appreciate your *patronage* and will endeavor to render you every possible service. / 日頃の御ひいきありがとうございます．Thank you for your *patronage* [*good favor*].

被害【*higai*】damage 例 台風は大きな被害を与えた．The typhoon caused a great deal of *damage*. / 事務所は火事で大きな被害を受けた．Our office suffered a lot of *damage* in [was badly *damaged* by] the fire. ‖ —者 a victim; a sufferer

控え【*hikae*】a note; a copy 例 この書類の控えをとっておきなさい．Make a *copy* of this document. ‖ —帳 a notebook [a memorandum (単数), memoranda (複)] ‖ —見本 duplicate sample ‖ —室 a waiting room; a lobby

控え目【*hikaeme*】：—に moderately; temperately; cautiously; with reserve 例 市場不安定のときは控え目にする方が賢明．When the market is unstable, it is wise to act *cautiously*. ‖ —の見方 reserved opinion ‖ —にいっても to say the least of it [at least; conservatively] ‖ —にする hold [hang] back 例 （相場が下がりそうなので）買い手は控え目にしている．The buyers *hold back*. / 国民は以前は大量の缶詰食品を消費していたが，現在はできるだけその消費を控えている．The people used to consume great quantities of canned foods, but now they *hold back* those consumption as much as possible.

比較【*hikaku*】comparison ‖ —にならない cannot compare; beyond comparison 例 AとBは比較にならない．A *is nothing to* B. / ～の点ではAとBは比較にならない．A *is no match for* B in ～. / これとあれでは比較にならない．There is no *comparison* between this and that. This cannot *be compared with* that. ‖ —する compare 例 貴社が当社の値段と条件を他の製造業者申し出のそれと比較されるなら，当社のものが一番有利なことがおわかりでしょう．If you *compare* our prices and terms with those offered by other makers, you will find ours will be most advantageous [more favorable]. ‖ —すると as compared with; in comparison with 例 この商品に対する貴社の申し込み値段は英国製品のそれと比較すると5％高い．The price you offer for this article is higher by 5% when *compared with* that of English make.

比較的【*hikakuteki*】comparative; relative **例** 比較的重要な事実 a fact of *comparative* [*relative*] importance ‖ —に in comparison; comparatively **例** 成績は比較的よい. The results are excellent *in comparison* [*comparatively* excellent].

悲観【*hikan*】pessimism ‖ —的 pessimistic **例** 悲観的見方 *pessimistic* views / 悲観的な口調でそういった. They said so in a *pessimistic* air. / 形勢は悲観せざるをえない. We have to take a *pessimistic* view of the prospects.

引き合い【*hikiai*】inquiry **例** トランジスタ・ラジオに対して引き合いをいただきありがとうございます. Thank you for your *inquiry* about our Transitor Radios. / 4月1日付貴引き合いに対する御返事としてさらしポプリンの見本に値段表31号を添えて送りました. In reply to your *inquiry* of 1st April, we have sent you a sample of Bleached Poplin and a Price List No. 31. / 取引先から時々レディメード洋服の引き合いを受けておりました. We have from time to time had *inquiries* from our friends for Ready Made Clothing. ‖ 〜について—する have [make] an inquiry for; inquire for ‖ —を受ける receive inquiries for ‖ —を求める invite one's inquiry for 〜 ‖ —について商談をまとめるため尽力する work on an inquiry ‖ —を始める start working ‖ —中 under negotiation; negotiating; working

引き合う【*hikiau*】(値段が) competitive; workable; pay **例** 自転車は高すぎて引き合わない. Bicycles are *unworkable*. / この仕事は引き合わない. The work does not *pay*.

引き当て【*hikiate*】cover ‖ —に for; against; designed for; covering ‖ —る keep (in reserve) for; appropriate; apply; cover; arrange to meet; earmark **例** 退職金の引き当てに100万円を留保してある. We have reserved one million yen to *cover* the retiring allowance. ‖ —金 reserve

引き受け【*hikiuke*】acceptance; undertaking(請負) ‖ 為替手形を—る accept a draft [bill of exchange] ‖ 〜からのオファーを

—る accept an offer from ~ ‖ (~からの注文を)—る accept (an order from ~); take over 《business》 例 このような安い値段では貴注文を引き受けることはできません. We deeply regret that we are unable to *accept* your order at such a low price. / 貴注文同封売約書第35号のとおり喜んで引き受けます. We are glad to *accept* your order as per [according to] enclosed Sales Note No. 35. ‖ 電信 (電報, テレックス) による — acceptance by cable (telegram, telex) / この仕事は当社で引き受けよう. We will see to the work. We will take over the work. / 当社は送り状金額に対し, 一覧後60日払いの為替手形を貴社あてに振り出します. 呈示ありしだい手形の引き受け支払いをしてくださることを信じます. We will draw a draft upon you for the amount of the invoice at 60 d/s and trust you will meet the bill [protect (honor) our draft] on presentation. / 万一この申し込みを引き受けないならば, 当分この品物は手に入らない. If you fail to *accept* the present offer, you will be unable to get the goods for some time. ‖ 手形の— acceptance of a bill ‖ 注文の— acceptance of an order ‖ 注文書の受け取り (受け取っただけ で引き受けるかどうかは未定) receipt of an order ‖ 手形—(支払い) protection of a draft ‖ —を拒絶する dishonor a bill ‖ —拒絶 nonacceptance

引き換え【*hikikae*】exchange; change; conversion ‖ —に in exchange for; alternatively; against; on; cash on delivery (代金引換払); against payment (支払いと同時に) 例 受取証と引き換えに現金を渡す hand over the money *in exchange for* the receipt / 現金と引き換えに品物を渡す deliver the goods *in exchange for* cash / 弊店は代金引き換えで品物をお渡しすることにしています. We make it a rule to deliver goods *in exchange for* the payment. ‖ —る exchange; cash (現金を) 例 その品を金に換えた. We *exchanged* the goods for money. / 銀行で小切手を現金に引き換えた. We *cashed* the check at the bank.

引き下げ【*hikisage*】lowering; reduction; cut ‖ 物価の— reduction in prices ‖ 賃金の— reduction in wages 例 賃 (銀の引

き) 下げを受けいれないだろう. The workers will not accept a *reduction in wages*.

引き出す【*hikidasu*】 draw 例 銀行から10ドルを引き出した. He *drew* 10 dollars from the bank. / このごろは預け入れる者より引き出す方が多い. More people *draw* money than deposit it. ‖ 情報を— obtain information ‖ 貯金を— draw one's savings

引き立て【*hikitate*】 →ひいき

引き継ぎ【*hikitsugi*】 business transfer; succession; taking over charge 例 引き継ぎ完了次第 on completion of *official business transfer* / 事務引き継ぎ *taking over charge* of an office / だれが君の後を引き継ぎますか. Who will *succeed* your office? Who will *take your place*?

引き続き【*hikitsuzuki*】 still; continually; successively; in succession; 連休 consecutive holidays 例 6時間引き続いて働く. He works six hours *at a stretch*. / 十年引き続いてこの仕事に従事している. We have been working on this project *in succession* for 10 years. / あれから引き続いてここにいます. I have been here *ever since*. / 2日間引き続いて休んだ. He was absent for 2 *consecutive days*.

引き続く【*hikitsuzuku*】 continue; last; persist; follow; ensue 例 市況は引き続き手堅く, 在庫は少ない. The market *continues* to be firm and so stocks are scarce.

引き船【*hikibune*】 a tugboat; a tug 例 引き船は港の入口でタンカーを迎える. *Tugs* meet tankers at the port entrance.

罷業【*higyō*】 →スト

引き渡し【*hikiwatashi*】 delivery 例 引き渡し日 *delivery* date / 値段が妥当であり, 引き渡しが信頼できれば, 貴社からの申し込みを待つ. We look forward to further offers from you as long as prices are reasonable and *deliveries* reliable. ‖ 引き渡す deliver; hand over; transfer; turn over 例 荷物を引き渡す *deliver* goods / 書類を引き渡す *hand over* document / 財産を息子に引き渡して引退した. He *transferred* his property to his son and retired from work. / 店を債権者に引き渡した. He *turned over* [*surrendered*] his business to his creditors. /

貴社商品至急入用ですから引き渡しのできる最も早い日時を教え
てください. State the earliest date you can *deliver*, as your
goods are urgently needed.

引く 【*hiku*】: 値を— reduce [lower; lessen] the price; make
~ cheaper 例 現金なら1割引きます. We shall *take off* 10
percent for cash. ‖ 人目を— attract notice ‖ 減ずる subtract
例 10から3引くと7 subtract 3 from 10 leaves 7 ‖ 水道を—
lay on city water ‖ ガスを— lay on gas ‖ 電話を— install the
telephone ‖ 身を— retire; resign ‖ 注意を— attract 例 この問
題が世間の注意を引いている. The problem is *attracting* public
attention.

否決する 【*hiketsu suru*】 reject; throw out; turn down 例 委
員たちは私の提案を否決 した. The committee members *rejected* my suggestions. ‖ 否決権 a negative voice [veto]

備考 【*bikō*】 note(s); remarks 例 会議についての備考を読んで
ください. Please read your *notes* to the meeting. ‖ —欄 a
remarks column

非公式の 【*hikōshiki no*】 unofficial; informal; private; unconfirmed 例 非公式の報道によると社長は引退したそうだ. *Un-
confirmed* reports suggest the president has resigned.

ビザ 【*biza*】 visa 例 大使館は3日以内にビザ申請を処理するだ
ろう. The embassy will process your *visa* application within
three days. ‖ —を下付する grant visa

非常 【*hijō*】 *emergency* 例 非常手段 an *emergency* measure / 非
常口 an *emergency* [a fire] exit / 非常のさいにはこのドアをあ
けなさい. Open this door in (case of) an *emergency*.

日付 【*hizuke*】 a date ‖ —を書く date 例 その手紙は3月10日の
日付でした. The letter was *dated* 10th March. / 4月1日付の
お手紙ありがとう. We thank you for your letter *dated* [of]
1st April. / その手紙は日付がない. The letter is *undated*. ‖ —
変更線 the (international) date line

必至 【*hisshi*】 inevitable 例 コストの上がるのは必至. Cost will
inevitably rise.

必需品 【*hitsujuhin*】 necessaries; necessities 例 生活必需品 the

0

necessities of life / その会社は補償の一部として生活必需品を提供するだろう. The company will provide the *necessities of life* as part of its compensation.

必須【hissu】 indispensable; inevitable; essential; vital 圀 彼は長となるのに必須の徳を欠いている. He lacks the qualities *requisite* to a chief [ruler]. / 彼は当社には必須の人物. His services are *indispensable* to our company. ‖ ―条件 prerequisite; essential conditions ‖ ―科目 compulsory course

匹敵する【hitteki suru】 rival; equal; be equal to; be equivalent to; match 圀 貿易実務では彼に匹敵する者はない. He has *no equal* [*no rival*] in his knowledge of foreign trade practices.

必要【hitsuyō】 necessity; need ‖ ―とする require; need; necessitate 圀 金が必要だ. We *need* [*are in need of*] money. / これは必要に迫られたとき使える金だ. The money is to be used only under *pressing* circumstances. / 荷渡しするには，3 週間の事前通知が必要. Three weeks' notice is *required* before delivery can be effected. ‖ ―条件 necessary condition ‖ ―な necessary; required; indispensable; essential 圀 外国へ行きたいが，必要な資金がない. I wish to go abroad, but I don't have the *necessary* means. / 必要な資金はどうして金策をするか. How will you find the *necessary* means? ‖ ―の場合には in case of need; when [if] necessary 圀 必要の場合には御自由にお使いください. Please use it at your pleasure *in case of need* [*when necessary*].

―押しする【hito-oshi suru】 press for; prompt; persuade; promote 圀 毎春従業員は賃上げを求めて一押しする. Every spring the workers *press for* higher pay.

―口にいって【hitokuchi ni itte】 in short 圀 一口にいって今年は非常に成功の年だった. *In short*, this has been an extremely successful year.

―そろい【hitosoroi】 a full set; a range of; a line of 圀 当社製品の一そろいの見本を喜んで送ります. We shall be glad to send you *a full set of* samples of our products. / 御請求に従い定価表を添えて一そろいの見本をお送りいたします. In accordance with your request, we are sending you the *whole range of* our sample together with the price-list.

一通り 【*hitotōri*】 briefly; generally ‖ ―説明する give a brief explanation; roughly explain; give an outline **例** この製造工程を一通り説明ねがいます. Please *give a brief explanation* of the manufacturing process.

一まとめにして 【*hitomatome ni shite*】 [一括して] in a lump; in mass; in a bundle **例** 一まとめに支払ってもらいたい. We prefer to be paid *in a lump* sum.

一人当たり 【*hitori atari*】 per capita; per head **例** 欧州に比べてアメリカの研究, 開発に対する支出額は一人当たり10倍となっている. The U.S. spends about ten times more *per capita* on research and development than Europe.

非難 【*hinan*】 blame; criticism **例** 彼の行動は非難の余地がない. His behavior is *above criticism* [*blameless*]. / その声明は非難の的となった. The statement became the focus of *criticism.* ‖ ―する blame one for; criticize; reproach; accuse **例** 悪い行為を非難した. We *reproached* [*accused*] them for their bad conduct.

否認 【*hinin*】 denial ‖ ―する deny; disapprove; veto; repudiate **例** 彼は自分の行為を否認している. He *denies* his own action. / 排日案を否認した. They have *vetoed* the anti-Japanese legislation.

日延べする 【*hinobe suru*】 postpone; put off; defer; extend [the term] **例** 荒模様につき日延べ. *Postponed* owing to the stormy weather. / 開会1週間日延べ. The session is to be *extended* by a week.

非番 【*hiban*】 off duty **例** わたしは5時に非番になる. I come *off duty* at 5. / いま非番です. I am now *off duty.*

備品 【*bihin*】 fixtures; furnishings; fittings **例** アパートは備品がそろうと完全になる. The apartment comes complete with all *fixtures.*

日歩 【*hibu*】 daily interest; interest per diem

備忘録 【*bibōroku*】 memorandum book; memo **例** 秘書はいつ

も約束の日時を備忘録に書きとめる. The secretary usually writes appointments in her *memorandum book*. ‖ —に記入する note on a memorandum

被保険 【*hihoken*】: —者 the [an] insured ‖ —物 insured property ‖ —額 the amount insured 例 被保険額は近年のインフレによりなお不十分. *The amount insured* is inadequate due to inflation in recent years.

秘密 【*himitsu*】 secret; confidence; privacy 例 貴社はこの情報を秘密にしてくださるでしょう. You will hold the information *confidential*. / それは公然の秘密だ. It is an open *secret*. / 秘密を明かした. They revealed *the secret* to us. ‖ —裏に secretly; confidentially; privately; with secrecy 例 ことは秘密のうちに運ばれた. The matter was plotted *secretly* [*in secrecy*; *in private*].

ひも付きの 【*himotsuki no*】 tied; restricted; strings attached; with a string on 例 このオファーにはひも付きはない. This offer has no *strings attached*. ‖ —契約 conditional contract ‖ —融資 tied loan

表 【*hyō*】 table; list; statement; chart; diagram 例 輸入品目を表にせよ. Make a *list* of (the item of) imports. ‖ —にする tabulate; list

費用 【*hiyō*】 expenses; expenditure; cost; fee 例 彼は会社の費用でアメリカへ行った. He went to America at the *expense* of the company. / 費用を切り詰めなければならぬ. We must cut down our *expenses*. / 費用はいくらで上がるか. What will the *expenses* amount to? / 費用は一文もかからない. It will not *cost a cent*. It will not involve any *expense*. / 費用を半分ずつもとう. Let's go halves in the *expenses*. / だいぶ費用を使った. We have incurred *a lot of expense*. It *cost* a great deal.

評価 【*hyōka*】 valuation; estimation; appraisal 例 高く(安く)—する rate anything high (low) ‖ —額 appraised [estimated] value ‖ —する value; estimate; appraise; appreciate ‖ 品物を—する appraise [appreciate] goods 例 品質を高く評価しています. We *have high respect* for its qualities. / 家は500万円

と評価してある. The house *is valued* at 5,000,000 yen.

表記 【hyōki】 inscribed on the face; declared; mention outside 例 表記金額正にいただきました. Received the sum *inscribed on the face.* ‖ 価格—郵便 declared value post

表現 【hyōgen】 expression 例 それはうまい表現だ. It is a good *expression.* ‖ —する represent; express 例 考えをはっきり表現すべきだ. You should *express* your opinion clearly.

標語 【hyōgo】 a motto; (団体政党の) a slogan; a maxim 例 われわれは国際友好の標語を賞金つきで募集しています. We offer a prize for the best *motto* concerning international friendship.

表示する 【hyōji suru】 express; indicate; describe; show 例 製造工程を表示してください. Please *describe* the production process.

標準 【hyōjun】 standard; a criterion (判断の) ‖ —値段 standard price ‖ —化 standardization ‖ —以下の below standard ‖ —時 the standard time ‖ —を上げる (下げる) raise (lower) the standard ‖ —に達する come up to standard 例 わが国の鉄の生産高は標準に達しない. The iron production of our country does not come up to *standard.*

表題 【hyōdai】 title; heading; caption 例 論文の表題 the *subject* of thesis / この本の表題は「物価」です. The *title* of the book is "Price". The book *is entitled* "Price". / 新聞の表題は内容と一致しない. Newspaper *headings* [*captions*] do not represent their contents.

評判 【hyōban】 reputation; fame; credit 例 同社の評判や信頼性に関して, どんな情報でも貴社の御意見をお聞かせください. We shall be obliged if you will give us your opinion as to their *reputation* [*fame*] and trustworthiness. / 流れている情報がほんとうなら, その会社はたいへん評判を落とします. If the report in circulation is true, the firm in question is losing much *reputation.* ‖ —がよい(悪い) be (un)popular; be well (ill) spoken of 例 彼は評判がいい. He is *popular* among us. He is *well spoken* of by all. He is a man of *good reputation.*

He has a *good reputation.* / その商社は 1920 年来絹の輸出に
従事しており，大へんよい評判を得ています． They have been
engaging in the export of silk since 1920 and enjoy a very
good reputation.

表面【*hyōmen*】surface; face; exterior ‖ —に持ち出す bring to
the surface; disclose; expose ‖ —的に superficially ‖ —化する
come (up) to the surface　例　彼の悪事が表面化した． His evil
deed *came to the surface.*

平積無用【*hirazumi muyō*】Not to be laid flat.　Never lay flat.

比率【*hiritsu*】ratio; proportion; percentage　例　月曜，金曜の
労働者の欠勤率は他の日よりも高い．　The *proportion* of workers absent on Mondays and Fridays is higher than the
rest of the week.

肥料【*hiryō*】manure; fertilizer ‖ 化学— chemical manure ‖ —工
業 the fertilizer industry ‖ 畑に—をやる manure [put manure
on] the field

比例【*hirei*】proportion; ratio ‖ 〜に—して in proportion to　例
輸入と輸出は比例していなければならない． Imports should be
in proportion to exports. / 賃金は時間と比例すべきだ． The
wages should be *proportional* [*in proportion*] *to* the hours. /
速力は時間と反比例になる． The velocity *is inversely proportional to* the time. ‖ 正— direct proportion ‖ 反— inverse
proportion

披露【*hirō*】announcement　例　世間には昨日披露が行われた．
The *announcement* was made to the public yesterday. ‖ —す
る announce ‖ —状 a letter of introduction ‖ 開店— announcement of opening shops

広がる【*hirogaru*】pervade; spread; extend; expand; prevail
（普及，流行する）　例　組合の勢力範囲が次第に広がる． The
union's sphere of influence is gradually *widening.* / 当社は
イギリス市場に輸出入とも貿易を広げたいと望んでいます．　We
are desirous of *extending* our trade, both import and export,
with the British market.

品質【*hinshitsu*】quality; brand; （品質請け合い　quality warranted) 例 品質良好です. The goods are superior in *quality* [of superior *quality*]. / 品質は申し分ない. The *quality* leaves nothing to be desired. / 日本製品は品質がよくなった. Japanese goods have improved in *quality*. / 品質は必ず御要望にそうものと確信しております. We are sure that *the quality* will meet with your requirements. / 本品をお試しくだされば品質がいかに優秀かおわかりいただけます. A trial will convince the customer of the excellence of the *quality*. / 当社の商品は上等品質であり，最上の仕上げであることを保証します. We assure you that our goods are *of the first class quality* and of the best workmanship. / 見本で販売した商品の品質は到着地に到着したとき見本と正確に等しいものでなければならない. The *quality* of the goods sold on sample must exactly be equal to sample upon arrival at destination. / 品質不良につき釈明してください. For the inferior *quality* of the goods we would like to have your explanation. / 品質不良を証明するため鑑定人の報告書を同封します. To prove the inferior *quality* of the goods, we have enclosed a survey report by the surveyor.

品種 【*hinshu*】 kind; sort; variety; class 例 当社にはいろいろの品種の在庫があります. We stock a large *variety* of products.

便船 【*binsen*】 an available ship; next ship; first steamer 例 便船あり次第行く. I am going in *the next ship that sails* [by *the next available boat*; by *the first steamer*].

品目 【*hinmoku*】 commodity; article; item 例 この品目はマージンが大きいので他の品よりよく売れる. This *article* outsells all our others by a large margin.

【ふ】

風袋 【*fūtai*】 tare; package 例 正確な風袋を取るように特に留意ありたし. Be particular to get the correct *tare*.

封筒 【*fūtō*】 envelope 例 御返事には同封の封筒を御利用くださ

い. The enclosed *envelope* is for your convenience. / 当社の
住所入り封筒を同封いたしました. We enclosed a self-addressed
envelope.

増える【*fueru*】 increase; multiply　**例** 人口は5倍に増えた. The
poulation *increased* fivefold.

賦課【*fuka*】 imposition; levy‖ ― を受ける be imposed a tax of
例 ぜいたく輸入品のすべてに5%の税金がかけられてきた. A 5%
tax has been *imposed* on all luxury imports.

部下【*buka*】 a subordinate; a follower　**例** 彼は部下からその役
職に就くよう票決された. He was voted into office by his
subordinates.

不可解【*fukakai*】 mystery; beyond (one's) comprehension ‖ ―
な incomprehensible; hard to understand; unintelligible　**例**
その販売を取り逃した理由は不可解. Why we lost the sale is
beyond my comprehension.

不確認信用状【*fukakunin shinyōjō*】 unconfirmed letter of credit;
unconfirmed L/C

不可【*fuka*】: ― の wrong; improper; unacceptable; unadvisable
例 貴社条件は満足にはほど遠く不可である. Your condition is
far from satisfactory and therefore *unacceptable*. ‖ ― とする
be against ~; disapprove of; regard ~ as wrong

不可欠の【*fukaketsu no*】 essential; indispensable　**例** 注文品を
発送していただくことが不可欠の条件です. It is an *essential*
condition that you dispatch our order. / 計画を成功させるの
に貴社の援助は不可欠です. Your assitance is *indispensable* for
the success of the scheme.

不可抗力【*fukakōryoku*】 force majeure; irresistible force; beyond control　**例** これは不可抗力だ. It is a case of *force
majeure*. / 御注文は火災又は不可抗力のような異例でやむをえな
い事情により変更することがあるという条件付きでお引き受けし
ます. The order is accepted subject to the unusual, unavoidable conditions, such as fires or causes *beyond our
control*. / 船積みの遅延は不可抗力のせいである. The delay of
shipment is due to *force majeure*.

不活発 【*fukappatsu*】 depression; inactivity; dullness ‖ —な inactive; dull; flat 例 市況が不活発である. The market is *flat* [*dull*; *inactive*; *slack*; *quiet*]. / 当地市場相場は非常に不活発で, 実際ほとんど取り引きがありません. The market here is exceedingly *inactive* and practically no business being done.

不可分の 【*fukabun no*】 inseparable; indivisible 例 自由企業と資本主義は不可分である. Free enterprise and capitalism are *inseparable*.

付加料金 【*fukaryōkin*】 surtax; surcharges 例 運送費として付加料金が課せられた. A *surcharge* has been added to cover transport costs.

不完全 【*fukanzen*】 imperfection; incompleteness ‖ —な imperfect; incomplete; faulty 例 損傷は, 主として荷造り不完全のためのように見受けられます. The damage appears to have been caused by the *faulty* packing of the goods.

付記する 【*fuki suru*】 write in addition; add 例 信用照会先銀行を付記してください. *Include* your bank reference, please.

普及する 【*fukyū suru*】 spread; popularize; diffuse; pervade; propagate 例 テレビ広告が当社製品の普及に大いに役立った. TV advertising has done much to *popularize* our products. / ここ数年オフィス・オートメーションが全国的に普及した. During these few years Office Automation System has *spread* throughout the country. / コンピュータはますます普及しつつある. Computer is *becoming* more and more *popular*.

不況 【*fukyō*】 depression; slump; recession (一時的) 例 経済は不況に向かいつつある. The economy is heading towards a *depression*. / 目下貿易は非常な不況です. Now the serious trade *depression* is prevailing. / 世界的な不況のため業務を清算するのもやむなきに至りました. We have been forced to liquidate our business due to the worldwide *depression*. / 不況のため首を切られた. He was dismissed because of *bad business*. ‖ —の dull; bad 例 商売は不況である. Business is *bad* [depressed]. ‖ —時 depression period; bad times ‖ —の年 lean years ‖ 経済— economic depression ‖ 財界— financial depression ‖ —を克服する overcome [get over] the recession ‖ —のどん底にある be at the bottom of the depression

不均衡な 【*fukinkō na*】 unbalanced; unbalancing; out of proportion; topsided; disproportionate

不均等 【*fukintō*】 inequality; unevenness; disproportion 例 この会社の男女従業員の間にはいちじるしい不均等がある. There is much *inequality* between male and female employees in this company.

腹案 【*fukuan*】 a plan; a design

伏在する 【*fukuzai suru*】 lie concealed; be hidden; be latent 例 彼には活用しない多くの才能が伏在している. He has much *latent* talent that he doesn't use.

複雑な 【*fukuzatsu na*】 intricate; complicated 例 流通機構は複雑だ. The distribution network is rather *complicated*.

副産物 【*fukusanbutsu*】 by-product 例 副産物を再生利用する. We recycle *by-products* of our industrial processes.

複写 【*fukusha*】 copy; reprint; duplication 例 下に私の署名の複写を記しておきましたから御承知ください. Below you will find a *copy* of my signature.

副社長 【*fukushachō*】 executive vice-president

副書 【*fukusho*】 duplicate 例 船荷証券副書を封入申し上げます. We now enclose a *duplicate* B/L.

複製 【*fukusei*】 reproduction 例 不許複製. All rights reserved./ 会社の事前の承諾なしで複製は禁止. *Reproduction* is forbidden without the company's prior consent. ‖ —する reproduce; duplicate

副本 【*fukuhon*】 duplicate; copy 例 自分自身の参考のため副本をもっていた. He kept a *duplicate* for his own reference.

含み 【*fukumi*】 understanding ‖ —で with the understanding that 例 この協定は貴方の共同経営者もそれを尊重するという含みで結ばれた. This agreement has been made *with the undestanding that* your partner will also honor it. ‖ —おく bear in mind; understand; regard as 例 この水曜日は国の祝

日なので配達はその翌日となることを含みおきください. Please *bear in mind* that next Wednesday is a national holiday, and thus deliveries will be a day later.

含む 【*fukumu*】 include; involve; contain 例 値段は貴方口銭2分を含む. The prices *include* a commission of 2% for you. / 運賃は価格に含まれていない. The freight is not *included* in the price.

複利 【*fukuri*】 compound interest 例 複利率は年7.5分. The *compound interest* rate is 7.5% p.a.

不景気 【*fukeiki*】 depression; recession 例 商売の不景気 a *depression* in trade / 貿易はきわめて不景気である. Trade is in extreme *depression.* / 一般的不景気のため，お得意様よりの集金が大変難しくなっている. A general *depression* of business has made it very difficult for us to collect the sums due to us from our customers.

不経済な 【*fukeizai na*】 uneconomical; unthrifty; wasteful 例 車は不経済だから売れなかった. Because the car was *uneconomical* it didn't sell. / そんな風に使うのは不経済だ. It is *uneconomical* to use it in that way. / 安物を買うのは不経済だ. It is *uneconomical* to buy cheap goods. / こんなものを使っては甚だしい時間の不経済だ. The use of it means an intolerable *waste of time.*

符合する 【*fugō suru*】 agree with; correspond with; coincide with; accord with 例 彼らの実験結果は当社のと符合する. The results of their experiments *coincide* with mine. / 当社の見解は貴社と符合する. Our views *coincide with* yours. ‖ 符合しない be inconsistent (with) ‖ びったり— exactly correspond to ‖ 意見が— be in accord with one's views

不合理な 【*fugōri na*】 unreasonable; irrational 例 御要求の値引きはまったく不合理である. The deduction required by you is entirely *unreasonable.*

負債 【*fusai*】 debt; liabilities; dues ‖ 長期— long term liabilities 例 いかなる負債に対しても支払い能力がある. They are solvent for any *debt.*

無事【*buji*】 safe 例 トラックは昨晩無事戻った. The truck came back *safe* last night. / 貨物が無事到着するよう祈っています. We hope they will arrive in *good order and condition*.

不十分【*fujūbun*】 insufficiency; shortage 例 貧弱な事業予測により，目下原料不足に陥っている. Due to poor business forecasting, we currently have a *shortage* of raw materials.

不振の【*fushin no*】 inactive; stagnant; dull; quiet; lethargic 例 市場の流通は目下不振. Market trading is currently *inactive*. / 在荷ははなはだ多く，買い申し込み少ないため相場は不振. Stocks are very heavy, with but few offers, consequently prices are *flat*.

不振販売【*fushin hanbai*】 poor [stagnant] sales 例 不振販売が市場で見込まれる. *Poor sales* are expected in this market.

不正【*fusei*】 injustice

不正確な【*fuseikaku na*】 inaccurate 例 同商会が当社と取引を始めて2年になるという記述からして不正確 なものです. Even their statement that they have been doing business with us for two years is *inaccurate*.

不成立【*fuseiritsu*】 failure; unmaterialization ‖ ─となる fail; end in failure 例 もし貴社がこれらの値段を受け入れないならば取引は不成立に終わります. Unless you can accept these prices, the business will *end in failure*.

防ぐ【*fusegu*】 prevent; stop; ward off; defend 例 政府は景気の行きすぎを未然に防止した. The Government *prevented* business activities *from* going too far.

付せん【*fusen*】 a slip; a rider; a tag 例 簡単に区別できるようにカートンごとに付せんが入っている. Each carton contains *a slip* for easy identification.

不足【*fusoku*】 shortage; scarcity; deficiency 例 供給が不足だ. Supplies show a *deficiency*. / こん包品のすべては重量不足でした. We find that every bale shows a *shortage* in weight. ‖ ─する be [run] short of 例 在庫品は不足を告げた. The goods in stock have *run short*.

不測の【*fusoku no*】 unexpected; unforeseen 例 不測のできご

とで船積みは遅れた. Due to *unforeseen* events, the shipment was delayed.

不即不離の【*fusokufuri no*】neutral; impartial; varying; irregular 例 裁判所が不即不離(公平)の態度をとることを望む. We hope the court will hold an *impartial* attitude.

札つきの【*fudatsuki no*】notorious; ill-famed; ill-reputed 例 彼は札つきの不器用な人間. He is *notorious* for his ineptitude.

負担【*futan*】a burden; an obligation ‖ ―する bear 例 弊社はすべての諸掛かりを負担します. We will *bear* all charges. / 電信, 出張の費用はそれぞれの側で負担する. Cabling, travelling shall be *on the accounts of* the respective parties.

不注意【*fuchūi*】carelessness; negligence 例 貴店の不注意により注文を失っている有様です. We are losing orders through your *negligence.*

不調【*fuchō*】failure; rupture 例 取引の不調度は今月は非常に高い. The business *failure* rate is very high this month.

部長【*buchō*】the head (chief) of a section [department] 例 彼は販売部長に任命された. He has been appointed *the head of the sales department.*

部長代理【*buchō dairi*】acting department manager 例 松本氏は現在部長代理だ. Mr. Matsumoto is the *acting department manager* at present.

不通【*futsū*】no communication; no intercourse 例 79年以来同社とは音信不通です. There has been *no communication* with them since 1979.

普通の【*futsū no*】regular; common; ordinary; usual 例 普通のやり方で処理されよう. It will be processed in the *usual* way.

普通電報【*futsūdenpō*】ordinary telegram

物価【*bukka*】prices of commodities; commodity prices 例 現在物価は暴落している. *Commodity prices* are slumping at present.

物価指数【*bukka shisū*】price index 例 物価指数は昨年より10％上がった. The *price index* has risen by 10% over last year.

復航【*fukkō*】a return [an inward] voyage　例 乗客は復航のみ
運びます．Passengers are only carried on the *inward voyage*.

不都合【*futsugō*】inconvenience　例 不都合をおわびします．We
apologise for any *inconvenience* caused.

物納【*butsunō*】payment in kind　例 物納は受け入れません．
Payment in kind will not be acceptable. ∥ ─する pay in kind

物品税【*buppinzei*】commodity tax　例 政府は物品税を課す見込
み．The government is likely to impose a *commodity tax*.

不定期【*futeiki*】: ─の irregular ∥ ─航路 irregular service　例
この船会社は横浜まで不定期航路をもっているだけです．This
shipping company only offers an *irregular service* to Yokohama. ∥ ─航路船 tramp (ship)　例 不定期航路船の積み荷能力
は小さい．The *tramp ship* has only a small cargo capacity.

不定の【*futei no*】indefinite; undecided; uncertain　例 どの会
社にこの契約をするかは未定．We are as yet *undecided* as to
which company will be offered the contract.

不適当な【*futekitō na*】unsuitable; unfit; inadequate　例 包装
が不適当であることがわかった．The packing has been found
inadequate.

ふ頭【*futō*】quay; pier　例 積み荷はふ頭で陸揚げする．The ship
is being unloaded at the *quay*. ∥ ─渡し ex quay　例 サンフラ
ンシスコふ頭渡し *ex quay* San Francisco

不動の【*fudō no*】indestructible　例 この車は依然として米国で不
動の地位を占めている．This car still holds an *indestructible*
position in the U.S. market.

不得策の【*futokusaku no*】unwise; unadvantageous　例 貴社に
とっていくつかの商社と一度に取引されることは不得策です．It
will be *disadvantageous* for you to enter into business connections with some companies at a time.

船賃【*funachin*】passage; fare　例 契約終了次第，帰国の船賃は
会社が支払います．The company shall pay your *passage* home
on completion of the contract.

船積み【*funazumi*】shipment; loading; shipping　例 船積みは
11月中にできます．*Shipment* can be made during November. /

当社の電子計算機の船積みは来月初めに確定しました. The *shipment* of electronic computers of our company defined the first of next month. / 定期的な船積みを要求します. We shall require regular *shipments*. ‖ ─する ship; load; effect [make] shipment 例 弊社綿漁網は今日むさし丸に船積みされました. Our Cotton Fishing Nets have *been shipped* per M.S. "Musashi Maru" today. / 1カ月の間隔で2回に船積みせよ. *Ship* our goods in 2 lots at an interval of one month. / 船積手配は船積期間内に買い手によってなされるべきである. *Shipping* arrangements should be made by the buyers within the *shipment period*. / 御注文品は船積みいたしました. We have effected *shipment* of your orders. / 8月5日に船積みしたことを喜んでお知らせします. We are pleased to inform that we have made *shipment* on August 5.

船積係 【*funazumi kakari*】 shipping clerk 例 船積係が品目第10号品を船積みした. *Shipping clerk* shipped the goods of item No. 10.

船積指図書 【*funazumi sashizusho*】 shipping order; S/O 例 現品積み出し準備完了, 貴社の即時船積指図書待つ. Goods are now ready for shipment and we are awaiting your immediate *shipping order*.

船積諸掛 【*funazumi shogakari*】 shipping charges 例 機械化すれば船積諸掛は低減しよう. The mechanization will reduce the *shipping charges*.

船積書類 【*funazumi shorui*】 shipping documents 例 送り状その他の船積書類を同封いたします. We have the pleasure to enclose an invoice and other *shipping documents*.

船積代理業者 【*funazumi dairi gyōsha*】 shipping agents 例 S父子商会は当社の船積代理業者. Smith and Sons are our *shipping agents*.

船積通知 【*funazumi tsūchi*】 a shipping advice [notice] 例 船積通知喜んで確認申し上げます. We are pleased to confirm our *shipping notice* [*advice*].

船積通知書 【*funazumi tsūchisho*】 shipping note; S/N

船積払【*funazumi barai*】cash on shipment　例　船積現金払いねがいます．Please pay *cash on shipment*.

船積品【*funazumi hin*】shipments　例　船積品は契約に一致しない．The *shipments* are not in accordance with the contract.

船積見本【*funazumi mihon*】shipment sample　例　船積見本は航空便で急送されました．The *shipment samples* have been despatched by air mail.

船積明細書【*funazumi meisaisho*】shipping specifications　例　貨物は発送次第，送り状および船積明細書を送ってください．As soon as the goods are despatched, please forward to us the invoice and *shipping specification*.

船積申込書【*funazumi mōshikomisho*】shipping application　例　貴社の船積申込書は承認ずみ．Your *shipping application* has been approved.

船荷【*funani*】cargo　例　船荷の通関および受け渡しの御用を相つとめます．We offer you our services for the clearance of *cargoes* through the customs and delivery.

船荷証券【*funani shōken*】bill of lading; B/L　例　船荷証券1通本船で送られたし．Send one copy of *B/L* by the vessel carrying the goods. / 船荷証券は次便で御送付します．*B/L* will follow by the next mail. / 同封の船荷証券のとおり東京丸にて横浜まで送りました．We shipped to Yokohama by M.S. "Tokyo Maru" as per *B/L* enclosed. / 船荷証券は本船に品物が積み込まれたことを明示せねばならない．*Bill of Lading* must indicate that the goods were loaded on board the carrying vessel.

船荷証券代証【*funani shōken daishō*】letter of guarantee　例　取引銀行からの船荷証券代証が必要．We require a *letter of guarantee* from your bank.

船便【*funabin*】shipping service; ship service　例　この船便は推薦できる．This *shipping service* can be recommended. ‖ ― で by ship [steamer; sea]

船【*fune*】vessel; ship; steamer　例　弊社は最初に利用できる船舶に船積みしましょう．We will try to make shipment by the first available *vessel*.

腐敗しやすい 【*fuhai shiyasui*】 perishable 例 腐敗物注意.
Perishable goods. くさりやすいので，冷蔵庫に入れてください.
As the goods are *perishable*, please keep them refrigerated.

不必要な 【*fuhitsuyō na*】 例 needless; unnecessary; unessential
例 不必要な無駄が利益を減少させ ている. *Unnecessary* waste
is reducing our profits.

部品 【*buhin*】 parts; part 例 お取り替えした部品についてはお
代を頂きます. The *parts* replaced will be charged.

不文律 【*fubunritsu*】 an unwritten law [rule] 例 会社の不文律
the *unwritten rules* of the firm / この事態に対して当社には不
文律がある. There is an *unwritten law* in our company per-
taining to this situation.

不変の 【*fuhen no*】 unchanged; constant 例 昨年は売上水準は
不変だった. The level of sales has been *constant* for the last
year.

不本意 【*fuhon-i*】 reluctance; unwillingness ‖ ―な reluctant;
unwilling 例 当社にとって，このような高い値を示すのは不本
意です. It is *reluctant* for us to indicate such high prices. ‖
―ながら with reluctance; reluctantly; unwillingly; against
one's will 例 弊社は不本意ながら価格を下げます. We are *reluctantly* forced to cut our prices. / こう申すのは不本意ですが
~. It is very much *against our will* to say this to you, but
~. / 不本意ながら~の旨御通知申し上げます. It is *with regret
and reluctance* that we have to inform you that ~.

不満 【*fuman*】 discontent; dissatisfaction 例 当社のアフターサ
ービスには多くの不満がある. There is much *dissatisfaction*
with our after sales service.

不味 【*fumi*】 flat 例 市況は不味である. The market is very
flat.

不向き 【*fumuki*】 unsuitable; unfit 例 彼はこの地位には不向き
だ. He is *unsuitable* for this position.

部門 【*bumon*】 category; sector; division 例 輸出取引の管理は
2つの部門に分類される. The conduct of export transactions

can be divided into two *categories*.

冬物【*fuyumono*】(衣服) winter clothing; winter goods 例 冬物衣類は秋までには倉入れになる. The *winter clothing* will be in the warehouse by autumn.

プライスリスト【*puraisu risuto*】a price list 例 現在のプライスリストを送ってください. Please send us your current *price list*.

プラスチック【*purasuchikku*】plastic

ブランディ【*burandei*】brandy 例 ブランディには高い物品税がかかる. There is a high excise duty on *brandy*.

プラント【*puranto*】plant 例 このプラントでの生産はこの夏から始まる. Production at the *plant* will begin next summer.

~振り【~*buri*】mode; way 例 弊社はとくに同社の営業振りを知りたい. We are particularly interested to know their *mode* of doing business.

振り合い【*furiai*】relation; comparison; balancing ‖ 他との—を考える take others into consideration; have regard to 例 他店との振り合いもありますからそう安くは差し上げられません. We can't sell them so cheap, since we must *take* our fellow traders *into consideration*. / 世間の振り合いも考えなければならない. We must have *regard* to custom.

振替【*furikae*】transfer ‖ —口座 transfer account ‖ —える transfer [change] ((to one's account)) 例 当社勘定に振り替えてください. Please *transfer* [*change*] to our accout. / この金は貴勘定に振り替えられた. The money has been *transferred* to your account.

不履行【*furikō*】non-fulfilment; non-performance; breach of contract 例 約束どおり進めないなら契約不履行のかどで告訴します. We will sue your company for *breach of contract*, if you do not proceed as promised.

振り出す【*furidasu*】draw; issue 例 弊社は貴行あてに一覧払いの手形を振り出す. We *draw* (a draft) at sight on your account. / 常例のとおり貴社あてに為替手形を振り出します. We shall *draw* a bill upon you in the usual course. / 一覧払い手

形を振り出してください. You may *draw* on us at sight. / 当社は貴社あて一覧後30日払い1,000ドルの為替手形を振り出しました. We have *drawn* on you a draft at 30 d/s for $1,000.

不利【*furi*】inimical; unfavorable; disadvantageous 例 その契約条件は不利と考えます. We consider the terms of contract *unfavorable*.

不良【*furyō*】failure; bad condition 例 貴社にその商品を不良状態で船積みしてしまいました. We have shipped the goods in *bad condition* to you. ‖ —品 defective [wrong] goods 例 不良品は受け取れません. *Defective goods* will not be accepted. / 不良品は引き取るか5割引きにするか, どちらがよいかお知らせください. Please inform us which is more convenient for us to take the *wrong goods* or to allow you 50% discount.

古臭い【*furukusai*】old; antiquated; old fashioned; outdated 例 これらの商品は古臭いから売れそうもない. These products are *out of date* and thus are unlikely to sell. / そんな古くさい考えではだめだ. Such an *old fashioned* idea won't do any good. / 古くさい話をする. They tell an *outdated* story.

プレミアム【*puremiamu*】(insurance) premium 例 支払い要求が多すぎるので, 貴保険料プレミアムは上がりました. Your *insurance premium* has been raised due to excessive claims.

付録【*furoku*】supplement; appendix

不渡り【*fuwatari*】dishonor; nonpayment 例 不渡手形を受け取り, 当社は目下資金難である. We are short of capital by *dishonored* bill at present. ‖ —になる be dishonored 例 当方手形不渡りの場合は~に参加引受方依頼せよ. If our bill has been *dishonored*, ask ~ for acceptance. / 貴社手形は支払い拒絶により不渡りとなりました. Your draft has been *dishonored* by non-payment.

分割注文【*bunkatsu chūmon*】split order 例 まず第一に当社は分割注文を受ける権利がある. We are authorized to accept a *split order* in the first instance.

分割積み【*bunkatsu zumi*】split shipment; partial shipment; instalment shipment 例 商品の分割積みを毎月いたします. A *partial shipment* of the merchandise will be made monthly.

分割払い 【*bunkatsu barai*】 partial payment; instalment payment‖—販売法 (英) hire purchase, (米) instalment plan　例 分割払い購入がますます一般化しつつある．*Instalment plan* purchases are growing in popularity.‖—で on the instalment plan

文書 【*bunsho*】 a document; correspondence　例 私の秘書がすべての文書を取り扱う．My secretary deals with all *correspondence*.‖—で in [by] writing; in written form; in black and white　例 その報告は文書をもってしなければならない．The report should be made *in written form* [*in writing*].

分譲する 【*bunjō suru*】 sell in plots　例 不動産が分譲された．The real estate was *sold in plots*.

文書番号 【*bunsho bangō*】 reference number

分析証 【*bunseki shō*】 certificate of analysis　例 分析証は船積みごとに差し上げます．A *certificate of analysis* will be submitted with each shipment.

分損担保 【*bunson tanpo*】 with average; W.A.‖—にもとづいた保険証券 insurance policy on W.A. terms

分損不担保 【*bunson futanpo*】 free from particular average; F.P.A.

分配 【*bunpai*】 distribution; apportionment; allotment; division　例 当社代理店が当社商品の分配の責任をもちます．Our agent is in charge of *distribution* of our products.‖—する distribute; divide　例 利益は5人に分配された．The profits *were divided* among the five.

分布 【*bunpu*】 distribution　例 その分布はほぼ人口分布に対応している．Their *distribution* is roughly proportional to the distribution of population.‖—する be distributed; be scattered　例 これらの品物は広く分布している．These goods are widely *scattered*.

分野 【*bunya*】 facet; field; world　例 A氏は業務のすべての分野を知っている．Mr. A knows every *facet* of the business.

分量 【*bunryō*】 quantity　例 船積みの分量が多くなればそれだけ

船積み費用は安くなる. The larger the *quantity* we ship, the smaller gets the per unit shipping cost.

分類【*bunrui*】: —する classify; assort; divide into classes **例** 当社製品はいくつかのクラスに分類される. Our products are *divided into* various *classes*.‖ —棚 a filing cabinet; a chest of drawers‖ —表 a classified table

【ヘ】

平均【*heikin*】 average **例** 平均〜の売り上げをする make an *average* sale of / 各州の平均税額 *average* amount of state taxes / 平均出来高 *average* trading / 平均風袋 *average* tare / それは平均〜と見られる. It may be put on an *average* of 〜. ‖ —して on the *average* **例** 当社の従業員は平均週40時間働く. Employees in our company work 40 hours per week *on the average.*

平日【*heijitsu*】 working day; weekday **例** 当社社員は平日のみ働く. Our employees only work on *weekdays.*

平常[運転]在庫【*heijōzaiko*】 running stocks

閉鎖[廃業]する【*heisa suru*】 discontinue business; go out of business **例** あそこは廃業するらしい. It is likely that they will *go out of business.*

閉店【*heiten*】: —する close [shut up] business [shop] **例** 商店はクリスマスで閉店だった. The store *closed business* on the Christmas holiday.

米ドル【*bei doru*】 U.S. dollars **例** 契約書は米ドルで記入してください. Please write the contract in *U.S. dollars.*‖ —借款 U.S. dollar loan

別口【*betsukuchi*】 another item; different lot **例** 別口がもっと貴意にかなうことがわかるでしょう. You will probably find *another item* more to your satisfaction.

別紙【*besshi*】 separate sheet; enclosed sheet; attached sheet **例** 詳細は別紙に記入します. Details are given on the *enclosed sheet.*

別送する 【*bessō suru*】 send separately; send under separate cover 例 注文書は別送します. The orders will be *sent separately*.

別段の 【*betsudan no*】 special; specific; particular ‖ ―規定なき限り unless otherwise provided; if not specially provided

別途積立金 【*betto tsumitate kin*】 special reserve fund 例 当社は偶発事故にそなえて別途積立金をしています. We have a *special reserve fund* for any contingencies.

別便 【*betsubin*】: ―で under separate cover; by separate mail [post]; separately 例 弊社のカタログ別便にてお送りします. We are sending you *separately* a copy of our catalog. / 別便で主要製品のカタログをお送りします. You will receive *separately* some catalogs of the main products of our manufactures. / 貴社にカタログを今日別便でお送りいたしました. The catalog sent you today *by separate cover*. (電文) / 弊社は貴社に別便にて見積りを送りました. We are sending you *under separate cover* a quotation.

変化 【*henka*】 change 例 市場には変化がありません. There is no *change* in the market.

弁解 【*benkai*】 explanation; excuse 例 弁解として～といい張る urge as an *explanation* that ～. / ～から弁解を求める demand *explanation* from / に対してこれと同様の弁解は立たない the same *excuse* cannot be used for ～ / しかるべき弁解をする make appropriate *excuses* / 筋の立たない弁解 a groundless *excuse*

便宜 【*bengi*】 facility; convenience 例 に対してあらゆる便宜を与える afford every *facility* for / に対して適当な便宜を与える grant proper *facilities* for / について十分な便宜を与える give full *facilities* with regard to

勉強 【*benkyō*】: ―する（安く売る）sell cheap [at a small profit]; quote the lowest possible prices ‖ ―値段 a close [cut; keen; competitive] price; the best [lowest] possible price 例 当社の製品を勉強値にて供給します. We can supply you with our goods at *competitive prices*. / 値段は最も勉強している. The

price is the *very best*. / 弊社は優秀品質の商品を，勉強値にて供
給することができます. We are in a position to supply you
with excellent "goods at *competitive prices*. / 勉強値段を出し
ていただかねばなりません. We must ask you for a *keener
price*. / 下記商品に対し精々勉強値段をお知らせください. Please
quote us your best *prices* for the following goods.

偏見 【*henken*】 prejudice　例　右申し述べたことは偏見の記述では
ないことを御了承ください. Please note that the above statement is made without *prejudice*.

変更 【*henkō*】 change; alteration ‖ ─する alter; change; effect
alterations ‖ ─は認めない no alteration [change] is allowed;
unchangeable

弁済 【*bensai*】 payment; settlement; liquidation ‖ ─する repay;
pay; settle　例　至急弁済ねがいます. Please *settle* the account
at the earliest possible date. ‖ 代位─ payment for honor

返事 【*henji*】 response; reply; answer　例　至極巧妙で要領を得
た返事 a decided, clever and effective *answer* / すぐ返事をも
らう get an instant *answer* / 質問に対する十分な返事 a sufficient *answer* to one's question / 色よい返事をする return an
encouraging *response* / 満足な返事を得る meet with a gratifying *response* / 早急かつ好意的な御返事をお待ちしています. We
look forward to your early and favorable *reply*. / なるべく早
く御返事をねがいます. Please send us an *answer* at your
earliest convenience. We are awaiting your early *reply*. / こ
の返事が貴社のお役に立てるものと思います. We hope our *reply*
will be helpful to you. / 貴社の6月5日付の御要求にしたがっ
て船積みいたしました. In *response* to your request of June
5, we have made shipment. / 返信用に切手と住所を記入した
封筒を同封します. We enclose a stamped, self addressed
envelope for your *reply*.

変動 【*hendō*】 fluctuation　例　為替相場の激変 a sharp *fluctuation* in exchange / 物価の激変 a violent *fluctuation* in prices. /
弊社の価格は市価の変動にしたがう. Our prices are subject to
market *fluctuation*. / 本商品の市況は変動がきわめて激しくまた

急速である．The *fluctuation* in this line is so heavy and rapid. / 市価に変動がありますため，すべて値段は最終的な確認を条件とすることに御了承ねがいます．Due to market *fluctuations*, all prices must be considered subject to our final confirmation. / ひどい変動はないと思う．We do not expect heavy *fluctuations*.

返品 【*henpin*】 returned goods; returns 〖例〗 返品は領収書持参のこと．*Returned goods* must be accompanied by a receipt.

返礼 【*henrei*】 return ((present)); reciprocation ‖ ―する make a return; reciprocate 〖例〗 いつにても，喜んで御返礼いたします．We shall at all times be happy to *reciprocate*. / 貴社の御厚意に報います．We are pleased to *reciprocate* your courtesy.

【ほ】

貿易 【*bōeki*】 commerce; trading; trade 〖例〗 日米貿易は著しく発展した．The *trade* between Japan and America has grown remarkably. / ニューヨークは世界の貿易の中心である．New York is the *trading* center of the world. / 日本のインド貿易は近年躍進また躍進の状態だ．Japanese *trade* with India has lately grown by leaps and bounds. / 山本氏はニューヨークに輸出貿易拡張のため，まもなく赴きます．Mr. Yamamoto will shortly leave here for New York, with a view to extending his export *trade* there. ‖ ―自由化 trade liberalization

貿易会社 【*bōeki gaisha*】 a trading firm [company]; importers & exporters 〖例〗 貿易会社に勤めたい．I want to work in a *trading company* [*firm*].

法外な 【*hōgai na*】 exorbitant; unreasonable 〖例〗 売りさばき人が法外な高値をつけることには賛成しない．We do not favor the dealer's asking an *exorbitant* price. / 貴社の法外な指値には同意できない．We shall not agree to your *unreasonable* limit.

包括 【*hōkatsu*】 inclusion; comprehension ‖ ―する include; comprise ‖ ―的 comprehensive

放棄する【hōki suru】give up; disclaim; abandon; renounce 例 弊社はたいてい その権利を放棄するだろう. We will most probably *abandon* that right.

報告【hōkoku】a report; a statement; information 例 商品の売れ行きについて, 御報告ねがいます. We shall be happy to have your *information* of the sale of the goods. / 御報告の儀はもちろん極く内密にいたします. Your *information* will, of course, be treated in strict confidence.

忙殺される【bōsatsu sareru】busy oneself with [in; at; about] be very busily occupied; be kept busy (with; by); be very busy (doing; with work)

奉仕【hōshi】service 例 いつも喜んで貴社の奉仕につとめます. We are always pleased to be at your *service*.

方式【hōshiki】a formula; method 例 能率的な生産方式を採用している. We have adopted efficient production *methods*.

報酬【hōshū】a reward; a remuneration; recompense 例 弊社では奉仕に対してなんら報酬を受けません. We accept no *remuneration* whatever for our service.

包装【hōsō】package; packing; pack 例 天候好天しだい包装開始の予定. We will commence *packing* as soon as weather permits. / 適切な輸出用包装が施されるべきである. Proper export bale *packing* is to be carried out. ‖ ―指図書 packing instruction

法的【hōteki】legal ‖ ―手段をとる institute legal proceedings; take legal steps 例 迅速な処置がとられない限り, 当社は法的手段をとります. The company will *institute legal proceedings* unless immediate action is taken. ‖ ―根拠 legal basis [foundation]

暴騰【bōtō】sudden rise 例 生産費が暴騰した. The cost *rose suddenly.*

方面【hōmen】field; phase; sector 例 日本品が取って代わるまで英国品がその方面を独占していた. English goods held the *field* until they were superseded by imports from Japan. ‖ 各―に in every field; on various phases [sectors]

暴落【*bōraku*】 a sudden fall; a violent setback; a big fall 例 ニューヨーク銀行株が暴落した. There was *a big fall* in Bank of New York stock. ‖ —する fall sharply; slump 例 値段は暴落する. The price will *fall sharply*.

ほかに【*hokani*】 besides; other; else; except; but; in addition to 例 この原因のほかに *above and beyond* these causes / 前に頂いた注文のほかにもう一つ注文をいただきたい. Please send another order *in addition to* the order previously sent. / ほかに何もすることはない. We have nothing *else* to do. / ほかに説明の仕様がない. We can't explain it in any *other* way. / そうするよりほかに仕方がない. We have no choice [There is nothing for it] *but* to do so. / 給料のほかに少し収入がある. He has some income *besides* his salary.

保管する【*hokan suru*】 warehouse; take custody of 例 しばらく保管乞う. Please *warehouse* these goods for a while. / 貴社の返事を受け取るまでの条件で商品は当社が保管します. We shall *hold* the goods subject to your reply reaching us.

保険【*hoken*】 insurance 例 貴社と海上保険契約を結ぶ. We will make marine *insurance* contract with you. / その近海の戦時損害に対しては保険契約には応じない. *Insurance* is not accepted against war risks in those waters. ‖ —をつける insure; effect insurance; take insurance 例 品物は十分に保険がついている. The goods *are* fully *insured*. / 積み荷に保険をつけてください. Please *effect insurance* on a cargo. / アメリカの保険会社に海上保険をつける. We *take* marine *insurance* through American insurance firms. / 商品の保険は当社でかけます. We will *effect insurance* on our goods. / 汽船箱根丸の積み荷に対し金額3万ドルの単独海損担保の保険お引き受けください. Please *insure* us for W.A. on the shipment per M.S. "Hakone Maru". / 下記品物に対し全危険担保で保険の引き受けを願います. Please *insure* us on the following goods against all risks. Please *cover* for us the goods detailed below against all risks. Please *effect insurance* for us on the goods specified below against all risks.

保険会社 【*hoken gaisha*】 insurance company; insurance underwriters; underwriters　例 保険会社に〜の損害賠償のお手配ねがいます. Make a claim with the *underwriters* for damage for 〜.

保険証券 【*hoken shōken*】 insurance policy [I/P]　例 保険会社からの料金取り立てのため海上保険証券直送ありたし. Return the *Marine Insurance Policy* to enable us to collect premiums from the underwriters.

保険証書 【*hoken shōsho*】 insurance certificate [I/C]

保険約款 【*hoken yakkan*】 insurance clause　例 この保険約款は要求をするさい困難を伴うだろう. This *insurance clause* will cause difficulties in making your claim.

保険料 【*hoken ryō*】 premium; insurance premium　例 相当高い保険料を支払わねばならない. You must pay comparatively high *premiums*.

保護する 【*hogo suru*】 protect　例 それは細菌に犯されないように保護されている. It is effectively *protected* against the attacks of bacteria.

誇り 【*hokori*】 pride　例 われわれは誇りをもって〜を指摘する. We point *with pride* to 〜. ‖ —とする be proud of; take (a) pride in; pride oneself on

補償 【*hoshō*】 compensation; reparation　例 当社は一切補償をしない. We do not allow any *compensation*. ‖ に対して—を要求する demand compensation for ‖ に—を与える give compensation to ‖ —の請求をする put in a claim for compensation ‖ 損害— compensation for a loss ‖ 損害—を請求する demand reparation for the injury ‖ 損害—をする make reparation for damages ‖ の—として in reparation of ‖ —する indemnify; compensate　例 貴社の尽力に対し補償をせねばならない. We must *compensate* you for your services.

保証する 【*hoshō suru*】 assure; guarantee　例 この品はすぐ積み出すことを保証します. We *assure* you that these goods will be shipped at once. / 貴船積品は見本と同一であることを保証せねばならない. You must *guarantee* your shipments are exactly equal to the sample. / こういう事情ですから目下御注文の引き渡しは保証できません. Under the circumstances, we are unable to *guarantee* the delivery of your order at present. / 当社商品は最上の仕上げであることを保証できます. We can *assure* you that our goods are of best workmanship. / 貴社の決めた価格の範囲内ですむという保証は で き な い. We cannot *guarantee* to purchase the goods within the price limit set by you. / この色は保証されている. This color *is warranted*. ‖ —金 guarantee money (fund) ‖ —状 letter of guarantee (L/G)

補助金【*hojokin*】a grant; a subsidy; a subvention 例 同協会は年1万ドルの補助金を受けている. The Society has an annual *grant* of $ 10,000.

保税【*hozei*】(倉庫に入れる) bond 例 保税貨物は政府倉庫に保管される. *Bonded* goods will be stored at the government warehouse. ‖ —倉庫 bonded warehouse 例 貴社の積み荷を保税倉庫から倉出しした. We have cleared your shipment from *bonded warehouse*. ‖ —工場 bonded factory ‖ —地域 bonded area ‖ —輸送 bonded transportation

発足する【*hossoku suru*】set a foot; make a start 例 それはまだ発足していない. It has not yet *made a start*.

没頭【*bottō*】devotion; concentration ‖ —する be absorbed in; devote oneself to; be deeply engaged; concentrate on 例 彼はずっと原子力の研究に没頭している. He has *been absorbed in* the study of atomic energy.

骨を折る【hone o oru】strive for; strive strenuously; take trouble 例 その会社は市場獲得に骨を折っています. The firms are *striving strenuously* to capture the market.

賞める【*homeru*】admire; extol; praise 例 貴社の仕事に対して貴社を賞める. We *admire* you for what you have done.

保留【*horyū*】reservation 例 わが社は保留付でオーストラリア着運賃保険料込み値段の信用状を設立します. We shall establish letter of credit for C.I.F. Australia with the *reservation*. ‖ —する reserve; defer 例 この提案は保留しよう. Let us *reserve*

this proposal./ 彼の処罰は保留（延期）になった．His punishment was *deferred*. / その問題の決定は次回まで保留された．The decision of the question was *deferred* to the next meeting.

本位【*hon-i*】（貨幣の）standard; basis 例 金（銀）本位 the gold (silver) *standard* / 金本位の国 a *gold-using* country / 営利本位の事業 an enterprise *run for* profit / 日本は金本位である． The currency of Japan is on a *gold basis*. ‖ 品質— quality first 例 当店では品質本位です．*Quality first* is the motto of our firm.

本月【*hongetsu*】this month 例 本月1日付御請求にしたがい，貴社あて販売委託しました．In accordance with your request of the 1st *this month*, we have consigned sale to you.

本件【*honken*】this case [affair; matter]; the matter in question 例 本件について率直な御意見をお聞かせください．We shall be pleased to have [We would like to hear] your frank opinion about *this case*. / 本件についてなにとぞお知らせください．We shall be obliged if you will inform us of *this matter*. / 本件御容赦願います．Kindly excuse me for troubling you in *this matter*.

本状【*honjō*】this paper; this letter ‖ —により by the letter ‖ —御持参の方 the bearer of this letter ‖ —執筆時には up to the writing; at the time of writing 例 本状執筆時には，それ以上の発展はなかった．*At the time of writing*, no further developments have occurred.

本船【*honsen*】the steamer; the vessel ‖ —受取書 Mate's Receipt [M/R] ‖ —積込値段（本船渡し）F.O.B. (free on board) ‖ 故障付—受取証 foul M/R [dirty M/R] ‖ —積込費 loading charge 例 本船積込費は最近1割値上がりした．*Loading charges* have recently increased by 10%.

本店【*honten*】head office; main office 例 私は2年前大阪本店よりロンドン支店へ転任しました．I was transfered from Osaka *main office* to London branch office two years ago.

本場【*honba*】origin of production; center ‖ —物 genuine products 例 パリは流行の本場だ．Paris is the *center* of fashion.

本領【*honryō*】 ability; feature 囫 法律を解釈し適用するのが判事の本領です. It is the *duty* of the judge to interpret and apply the laws. ‖ —を発揮する display one's skill; exert one's ability

【ま】

マーク (荷印)【*māku*】shipping marks; case marks ‖ ―をつける mark　囫　包装には次のマークをつけること. Package to be *marked* as follows.

マージン【*mājin*】a margin; a profit; a profit margin　囫　その値段ではもうけのマージンがない. The price leaves no *margin of profit*.

前貸し【*maegashi*】advance　囫　手当の前貸しをする. We will give him an *advance* upon his allowance.

前払い【*maebarai*】advance payment; prepayment　囫　前払い注文に対しては2.5%の割引をする. We allow a $2\frac{1}{2}\%$ discount for *advance payment*.

前もって【*mae motte*】beforehand; in advance　囫　御親切なる御配慮をいただけるものと前もって感謝します. Thank you *in advance* for your kind consideration. / 初注文あるものと前もって感謝する. We thank you *in advance* for your initial order. / 前もって品質は指定はしません. We do not specify *in advance* the particular quality.

任す【*makasu*】entrust; authorize　囫　われわれはこの問題を貴社に任せたい. We would like to *entrust* you with this matter.

負かす【*makasu*】outrival; outcompete; beat　囫　その品を1個500円から300円に負かした. We *beat* down the price of the articles from 500 yen to 300 yen a piece.

負ける【*makeru*】get the worst of it; be beaten; be outcompeted ‖ けんかに― get [have] the worst of a quarrel　囫　最近の貿易戦争で松本商会は負けた. In the recent trade war, Matsumoto & Co. *got the worst of it*.

まさに【*masani*】duly　囫　5月10日付の御引き合い状正に受け取りました. We have *duly* received your inquiry of May 10.

勝る【*masaru*】be superior; surpass; excel; be better　囫　この価格で市場に出回っているどの品物より本品は勝っている. At the present price, our item *is superior to* any similar goods on the market.

増す 【*masu*】 increase; augment; enhance; rise; grow **例** 同会社は資本金を 1 万ポンドから 2 万ポンドに増した. The company has *increased* the capital stock from £ 10,000 to £ 20,000. / その商品の売れ高は年とともに増加しつつある. The sale of the goods has been *increasing* with the years.

まず第 1 に 【*mazu daiichi ni*】 firstly; first; in the first place; first of all **例** きみは第 1 に言葉づかいで判断される. You will be judged by your speech *first of all*.

ますます 【*masu masu*】 all the more; still more; the more ~ the more ~ **例** ますます興味あり *all the more* interested / あなたの説明を聞けば聞くほどますますわからなくなる. *The more* you explain, *the more* we are puzzled.

まだ 【*mada*】 still; yet **例** まだ話し中である. They are *still* talking. / まだ出港していない. It has not left port *yet*.

麻袋 【*matai*】 gunny [jute] bags **例** 頑丈だから麻袋が使われた. A *gunny bag* was used because of its strong fabric.

間違い 【*machigai*】 mistake; error; fault; oversight **例** 間違いは貴社の方にあります. The *error* is on your side.

間違っている 【*machigatte iru*】 be wrong; be at fault **例** 貴社の計算は約 40 万円間違っている. Your accounts *are wrong* by some ¥ 400,000.

まちまち 【*machi machi*】 —の (に) diverse(ly); various(ly); different(ly); divided **例** 意見がまちまちだ. They are *divided* in opinion. / 報告がまちまちだ. There are *various* [*different*] reports about it. ‖ —である vary; divide **例** 6 月における織物生産高はまちまちだ. Textile production *varied* widely in June. / この件に関しては意見がまちまちだ. Opinions *vary* on this point.

待つ 【*matsu*】 wait; look forward to **例** 早い御返事お待ちしております. We are *waiting* for your early reply. / 貴方からのお便りをお待ちしております. We are *looking forward to* hearing from you.

まとまった【*matomatta*】 sizable; appreciable **例** 貴社とまとまった商売をします. We do an *appreciable* business with your company.

間に合う【*maniau*】 be in time for; be available **例** 間に合う商品を船積みしました. We have shipped the goods that will *be available*. / その商品を間に合うように送ってください. Please send us the goods *in time*.

ままである【*mama de aru*】 unchanged **例** 市況は変動なくそのままである. The market remains *unchanged*.

守る【*mamoru*】 observe; keep; adhere (to); abide by **例** 日時は正確に守らなければならない. The date must be punctually *kept*. ‖ 秘密を— keep a secret

万一【*man-ichi*】 in case; in the event of **例** 万一遅れた場合にはお知らせします. *In the event of* some delay, you will be informed of same.

満期になる【*manki ni naru*】 expire; mature; come to an end; fall due **例** 本信用状は7月30日満期となる. This L/C *expires* on July 30. / 手形は本月10日満期となります. The bill will *mature* on the 10th. / 信用状は4月10日に満期となった. The letter of credit *came to an end* on April 10. / この手形は6月10日に満期となる. This draft *falls due* on 10th June.

満船【*mansen*】 a full cargo; a ship load **例** その船は約800トンの荷を積んで満船である. The ship has a *full cargo* of about 800 tons.

満足【*manzoku*】 satisfaction **例** 品質，価格ともに満足できるので，100箱注文する. As we have found both the quality and the price quite *satisfactory*, we are glad to place an order with you for 100 cases. / 採用いただければ，御満足のいくよう最善を尽くします. If you should decide to engage me, I should do my utmost to give you every *satisfaction*. ‖ —させる content; satisfy **例** バイヤーは満足していた. The buyer was *contented*. / 弊社はこれらの条件で満足です. We are *satisfied* with these terms. / 商品が無事貴地着の上，商品の品質に御満足されることを確信いたします. We trust you will *be satisfied*

with the quality of the goods when they arrive safely. / 当
社製品に御満足なさっていることをうれしく存じます. We are
delighted to hear that you *are satisfied* with the goods we
supplied. / 同社からの商品はいずれも弊社を満足させなかった.
No goods sent by them satisfied us.

満点【*manten*】full mark; excellent; perfect　例 100 パーセン
ト満点である. It is 100 per cent *perfect*.

【み】

見送る【*miokuru*】hold off; stop　例 その商品をテストするまで
買い入れを見送ります. We will *hold off* purchases until we
have tested the product.

見落とし【*miotoshi*】oversight; error; overlooking　例 貴社がこ
の見落としをしたとは信じられない. It is incredible that you
should have committed this *oversight*.

見返り【*mikaeri*】counterpart; collateral ‖ —資金 credit funds
例 見返り資金はいつも低い. *Credit funds* are at an all time
low. ‖ —担保 collateral security ‖ —輸入 counterpart imports

見切り売り【*mikiriuri*】bargain sale; clearance sale　例 見切り
売りで余分の仕入品を一掃した. The *bargain sale* cleared out
the excess stock.

未決の【*miketsu no*】pending; outstanding　例 弊社は未決のま
まのクレームを解決した. We settled the *pending* claim. / 未決
の勘定が多くある. We have many *outstanding* accounts.

見込み【*mikomi*】prospect; promises; outlook　例 十分成功の見
込みをもって開店しましたので社員を100人雇用したい. Having
established ourselves in business here with every *prospect* of
success, we wish to hire 100 employees. / 貴市場の将来の見込
みについてお知らせください. Please inform us of the future
prospects of your market. ‖ —利益 expected profit

見込みちがい【*mikomi chigai*】mistake; miscalculation ‖ —をす
る make a wrong estimate; miscalculate　例 仕事に要する時
間について見込みちがいをした. They *made a wrong estimate*

as to the time required for a job.

水先案内 【*mizusaki an-nai*】a pilot ‖ —料 pilotage 例 水先案内料は運賃に含まれている. *Pilotage* has been included in the transport charges.

未然に防ぐ 【*mizen ni fusegu*】nip in the bud; prevent (before it is too late) 例 悪いうわさは未然に防がなければならない. The bad publicity should be *nipped in the bud*.

未着 【*michaku*】nonarrival 例 荷物未着のため非常に迷惑しております. We are greatly inconvenienced through the *nonarrival* of the goods.

密接 【*missetsu*】: —な (に) (in) close 例 弊社は貴社と密接な関係を確立したい. We wish to establish a *close* connection with you. / 弊社は貴社と密接な関係にあります. We are *in close* connections with you.

見積もり 【*mitsumori*】quotation; estimation; calculation 例 貴見積もりは高すぎる, 競争者は安価にオファーしている. Your *quotation* is too high, and competitors are offering lower prices. / 弊社は貴社が現在の見積もりを受け入れることを強く勧めます. We strongly recommend that you accept the present *quotation*. ‖ —送り状 proforma invoice 例 弊社は喜んで見積もり送り状を同封します. We are pleased to enclose our *proforma invoices*. ‖ —書 estimate 例 同封した見積書からわが社の価格が低いことが分るでしょう. From the enclosed *estimate* you will observe that our prices are low. ‖ —注文書 proforma indent

見積もる 【*mitsumoru*】quote 例 貴社の最低価格で弊社に見積もりしてください. Please *quote* us your lowest prices. / 値段は御提案のように F.O.B. にもとづいて見積もってあります. The prices are *quoted* on F.O.B. as you suggested. / 下記商品について運賃保険料込最低値にて見積もり乞う. Please *quote* your rockbottom prices on a C.I.F. basis on following items. / 同封の値段表のように最善の条件を見積もりました. We have *quoted* our best terms as in the enclosed price list.

見通し 【*mitōshi*】a prospect; an outlook 例 長期の見通し a

long-range *outlook* [*prospect*] / 事業の見通し business *outlook* / 繊維工業の見通しはどうですか. What do you think of the *prospect* of fiber industry? / まだはっきり見通しがつかない. The prospect [*outlook*] is still dim. / 経済の見通しは一向に明るくない. The economic *outlook* is not promising at all. / 金融の見通しは上々と思われる. I consider the monetary *outlook* satisfactory.

認める【*mitomeru*】notice; find; admit; allow; permit; recognize 囲 それは法律で認められている. It *is allowed* by the law.

見直す【*minaosu*】give more credit 囲 彼の業績はもっと見直されるべきだ. He should be *given more credit* for his achievements.

見逃す【*minogasu*】overlook; neglect; ignore 囲 これらの商品はまったく見逃されてきた. The goods have been utterly *neglected*.

未払いである【*mibarai de aru*】be unsettled; be outstanding 囲 金 10 万円也の勘定は, ただ今 1 カ月間期限経過し, 未払いのままになっていることをお知らせします. Permit me to point out that my account for ￥100,000, now one month overdue, *is still unsettled*. ‖ 未払利息 interest payable

見本【*mihon*】a pattern; a sample; a specimen ‖ 原— original sample ‖ 控— duplicate sample ‖ 第三— triplicate sample ‖ 先発— advance sample ‖ 船積— shipping sample ‖ —帳 pattern book ‖ 買— buying sample 囲 同封の見本お受け取りください. Please find the *samples* that are enclosed. / 見本を受け取ったが, あまり少量で品質の判定ができない. *Sample* received, but it is too small to judge quality. / 貴社から返事があり次第多種多様の見本を送りましょう. Upon hearing from you, we will despatch a good variety of *samples*. / 見本を出していただかないと, 見積もりはできません. We cannot quote unless you can provide *a sample*. / 見本のうち, 一, 二のものは在庫がありません. We have no stock of one or two of the *patterns*. / 6 月 3 日に御送付いただいた見本を本日ありがたく受け取

りました．We have today received with thanks the *sample* you sent us on June 3. / 当社の買見本に相当する貴社の見本を航空便でお送りください．Please send us by air mail your *samples* corresponding to our buying samples.

見本市 【*mihon ichi*】 a trade fair　囫 見本市で貴展示品を拝見しました．We had opportunity of seeing a display of your products at the *trade fair*. / 見本市は大成功だった．The *trade fair* was a huge success.

民間会社 【*minkan gaisha*】 a private enterprise [firm;company] 囫 景気対策のため民間企業への課税は軽減された．Taxes on *private enterprise* have been reduced in order to stimulate the economy.

民間貿易 【*minkan bōeki*】 private trade; business on a commercial basis

【む】

無傷で 【*mukizu de*】 intact; unscathed; in good condition; unimpaired　囫 その商品は無傷で到着した．The goods have arrived *in good* [*perfect*] *condition*.

報いる 【*mukuiru*】 return; reward; reciprocate　囫 その返礼に弊社のできるだけのことをしましょう．In return we will *reciprocate* to the best of our ability.

向け 【*muke*】 for; scheduled for; destined for; bound for　囫 これらの品はアメリカ向けです．These goods are *destined for* America. / 品物はニューヨーク向けです．The goods are *bound for* New York.

無効の 【*mukō no*】 invalid; void　囫 その契約は無効と判定された．The contract was declared *void*.

矛盾 【*mujun*】 discrepancy; conflict; contradiction　囫 条件上に矛盾をきたす incur a *contradiction* in terms / 会計係が2つの計算書の間の矛盾を発見した．The accountant has found a *discrepancy* between the two accounts.

無条件で 【*mujōken de*】 at par; unconditionally　囫 無条件に彼

の申し出を受け入れた．We accepted their offer *unconditionally* [*without any condition*].

無償物資【*mushō busshi*】grant 例 政府は無償物資 50 万ドルをタンザニアに急送した．The government has dispatched *grants* worth \$500,000 to Tanzania.

結ぶ【*musubu*】conclude; close ((a contract)) 例 小麦に対し金 80 万円の保険契約を結んでください．Please *close* insurance on the wheat for ¥800,000.

無税【*muzei*】：—品 free goods ‖ —で free of duty; duty free ‖ —の free; tax-free; duty-free; taxless 例 空港には出国乗客用の免税店がある．The airport has a *duty-free* shop for outgoing passengers.

無責任【*musekinin*】irresponsibility 例 無責任を責められた．He was accused of *irresponsibility.* ‖ —な irresponsible 例 無責任なやり方だ．It is *irresponsible* way of doing business. 無責任な人だ．He is an *irresponsible* man.

無断で【*mudan de*】without notice 例 この目録に掲げてある定価は無断で変更することがあります．The prices in this catalog are subject to change *without notice.*

無理【*muri*】：—な unreasonable; impossible; impracticable 例 それは無理とみなされている．It is regarded as *impossible.* ‖ —はない reasonable; (quite) natural; it is no wonder that ～ 例 先方が怒るのも無理はない．It *is no wonder that* they should get angry. / 無理に彼を大阪へやった．We *forced* him to go to Osaka. We sent him to Osaka against his *will.*

無料で【*muryō de*】free of charge; without charge 例 売り手は買い手に見本を無料で提供します．The sellers are to supply the buyers with samples *free of charge.* / 見本は無料で送付します．We send samples *free of charge.* / 当店でお買い上げの品は市内に限りすべて無料で配達します．Every article you buy at this store will be delivered *free of charge* within city limits. / 無料でこの品を配った．They distributed the goods among us *for nothing.* ‖ 入場— admission free ‖ 運賃— freight free

【め】

盟外船【*meigaisen*】non-conference vessel

銘柄【*meigara*】brand (商標); description (品名); an issue (株式) 例 この銘柄は10年間市場のリーダーでした。This *brand* has been the market leader for 10 years.

名義【*meigi*】name ‖ ―変更 transfer of name ‖ ―で under the name of 例 世間に知られることを避けて，スミス名義で記載した。To avoid publicity, he is registered *under the name of* "Smith". ‖ ―上 nominally; tentatively

明細【*meisai*】particulars; details; description 例 貴船積品は明細と一致しない。Your shipments do not agree with *description.* / 弊状受け取り次第明細のすべてをお送りください。We ask you to send us, on receipt of this letter full of your *details.* / 納期の明細を通知する。We will advise you in *detail* as to the time of shipment. / 明細は電信する。We will cable you *full particulars.* / 通関用として価格などに関する必要な明細書を貴社に差し出すよう同社に指図しました。We have instructed them to furnish you with necessary *particulars* as to value, etc., for customs purposes. ‖ ―書 specification 例 表の全項目に対する完全な明細書をお送り願います。Please give us complete *specifications* for all the items listed.

迷惑【*meiwaku*】inconvenience; trouble; annoyance 例 迷惑をかけておわび申し上げます。We apologize sincerely for any *inconvenience.* We are sorry to have *troubled* you in this matter. We are sorry that we have caused you *inconvenience.* We are sorry you have been put to *inconvenience.*

メーカー【*mēkā*】manufacturer; producer 例 メーカーと代理店について交渉してみます。We will approach the *manufacturers* about their agency.

目立った【*medatta*】marked; striking; conspicuous; remarkable; noticeable 例 同社の本年度の業績は目立った。Their business for this year was *remarkable* [*noticeable*]. / それをよ

く目立ったところにおきなさい。Place it in a *conspicuous* [*noticeable*] place.

綿花【*menka*】raw cotton 例 綿花50こりに関する当社注文書第25号を同封します。We are enclosing our Order No. 25 covering 50 bales of *cotton*.

面会【*menkai*】interview 例 御都合のよい折に面会くださいますよう。I should welcome a *personal interview* at your convenience. I can come to *see you* at any time suitable for you. / 面会御希望なら指定どおりいつでも参上します。Should you desire an *interview* [If you care to *see*], I should be most pleased to call on you at any time you may appoint.

綿糸【*menshi*】cotton yarn 例 30番手綿糸 *30s yarn* [*count* cotton yarn] / 弊社は綿糸を提供できます。We can offer you the *cotton yarn*.

免税【*menzei*】tax exemption; immunity ‖ ―品 tax free articles; duty-free articles [imports] 例 〜の免税を保証できますか。Can you guarantee *immunity* for 〜? / 免税あるまで倉出しするな。Leave the goods in bond until *immunity* is obtained. ‖ ―になる be exempted from taxation

綿製品【*menseihin*】cotton goods 例 船積みする綿製品5箱あり。We have five cases of *cottons* for shipment. / 綿製品は非必需消耗品に該当する。*Cotton goods* are under non-essential consumer goods.

免状【*menjō*】permit ‖ 輸出― export permit 例 輸出免状が出るまで、出荷日をお知らせできない。Until *export permit* is granted we cannot quote the delivery date.

免責【*menseki*】: ―条項 escape [exemption clause] 例 契約書には災難の場合の免責条項が含まれる。The contract contains an *escape clause* in the event of mishaps. ‖ ―歩合 franchise ‖ ―歩合約款 memorandum clause

面目【*menmoku*】honor 例 彼はわが社の面目を汚した。He disgraced the *honour* of our company. / 面目にかけてそれをやります。I will carry it *on my honor*. / 彼らはそれで大いに面目を施した。It did great *credit* to them. ‖ ―を一新する undergo reformation; present a new aspect ‖ —を失する lose one's face ‖ —を保つ save one's face; preserve one's honor ‖ —に かかわる endanger one's honor; react unfavorably on; bring discredit on

【も】

もうけ【*mōke*】margin; profit; gains; earnings 例 貴社の指 値ではもうけがありません. Your limit leaves us no *margin* for profit. / この仕事で毎日5万円のもうけがある. We make a *profit* of 50,000 yen a day out of this job. / この商売は大も うけになる. The business will bring a huge *profit*. ‖ もうかる 商売 a profitable business 例 この商売はもうけがない. This business is *unprofitable* [*does not pay*].

申し込み【*mōshikomi*】application; proposal; offer; request 例 申し込みを承知した. We accepted an *offer*. / 申し込みに応じ ます. We will accept your *offer*. / お申し込みありしだい見 本を送る. Sample will be sent *on application*. ‖ 確約— firm offer ‖ 反対— (返りオファー) counter-offer ‖ 確約なしのオファ — offer without engagement ‖ 売り違い御免のオファー offer subject to being unsold ‖ 先売御免付オファー offer subject to prior sale ‖ 実見提供 offer on approval ‖ 申し込む offer; apply (for); make an application [offer] (for) 例 当社製品の申し 込みは半年前にねがいたし. Please *offer* the products of our company before half a year at the latest. / 1千万円の火災保険 を申し込む. We *apply* for a fire insurance for ¥10,000,000. / 小麦に対し金額50万円の保険を申し込みください. Please *open* insurance on wheat for 500,000 yen. / 彼は保険会社に就職の 申し込みをした. He has *made application for* a position in the insurance company. / 会計係の地位に申し込みをします. I wish to *apply* [*make application*] *for* the position of ac- countant. / 貴電受け取り次第売り違い御免の条件でこれら商品の 確約申し込みをします. We *offer* you firm these goods subject to their being unsold on receipt of your reply by cable. / 1

トンにつき 6 ポンドで反対申し込みをします. We *make* you a counter *offer* at £6 per ton.

申し添える【*mōshi soeru*】add **例** この際～ということを申し添えます. At this time we should *add* that ～.

申し出【*mōshide*】proposal; request; offer ‖ ━る propose; request; offer **例** パンフレット御入用の方はお申し出ください. Any one who wants the pamphlet should *apply* to our office.

申しわけ【*mōshiwake*】apology; excuse ‖ ━する make an *apology* to; excuse ‖ ━ない be sorry; regret; it is indeed regrettable; we (would) apologize to you **例** この過失を犯し申しわけありません. それには十分責任をとります. We *are sorry* we made this error, and accept full responsibility for it.

目的【*mokuteki*】purpose; aim; object; end **例** 訪問の目的は何ですか. What is the *purpose* [*object*] of your visit? / 彼の目的はできるだけ早くそれを入手することだった. His *aim* was to get it as soon as possible. / 何の目的でそれが御入用ですか. *For* what *purpose* do you want it? ‖ ～の━で with a view to; with an intention of; for the purpose of; to the end; aiming at **例** その目的で金を貯めている. We are saving money *to that end*. ‖ ━地 landing port; destination **例** 旅行の目的地はシカゴだ. The *destination* of this journey is Chicago. ‖ ━にかなう answer [serve] the purpose

目標【*mokuhyō*】aim; object; mark; target **例** 輸出は1億2千万ドルの目標に向けられた. Exports were headed for the $120 million *target*. / 今月の目標額は2万トンです. The *target figure* for this month is two million tons.

模造【*mozō*】imitation **例** 模造品は弊社商品と品質やデザインの点で見分けることができます. You can tell our merchandise from the *imitation* by its quality and design. ‖ ━宝石類 imitation jewels

保合【*mochiai*】(市場) quiet; steady; no change; unchanged; (市価) maintained **例** 相場は保合である. Prices *are steady* [*remain stationary*; *maintain* equilibrium]. / 市場は保合である. The market *remains unchanged* [*stationary*]. ‖ 強(弱)━

steady with an upward [downward] tendency

持ち越し 【*mochikoshi*】 (前から) brought forward; (次へ) carried forward ‖ —ストック carry-over 例 持越品を投げ売りするのは当社の方針に反します. It is against our policy to sell carry-over below cost.

持ち直す 【*mochi naosu*】 (市場) improve; recover; rally; revive 例 昨日の株式市場は値を持ち直した. Prices *recovered* fairly on the stock exchange yesterday. / 少し景気が持ち直した. Business is *improving*. / 相場はじきに持ち直すだろう. The market will soon *rally*.

元帳 【*motochō*】 ledger 例 この項目はまだ元帳に転記してありません. This item has not yet been carried into the *ledger*.

基づく 【*motozuku*】 based on; owing to; on; in accordance with 例 この注文は弊社見本 No. 10 に基づく. This order *is based on* our Sample No. 10. / この計画は彼の考えに基づく. This plan *is based on* his idea. / それは商売の不振に基づくものだ. It is owing to the dull business. / 彼は自分の主義に基づいて行動する. He acts *on* his own principle. / 規定に基づいて処罰された. They were punished *in accordance with* the regulations. / すべての取り引きは次の条件に基づいて行われること. All business shall be conducted *on* the following terms and conditions.

元値 【*motone*】 cost ‖ —を切る sell at below cost; sell at a loss; take a loss (損をする) 例 いま元値を切っても売った方がいい. You had better *sell* them *at below cost* now. / 元値で売ろう. We will *sell* you this article *at the cost price* [*at cost*].

求める 【*motomeru*】 demand; ask; look for 例 乳牛を数頭求めている. We *are in the market for* some cows. / 私の意見を求めた. He *asked* my opinion about it. / 彼らは就業時間の短縮を求めた. They *demanded* shortening the working hours. / 彼は職を求めている. He is *looking* [*hunting*] *for* a job. / 援助を求めた. They *asked* us *for* help. ‖ お求めにしたがい according to [in accordance with; in compliance with] one's request

物 【*mono*】 thing; substance; article; goods; commodity; one's belongings; property; one's effects 例 会社の物を私用しては いけない. You must not use the *property* of the company for private purposes. / 戦後は物がなくて困った. After the war we suffered from the shortage of *goods*. / あの店は質のいい物を 売っている. They sell *things* [*articles*; *goods*; *commodities*] of good quality at that store. / 身の回りのものを預ってもらう よう頼んだ. We asked them to take charge of our *personal effects*. We left our *belongings* in their care.

模倣 【*mohō*】 imitation 例 弊社の製品は外国品の模倣ではありま せん. Our goods are not *imitations* of foreign articles.

模様入り 【*moyō iri*】 with designs 例 模様入りテトロンポロシャ ツ polyester polo shirts *with designs*

問題 【*mondai*】 subject; issue; problem; matter; question 例 問題はそのままになっている. The *problem* remains unsettled./ それは重大な問題だ. That is a serious [grave] *matter* [*question*; *problem*]. / それは問題にならない（もってのほか）. It is out of the *question*. / 大したことはない. It *matters* little. / 問 題はこうだ. The *question* [*point*] is this. / お申し込みの値段 の値引きはまったく問題になりません. The reduction of price mentioned is quite out of the *question*. ‖ —にぶつかる en- counter [meet; confront] a problem ‖ —を生ずる cast [give rise to] a question ‖ —化する come into question ‖ —の in question; under review; the matter referred to

【や】

ヤード【*yādo*】yard 例 商品の中にはヤードで売るものがある.
Some goods are sold by the *yard*.

やがて【*yagate*】before long; in no time; in due course 例 や
がて貴簡のお返事をします. Your letter will be answered *in
due course*.

役員【*yakuin*】director; officer; staff; board 例 役員は決議の
すべてを裁定しなければならない. *The director* must ratify all
decisions.

約定【*yakujō*】promise; engagement; contract; arrangement
例 いつ, 約定品を引き渡せるか. When can you deliver our
contracts? / 約定品を船積み次第通知ください. Please advise us
as soon as you ship our *contracts*. ‖ —する make agreement;
promise; stipulate 例 売約書にはロンドン経由でマンチェス
ター向けの積み出しを約定してある. This contract of sale *stipulates* that the goods should be shipped via London to Man-
chester.

約束【*yakusoku*】promise; engagement 例 約束は実行します.
We will carry out our *promise*.

約束手形【*yakusoku tegata*】(promissory) note 例 約束手形を割
引してもらえるか. Can you get *promissory note* discounted? ‖
—を振り出す issue a promissory note ‖ —振出人 promiser

役に立つ【*yakuni tatsu*】be of use; be helpful; be serviceable
例 この報告がお役に立つことを期待いたしております. We trust
that this information may *be of use* to you. / 今後とも貴社の
お役に立ちたいと思います. We hope that you will continue
to allow us to *serve* you.

屋号【*yagō*】a firm name

安い【*yasui*】low; low-priced; inexpensive; moderate 例 す
ぐれた品質にしては, 価格が安いことに御同意いただけるでしょ
う. You will agree that the *price* is extremely *low* for such
excellent quality. ‖ —値段 competitive [reasonable] prices 例

安い値段で商品を売ることを保証します. We can assure you that we sell our goods at *competitive prices.* ‖ 安すぎる too low; unrealistic; impracticable ‖ 安く売る sell cheap ‖ 安くする cheapen; cut [reduce] the price ‖ 安くなる go down in price; prices come down 例 安く品物を提供しましょう. We will offer you the goods *at low prices.* / 値段はいくぶん安くなるだろう. The prices will be somewhat *reduced.*

休む 【*yasumu*】 rest 例 彼は一週間仕事を休んだ. He *rested* from work for a week.

厄介 【*yakkai*】 trouble 例 ご厄介をおかけしてまことに相すみません. Please excuse us for the trouble we are giving you.

雇い入れ 【*yatoiire*】 employ; hire 例 経験のある婦人タイピストを至急雇い入れたい. An experienced lady typist is open for immediate *employment.*

やむなく 【*yamunaku*】: ―する have to; be compelled to; be obliged to 例 やむなく取り消しします. We *are obliged to* cancel.

【ゆ】

優位 【*yūi*】 position of advantage; dominant position 例 当社のもうけは貴社のもうけより優位に立っています. The profits of our company gain *advantage over* that of yours.

優遇 【*yūgū*】 cordial reception; hearty welcome; favorable treatment ‖ ―する give a warm reception; treat a person favorable; extend a favor to 例 この貿易会社では女子を比較的優遇する. Women *are* comparatively *well paid* in this trading company.

有限 【*yūgen*】 limit ‖ ―会社 limited company ‖ ―責任 limited liability 例 有限責任のみを受け入れよう. They will only accept *limited liability.*

有効 【*yūkō*】 (な) valid; effective 例 すべての確定売り申し込みは打電の時から 72 時間有効である. All firm offers shall be *valid* for 72 hours from the time dispatched. / このオファーの

有効期限は見積書日付より 1 カ月です．The *validity* of this offer is for one month from the date of estimate. / 覚書の有効期間は契約日付より 2 カ年間とする．Duration of memorandum is to be *effective* for two years after contract. / 本信用状は 7 月 30 日まで有効です．This L/C is *effective* until July 30. ‖ —期限 expiry time

融資 【*yūshi*】 financing; advance of funds; a loan ‖ —する finance 囲 銀行は確実な会社に融資する．Banks *finance* reliable firms.

優先 【*yūsen*】 priority; preference 囲 3 日以内に御返事到着すれば貴方を優先します．We shall be pleased to give you *priority* if your reply reaches us within 3 days. / 当方に優先権を賜わりありがたく存じます．We thank you for *the preference* you have given to our house. ‖ —を与える give priority to ‖ —措置を講ずる accord preferential treatment ‖ —を得る take priority of; take precedence over

郵送 【*yūsō*】 post; mail 囲 貴社に見本を郵送した．We *posted* a sample to you. ‖ —証明書 certificate of mailing ‖ —料 postage

郵便 【*yūbin*】 post; mail 囲 郵便で知らせます．We shall let you know by *post*. / 当社は郵便で信用状を開設しました．We have established a letter of credit by *mail*. / 20 万円の郵便為替を同封しましたからお受け取りください．Enclosed please find a *postal* money order for ￥200,000. ‖ —振替 mail transfer ‖ 書留— registered mail ‖ 航空— air mail ‖ 船— surface mail ‖ 印刷物 printed matter ‖ 返信 return mail ‖ —で送る send by mail; post; mail ‖ —私書箱 post office box [POB; PO Box] ‖ —貯金 postal savings ‖ —注文 mail order ‖ —為替 postal money order [P.M.O.] ‖ —切手 postage stamp ‖ —切手を貼る affix a stamp to a letter ‖ —日数 mail days ‖ —小包受取書 parcel receipt

有望 【*yūbō*】 bright prospect ‖ —な hopeful; promising 囲 あの会社は前途有望である．That company has a *bright prospect* [is *promising*].

有名な【*yūmei na*】 famous **例** 日本は船舶建造においては世界的に有名です. Japan *is famous* the world over *for* building ships.

猶予【*yūyo*】 grace (支払い); postponement; extension of time **例** もし貴社がもう少し猶予をくださるならありがたく思います. We shall be much obliged if you will give us a little *more time.* / 貴社が通常の猶予をくださるものと信じています. We trust you will give us the usual period of *grace.*

有利【*yūri*】 profitability; favor; advantage **例** 計画は有利に展開しよう. This plan will turn to *advantage.* ‖ ―な profitable; favorable; advantageous **例** 双方の利益に有利な取り引きであることがわかるでしょう. It will turn out to be a *profitable* business to our mutual benefit. / 当社の品物で有利な商いのできることはおわかりのことと思います. You see a possibility of a *profitable* business in our goods.

優良【*yūryō*】 superiority; excellence ‖ ―品 excellent goods; articles of superior quality ‖ ―な superior; excellent; competent **例** 品質が優良なら自然と需要が増える. The *superior* quality creates its own demand.

有力な【*yūryoku na*】 reliable **例** 当地における有力な商社をいくつか御紹介します. We will be sure to introduce to you some *reliable* firms here.

輸出【*yushutsu*】 export; exportation **例** 最近当社は輸出課を開設しました. We have recently opened *the export* section. / 私は3年間輸出業に従事していました. I have had three years' experience in *export* business. ‖ ―する export **例** 弊社の商品はフランスに輸出された. Our goods were *exported* to France. ‖ ―商 an exporter **例** 当社は日本製商品の輸出入商として開業しました. We have commenced business as Importers and *Exporters* of Japanese goods. / 当社は自転車および部品の輸出商で世界各地に輸出しています. We are *exporters* of bicycles and parts and have been shipping them to all parts of the world. ‖ ―運賃 export freight ‖ ―契約書 export contract sheet ‖ ―申告 export declaration ‖ ―信用保険 export credit insur-

ance ‖ —税 export duties ‖ —代理店 export agent ‖ —通関 export clearing ‖ —手続 export procedure ‖ —割引 export discount ‖ —割当 export quota ‖ —禁止 embargo

譲り受け【yuzuriuke】 transfer ‖ —人 assignee; transferee 例 その譲受人はその特許の以前の所有者がもつすべての権利をもちます. The *assignee* has all the rights possessed by the former holder of the patent.

輸送【yusō】 transportation; transit; traffic ‖ 海上— transport by sea ‖ 陸上— land transport ‖ —中の in transit ‖ —する transport 例 われわれは米を船で輸送した. We *transported* the rice by ship.

輸入【yunyū】 import; importation 例 貴社は日本製雑貨の輸入に関心をおもちかどうかお尋ねします. We inquire whether you are interested in the *import* of Japanese sundry goods. ‖ —関税 import duties ‖ —許可 import admission ‖ —許可書 import license ‖ —禁止 import prohibition ‖ —制限 import restriction 例 わが国には近い将来輸入制限が実施される様子はありません. There is no likelihood of *import restrictions* being imposed in our country in the near future. ‖ —手続 import procedure ‖ —統制 import control ‖ —保証金 import collateral ‖ —割当 import quota 例 輸入割当を入手するために複雑な手続きが必要です. You must take the complicated procedures to obtain *import quota*. ‖ —商 importer 例 Y貿易は信頼のおける一流の綿製品の輸入商社です. Y trading company is a reliable firm and one of the leading *importers* of cotton goods here.

許す【yurusu】 permit; allow; grant; admit; acknowledge; forgive; excuse 例 貴商品の船積みが遅れたことをお許しください. Please *excuse* the delay in shipment of your goods. ‖ 許しを乞う beg one's pardon; request one's permission

ゆるめる【yurumeru】 loosen; modify; relax; ease; relieve ‖ ゆるみ relaxation ‖ ゆるむ become loose; lessen; ease off 例 来年から輸入制限がゆるめられる. Import restrictions will be *eased* from next year.

【よ】

良い 【yoi】 good; fine; favorable 例 品質が良い. The quality is *good* [*fine*].

用 【yō】 business; affairs; engagement 例 彼女は用でアメリカ へ行っています. She is in America *on business.*

用意 【yōi】 preparation; readiness; provision; precaution ‖ ― する prepare [provide; arrange] for ‖ ―がある be prepared [ready] for 例 5分の特別現金割引をする用意があります. We *are prepared to* allow you a special cash discount of 5%. / 品物は船積みの用意ができております. The goods *are now ready for* shipment. / 貴社お申し込みの取り引きに入る用意があ ります. We *are ready* to enter into the business which you propose.

容器 【yōki】 container; pack ‖ 木箱 wooden case [box] ‖ ボール 箱 carton (box) ‖ 俵 bale ‖ つぼ jar ‖ たる barrel ‖ セメントだ る cask ‖ 缶 can ‖ ドラム缶 drum ‖ 錫内張り箱 tin-lined case ‖ 袋 bag ‖ 紙袋 paper bag ‖ フラスコ flask ‖ かご basket ‖ 釘だる keg ‖ おり cage; pen ‖ ふじ巻きびん demijohn ‖ 茶箱 chest ‖ 大だる hogshead ‖ ばらで in bulk

要求 【yōkyū】 request; requisition; demand 例 御要求あり次第, 御報告いたすつもりです. We will inform you upon *request.* ‖ ―物 requirement ‖ ―者 demandant; claimant ‖ ―する re- quire; request; demand; claim; ask for 例 貴社の御要求通 りに御注文を引き受けることはできない. We are unable to ac- cept your order exactly as you *desired.* ‖ 損害賠償を―する claim for the damage ‖ ―に従い upon demand; at one's re- quest ‖ ―にかなう meet the requirement

要件 【yōken】 important matter; requisite 例 重要要件を処理し た. We dealt with the *important matter.*

溶鉱炉 【yōkōro】 a blast furnace 例 溶鉱炉は鉄鉱石の処理に使 う. The *blast furnace* is used to process iron ore.

容積 【yōseki】 measurement ‖ ―重量明細書 measurement and

weight list

用船【yōsen】 chartered vessel ‖ —料 charterage ‖ —契約書 charter party ‖ 裸— bare charter ‖ —する charter **例** 1万トンの船をいくらで用船できますか. At what rate can you *charter* a vessel of about 10,000 tons? ‖ —者 charterer **例** 用船者は一流と思われますが, 当方としては保証できかねます. The *charterers* are considered first class, but we cannot guarantee them.

要望【yōbō】 demand; needs; requirement **例** 商品は貴社の御要望にそうものであることを確信しております. We are confident that the goods will meet your *requirements*.

用命【yōmei】 order; command; requirement **例** お得意様からの御用命はなんなりと直ちに調達します. We are in a position to fill all *requirements* of our customers at once.

羊毛【yōmō】 (の) wool(en) **例** オーストラリアの羊毛市場は急騰しました. The Australian *woolen* market has had a big rise.

要領【yōryō】 point; main point; essentials; outline; summary ‖ —を得た relevant; pertinent ‖ —を得ている be to the point [purpose] **例** 先方の提案は要領を得ている. Their proposal is *to the point.* ‖ —を得たことをいう speak to the point ‖ —を得ない be off the point; be nothing to the purpose

予告【yokoku】 previous notice; notice **例** 定価表の値段は予告あるまでは有効です. The prices given in the list are good till further *notice.* ‖ —なしに without notice **例** この配船予定は予告なしに変更することがあります. This shipping schedule is subject to change *without notice.* ‖ —期間の満了 expiration of a notice ‖ —する give a person a notice; notify beforehand **例** 1カ月前に予告する *give a person a* month's *notice*

余剰【yojō】 excess; extra; surplus ‖ —の spare [extra] ‖ —物資 surplus materials **例** ある種の余剰品は値段表の半額引きで片づけられることになる. Certain *surplus lines* will be going at 50% off list-prices.

余地【yochi】 room; margin **例** この取り決めは改善の余地がある. This agreement has some *room* for improvement. ‖ —な

└leave no room for ～; admit of no ～

予定【*yotei*】 schedule; plan; program ‖ —額 estimated amount ‖ 船舶— 出帆日 estimated time of departure [ETD] ‖ 船舶— 到着日 estimated time of arrival [ETA] ‖ —する be scheduled to; be expected to; plan; intend to arrange　例 大和丸は明日横浜に入港の予定です. The Yamato Maru *is scheduled* to reach [get to; make port in] Yokohama tomorrow. / 三宅丸は9月20日横浜出港の予定である. The Miyake Maru *is to* leave [sail, set sail from] Yokohama on the 20th of September. ‖ —より早く before the schedule ‖ —より遅れて behind the schedule ‖ —の expected; scheduled; estimated; appointed ‖ —保険証明書 certificate of insurance

予約【*yoyaku*】 reservation; previous booking; advance order ‖ 為替の— exchange contract ‖ —者 subscriber ‖ —済みの reserved; engaged ‖ —販売 advance sale ‖ 購読— subscription ‖ —する reserve; book　例 船腹を予約しなければならない. We have to *reserve* space. / 指定船は満載のため船腹予約ができない. We cannot *reserve* space as the named vessel is filled up. / 船会社は特定の船について輸出業者の予約を受け付ける. The shipping company *books for* the exporter on a particular vessel.

余裕【*yoyū*】 room ‖ —がある ((can)) afford　例 休暇をとる余裕がない. I cannot *afford* a holiday.

喜んで【*yorokonde*】 with pleasure　例 同様の場合がありましたときはいつでも喜んでご用達申し上げます. Always *with pleasure* at your service in similar cases. ‖ 喜ぶ be glad (of); be delighted (at); be pleased at ‖ —知らせる be pleased to inform a person that ～ ‖ —する be happy to; be willing to; be prepared to; take pleasure in ～ing　例 貴社と取り引きを始めることを非常に喜んでいます. We *are* quite *willing to* open an account with you.

弱気【*yowaki*】 (弱含み) weak tone; bearish tendency (弱保合 [横ばい]) standstill with bearish trend　例 市況は弱気である The market situation is *weak.*

【ら】

落札する【*rakusatsu suru*】win a bid for ~ ; win in the tender ;
be successful in tender ; have one's tender accepted 例 ブラ
ウン会社が橋梁建造の契約を落札するだろう. Brown & Co. will
win the bid for the contract to build the bridge. ‖ 落札者 successful tenderer ; winner in the tender

落成する【*rakusei suru*】be completed ; be finished 例 この倉
庫は今月末までに落成する予定です. This warehouse is *to be
completed* by the end of this month.

欄外【*rangai*】margin 例 左の欄外に摘要が記載されています.
Remarks are given in the left *margin*. ‖ —の見出し running
title [head]

【り】

利益【*rieki*】profit (margin) ; returns ; gains ; advantage ; benefit
例 当社の値段はごくわずかの利益しか見込んでおりません. Our
prices allow only a very small *margin*. / このオファーを即時
引き受けられることが貴社の利益です. It is to your *advantage*
to accept this offer without delay. / この金額には希望利益が
一割含まれています. Ten per cent for an imaginary *profit* is
included in this amount. / 本通信が貴我双方の利益となること
と思います. We trust this writing will be for our mutual
benefit. ‖ —金 profit ‖ —と損失 profit and loss ‖ 総—金 gross
profit ‖ 純— net profit ‖ 見越(希望)— imaginary profit ‖ —の
ある profitable [paying] ‖ —のない unprofitable ‖ —を生む
yield profit ‖ —を得る make [obtain] profit of ‖ 少ない—
narrow margin of profit ‖ —を与える benefit ‖ —配当 distribution of profits

利害【*rigai*】advantages and disadvantages ; interests ; concern
例 イギリスの利害はアメリカのそれときわめて密接に関係して
いる. The *interests* of England are closely bound up with

those of America. ‖ —関係 interests ‖ —を同じくする have common interests ‖ 利害関係がある have a concern [an interest] in

陸揚げ 【*rikuage*】 landing; discharge; unloading **例** 要償は商品の陸揚げ後15日以内に打電すべきこと. Any claim is to be cabled within 15 days from the date of final *discharge* of goods. ‖ 船荷の— the discharge of cargo ‖ —手続 landing formalities ‖ —港 port of discharge ‖ —未済貨物 goods afloat ‖ —費 landing charges ‖ —港不定貨物 optional cargo ‖ —する land cargo; unload a ship; discharge **例** これらの貨物は1時間で陸揚げされるでしょう. These goods will *be landed* in an hour. ‖ —代理人 landing agent ‖ —重量 landed weight ‖ —期間 days for landing

履行 【*rikō*】 performance of a duty; fulfillment of a promise; execution of contract **例** 買い手は契約の履行を主張する. Buyers insist on the *performance* of this contract. / 契約の適正履行のための保証を得なければならない. A security must be obtained for the due *performance* of the contract. ‖ —する perform; fulfill; execute **例** 貴社に支払いを履行するつもりでいます. We will *execute* the payment for you. / この注文が満足に履行されるなら, 喜んで再注文しよう. If this order is *executed* in a satisfactory manner, we shall be glad to send you repeat order. / 貴注文をもっと早く履行するようあらゆる努力をすることを請合います. We assure you that every effort will be made to *execute* your order earlier.

利ざや 【*rizaya*】 margin of profit **例** この品でかなりの利ざやが得られます. This will give you a fair *margin of profit*.

利子 【*rishi*】 interest **例** 預金には6分の利子を付けます. Six per cent *interest* is allowed on deposits. ‖ 延滞— overdue interest ‖ 未払— unpaid interest ‖ ～%の—がつく yield interest at ～% ‖ —平衡税 interest equalization tax

利息 【*risoku*】 interest **例** 5分の利息で金を借りる borrow money at 5% *interest* / 国債に年8分の利息がつく. The national bond carries *interest* at 8% per annum. ‖ 前受— interest prepaid

理由【*riyū*】 reason; cause **囫** 買い手は次の理由をあげた．The buyer gave the *reasons* as follows.‖ の— reason for ‖ 正当な — justifiable reason ‖ もっともな rational reason ‖ 明白な— obvious reason ‖ —書 statement of reasons ‖ 十分の—がある there is a good reason for ~ ‖ いろいろの—で for several reasons ‖ どんな—で for what reason; on what ground

流行【*ryūkō*】 fashion; vogue ‖ —する be in fashion; be popular ‖ —に遅れる be behind the fashion; be going out of fashion ‖ —遅れの out of fashion; old-fashioned **囫** 最近の好みは変わりつつあり，貴社御要求の品物はいまは流行遅れです．Recent tastes are changing and the goods you require are now *out of fashion.* / こういう自動車はもう流行遅れだ．These cars are now *out of fashion.* / それは最新の流行です．It is the *latest fashion.*

隆盛【*ryūsei*】 prosperity **囫** 弊社は年々隆盛を続けています．We are enjoying *prosperity* year after year.

流通【*ryūtsū*】 negotiation; circulation ‖ —する circulate; flow ‖ —性 negotiability ‖ 流通手形 negotiable bill ‖ —証券 negotiable document ‖ —機構 distribution structure ‖ —ルート (商品の) distribution channel

履歴書【*rirekisho*】 curriculum vitae; personal history **囫** 履歴書を御持参ください．We hope that you will bring a *curriculum vitae* [*personal history*] with you.

利用【*riyō*】 availability; utilization; use **囫** 時間と金を大いに利用せよ．Make the best *use* of your time and money. / 目下のところ直行船は利用できません．No direct vessel is available at present.

了解【*ryōkai*】 understanding; comprehension ‖ —がつく come to an understanding ‖ —する understand; realize **囫** 弊社は船積みの遅延はやむを得ないことを十分に了解します．We fully *realize* that the delay in shipment is inevitable. / どうして異状が起こったか了解に苦しみます．We cannot *understand how* it should have gone out of condition.

料金【*ryōkin*】 charge; rate; fare **囫** 料金は 11 月 15 日現在で上

がる. The *rate* will rise as of November 15. ‖ ―表 tariff ‖ ―値上げ raise of charge ‖ ―値下げ reduction of charge ‖ 料金先方払 charge forward

領事送り状【*ryōji okurijō*】 consular invoice 囫 ベネズエラ向船積には領事送り状が必要です. *Consular invoices* are required for shipment to Venezuela.

領収【*ryōshū*】 receipt ‖ ―者 recipient; receiver ‖ ―する receive; be in receipt of ‖ ―書 receipt; acknowledgement 囫 御請求により右金額にたいする領収証を同封しましたからお受け取りください. Enclosed please find a *receipt*, as requested for the amount. ‖ 仮―書 interim receipt

旅客【*ryokaku*】 passenger 囫 この飛行機は150人の旅客を運べる. This plane can carry 150 *passengers*.

旅券【*ryoken*】 passport ‖ ―査証 passport visa ‖ ―を申請する apply for a passport 囫 旅行の少なくとも2週間前に旅券の申請をしなければならない. You should *apply for a passport* at least two weeks before you travel.

利率【*riritsu*】 rate of interest 囫 利率は年1割. The *rate of interest* is 10% p.a. ‖ ―で at the rate of ‖ ―の引き上げ(引き下げ) raise (reduction) in interest rate

【る】

累計【*ruikei*】 total; aggregate; grand total ‖ ―して in total; in the aggregate 囫 累計は2万ドル. The grand total is $20,000.

類似【*ruiji*】 resemblance; similarity ‖ ―のもの similar [the like] ‖ ―する be similar to; alike 囫 両者は類似する点が多い. The two of them *are alike* in many respects.

累積【*ruiseki*】 accumulation ‖ ―する accumulate 囫 滞貨が倉庫に累積している. Goods are *accumulated* in the warehouse.

ルート【*rūto*】 route; course ‖ 販売― distribution [sales] channel ‖ 正規の― regular course; legitimate channel ‖ 直販― direct selling route 囫 直販ルートがいちばん安い. The *direct*

selling route is the cheapest.

【れ】

例外的【reigaiteki】(に) exceptional(ly) 例 これは例外的な低率です。This is an *exceptionally* low rate.

冷蔵庫【reizōko】 refrigerator 例 冷蔵庫を生産しております。We produce *refrigerators*.

劣等品【rettōhin】 inferior goods; goods of inferior quality 例 買い手は劣等品質を理由に1割の値引きを要求する。Buyers claim an allowance of 10% for *inferior quality*.

廉売【renbai】 bargain sale; clearance sale; sacrifice sale; dumping 例 それは廉売品です。Those goods are offered at a *bargain*. ‖ ―する sell at a bargain; sell cheap; clear; sell at sacrifice

連絡【renraku】 contact; touch; connect 例 鉄鋼の仕入れについて貴社と御連絡がつき喜んでいます。We are pleased to get in *touch* with you for the supply of steel. / 当社の代理店をしてくれる会社と連絡をつけたい。We should like to have a *contact* with a firm who would be willing to represent us.

【ろ】

漏損【rōson】 leakage; leakage loss 例 漏損は売り手負担のこと。*Leakage* is to be borne by seller. / コンテナは完全密封で漏損には保証つき。The containers are completely sealed and are guaranteed against *leakage*.

労働【rōdō】 labor ‖ ―不足 labor shortage ‖ ―条件 working conditions 例 労働条件はこの20年間著しく改善された。*Working conditions* have improved markedly over the last twenty years. ‖ ―組合 labor union ‖ ―市場 labor market ‖ ―時間 working hours ‖ ―争議 labor dispute ‖ ―罷業 strike

論争【ronsō】 debate; dispute 例 この問題について大衆論争があろう。There will be a public *debate* on the issue.

論評【*ronpyō*】criticism; comment ‖ —する criticize; comment on 例 首相はこの問題について論評を避けた. The Prime Minister refused to *comment on* the issue.

【わ】

わいろ【*wairo*】bribe 例 わいろをやり取りするのは悪いことです. It is bad custom to offer or take a *bribe*.

渡し【*watashi*】delivery ‖ 直— prompt [immediate] delivery 例 直渡しを保証します. You can be assured of *immediate delivery.* ‖ 代金引換— cash on delivery [C.O.D.] ‖ 書類引受— documents against acceptance [D.A.] ‖ 書類支払— documents against payment [D.P.] ‖ 工場— ex factory ‖ 貨車— ex rail ‖ 倉庫— ex warehouse [godown] ‖ 船側— free alongside ship [F.A.S; ex ship] ‖ 甲板— free on board [F.O.B] ‖ 保税倉庫— ex bond ‖ はしけ— ex lighter; delivery in lighter

渡す【*watasu*】hand; give: provide 例 この手紙は山田氏から貴方に渡されるでしょう. This letter will be *put* in your *hands* by Mr. Yamada. / 商品は当地の代理店に渡したときは完全な状態でした. The goods were in perfect condition when *handed* over to the agent here.

割り当て【*wariate*】allocation; quota; allotment; assignment 例 輸入割当を入手するためには複雑な手続きが必要である. You must carry out complicated procedures to obtain import *quotas.* ‖ —制 quota [allocation] system ‖ —金 allotment ‖ —る assign; allocate; divide between; prorate

割引【*waribiki*】discount; reduction; rebate 例 送り状金額から1割引をします. 10% *discount* will be allowed on invoice amount. / 見積もり価格は通常2% の割引がされています. The prices quoted are subject to usual *discount* of 2 %. / この注文は大口なので数量割引を願います. This order is quite large and we would request you to make a *quantity discount.*/ これらの機械の業者割引率, 数量割引率と価格をお知らせください. We would appreciate your letting us know the prices as well as the *trade and quantity discount* rate for these ma-chines. / 貴社の特別割引価格を呈示ください. We would appre-ciate your special *discount.* ‖ 再— rediscount ‖ 現金— cash discount ‖ 仲間— trade discount ‖ 手形の— bill discount ‖ 値段の— discount off [on] the price ‖ —値段 reduced price ‖ —率 discount rate ‖ —手形 discounted bill ‖ —する give [al-low, make] a discount; reduce; give [allow; grant] a reduc-tion 囫 従来の価格より 10%割引します. We will make *a dis-count* of 10 per cent on the prices previously quoted. / 弊社は貴社にとくに 5 分の割引をします. We will offer you a spe-cial *discount* of 5%.

割り増し【*warimashi*】extra charge; premium 囫 割増運賃(船)として 1 割の料金が課せられる. A charge of 10% is made for *extra freight.* / 別の包装をお望みでしたら, 割増価格をお支払いください. If you want different packing, please pay *extra* for it. / 高い割増金を支払わなければならない. You must pay high *premiums.* ‖ —をする pay [give] an extra [a premium] ‖ —金 premium [bonus]

割り戻し【*warimodoshi*】rebate (料金); drawback (税金); bo-nus (保険) 囫 横浜からロンドンまでの運賃にいくらの割り戻しを出していただけるのですか. What *rebate* will you allow us for freight from Yokohama to London? ‖ 延期払い— deferred rebate ‖ 仕入れ— purchase rebate ‖ 売り上げ— sales rebate

編者略歴

三 好 章 六 （みよし・しょうろく）
昭和16年東京外語大卒。群馬県立女子大教授。

教歴: 東京外語大，専修大，神奈川大など。
　　　英語検定協会検定委員。
　　　日本商工会議所商業英語検定委員。

著書:『貿易英語活用辞典』（神奈川県庁発行）
　　　『アンカー英作文辞典』（学研発行）など

昭和59年 4 月10日　初版発行

コンパクト貿易英語活用辞典

Ⓒ

編　者　三　好　章　六

発行者　株式
　　　　会社 北 星 堂 書 店
　　　　代表者　山　本　雅　三

発行所　株式
　　　　会社 北 星 堂 書 店
〒101 東京都千代田区神田錦町 3-12
電話 294-3301 振替口座東京 8-16024

印刷: 住友出版印刷　製本: 大成社

THE HOKUSEIDO PRESS
12, 3-chome, Nishikicho, Kanda, Tokyo, Japan